Art Glass, Pottery & Decorative Arts
featuring the Dot Talbert Collection
Heritage Signature Auction #614
March 20, 2005 • Dallas

Bryan Abbott, Director of Acquisitions • Ext 320 • Bryan@HeritageGalleries.com
Jared Green, V.P. of Business Development • Ext 279 • JaredG@HeritageGalleries.com

PUBLIC LOT VIEWING
Saturday, March 19, 2005
9:00 AM — 5:00 PM CT

PRIVATE LOT VIEWING
Wednesday-Friday, March 16-18, 2005
by appointment only
Please provide lot numbers for all items to be viewed ahead of time by contacting our Customer Service Dept. at 800.872.6427 ext. 150

Heritage Galleries & Auctioneers
3500 Maple Avenue, 17th floor
Dallas, Texas 75219
800.872.6467

ABSENTEE BIDS BY FAX
Deadline: Friday, March 18, 2005
12:00 noon CT • fax: 214.443.8425

LIVE TELEPHONE BIDDING
Must be arranged on or before Friday, March 18, 2005
800.872.6467 • Customer Service Dept. (ext. 150)

AUCTION SESSIONS
Session I
Sunday Morning, March 20, 2005 at 10:00 AM CT
Lots 30001 — 30426

Session II
Sunday, March 20, 2005, approx. 2:00 PM CT
Lots 30427 — 30977

AUCTIONEERS
Sam Foose, TX License #00011727
Leo Frese, John Petty, Scott Peterson

AUCTION RESULTS
Immediately available at: HeritageGalleries.com

ABSENTEE BIDS BY INTERNET
www.HeritageGalleries.com
bid@HeritageGalleries.com
Internet bidding closes at 10:00 PM CT
Saturday, March 19, 2005

LOT PICK UP
Lot pickup Monday, March 21, 2005 9:00 AM — 5:00 PM, by appointment only

Catered meals will be served on Sunday
Lots are sold at an approximate rate of 80 — 100 lots per hour
View lots online at HeritageGalleries.com

HERITAGE
Galleries & Auctioneers

3500 Maple Avenue, 17th Floor • Dallas, Texas 75219-3941
214.528.3500 • 800.872.6467 • 214.443.8425 (fax)

Catalogued by: Bryan Abbott, Stuart R. Lee, Elaine Miller and Don Darnell • Edited by: Deborah Scott
Production and Design by: Mandy Bottoms, Cindy Brenner, Carlos Cardoza, Keith Craker, Cathy Hadd, Mary Hermann,
Matt Pegues, Michael Puttonen, Marsha Taylor and Carl Watson
Catalog and Internet Imaging by: Lucas Garritson, Jamie Graham, Steve Robinson, Collette Warren and Tony Webb
with thanks to Reyne Haines and Danny Gipson for their expertise in vetting this auction
and special thanks to Karen Fedri

Steve Ivy
CEO
*Co-Chairman
of the Board*

Jim Halperin
*Co-Chairman
of the Board*

Greg Rohan
President

Bryan Abbott
Director

Lucas Rigby
Consignments

Jared Green
*Vice President
Business Development*

Ed Jaster
Consignments

HERITAGE
Galleries & Auctioneers

3500 Maple Avenue, 17h Floor
Dallas, Texas 75219-3941
214.528.3500 • 800.872.6467 • 214.443.8425 (fax)

HERITAGE
Galleries & Auctioneers

Dear Fellow Collector:

I'm truly excited about this, our latest auction of exquisite art glass. There are some magnificent pieces in this sale, pieces I'm sure you are going to want to add to your own collection.

The majority of this sale features material from the collection of Dorothy Talbert. "Dot," a well-known collector and dealer since 1971, and proprietor of **Show and Tell Antiques** of Waco, Texas, has amassed an impressive collection of art glass. Looking through this catalog, I'm sure you will see the love and care that went into the selection of each piece in the collection. It's a collection that was clearly put together by someone with an eye for quality and a love for art glass.

If I had to chose just a few favorites out of the entire collection, I think that the internally-decorated Tiffany Studios floral paperweight vase would be right up there at the top of my list. A piece that is as important as it is beautiful, this would certainly be the highlight of any quality collection.

Another outstanding piece is the signed Thomas Webb & Sons Oriental motif carved rock crystal vase. Again, beauty and significance wrapped up in one piece. How could you go wrong?

Of course, I wouldn't want to overlook the rare Muller art nouveau form pitcher with an orange and metallic autumn leaf theme, or the selection of Royal Copenhagen's Flora Danica porcelain, including an oval covered soup tureen and underplate. I'm sure you will agree that these lovely pieces are truly worthy of your time and consideration.

Whatever your collecting interests, I believe you will find something in this catalog to tempt you. Of course, if there is ever any way in which I can assist you in your collecting pursuits, please feel free to contact me.

Best regards,

Bryan Abbott
Director of Antiques and Decorative Arts
Heritage Galleries & Auctioneers

Terms and Conditions of Sale

AUCTIONEER AND AUCTION:

1. This auction is presented by Heritage Numismatic Auctions. Inc. or its subsidiary Currency Auctions of America, Inc. or their affiliate, Heritage Auctions, Inc. through its divisions Heritage Comic Auctions, or Heritage Sports Collectibles Auctions, as identified with the applicable licensing information either on the title page of the catalog or on the Internet site (the "Auctioneer"). The auction is conducted under these Terms and Conditions of Auction and applicable state and local law.

BUYER'S PREMIUM:

2. On bids placed through Heritage, a Buyer's Premium of fifteen percent (15%) for Heritage Numismatic Auctions Inc, Heritage-CAA, Heritage-Slater Americana and Heritage Comics Auctions or nineteen and one-half percent (19.5%) for Heritage Sports Collectibles, Heritage-Odyssey and Heritage Galleries & Auctioneers of the hammer price will be added to the successful bid. If the bid is placed through eBay Live a Buyer's Premium equal to the normal Buyer's Premium plus an additional five percent (5%) of the hammer price will be added to the successful bid. There is a minimum Buyer's Premium of $9.00 per lot.

AUCTION VENUES:

3. Exclusively Internet, CurrencyAuction.com, Amazing Comics Auctions, and Bullet Auctions are auctions conducted on the Internet. Signature auctions accept bids on the Internet first, followed by a floor bidding session. Bids may be placed prior to the floor bidding session by Internet, telephone, fax, or mail.

BIDDERS:

4. Any person participating in or who registers for the auction agrees to be bound by and accepts these Terms and Conditions of Auction ("Bidder(s)").
5. All Bidders must meet Auctioneer's qualifications to bid. Any Bidder who is not a customer in good standing of the Auctioneer may be disqualified at Auctioneer's sole option and will not be awarded lots. Such a determination may be made by Auctioneer in its sole and unlimited discretion, at any time prior to, during, or even after the close of the auction.
6. If an entity places a bid, then the person executing the bid on behalf of the entity agrees to personally guarantee payment for any successful bid.
7. Auctioneer reserves the right to exclude any person it deems in its sole opinion is disruptive to the auction or is otherwise commercially unsuitable.

CREDIT REFERENCES:

8. Bidders who do not have established credit with the Auctioneer must either furnish satisfactory credit information including two collectibles-related references well in advance of the auction date or supply valid credit card information. All Bidders must meet Auctioneer's qualifications to bid. Any Bidder who is not a customer in good standing at Auctioneer may be disqualified and will not be awarded lots. Auctioneer reserves the right to disqualify any Bidder even after the close of the auction. Bids placed through our Interactive Internet program will only be accepted from pre-registered Bidders. Bidders who are not members of HeritageGalleries.com should pre-register at least two business days before the first session to allow adequate time to contact references.

BIDDING OPTIONS:

9. Bids may be placed for a Signature Sale as set forth in the printed catalog section entitled "Choose your bidding method." For Exclusively Internet, CurrencyAuction. Com, Amazing Comics Auctions, and Bullet auctions see the alternatives shown on each website. Review at HeritageCoin.com/Auctions/howtobid.asp.
10. The Auctioneer cannot be responsible for your errors in bidding, so carefully check that your bid is entered correctly. When identical mail or FAX bids are submitted, preference is given to the first received; Internet bids are evaluated as received first. The decision of the Auctioneer and declaration of the winning Bidder is final. The Auctioneer is not responsible for executing mail bids or FAX bids received on or after the day the first lot is sold, nor Internet bids submitted after the published closing time; nor is the Auctioneer responsible for proper execution of bids submitted by telephone, mail, FAX, e-mail, Internet, or in person once the auction begins. To ensure the greatest accuracy, your written bids should be entered on the standard bid sheet form and be received at the Auctioneer's place of business at least two business days in advance of the auction date. Internet bids may not be withdrawn until your written request is received and acknowledged by Auctioneer (FAX: 214-443-8425); such requests must state the reason, and may constitute grounds for withdrawal of bidding privileges. Lots won by mail Bidders will not be delivered at the auction unless prearranged in advance. Bid increments determine the lowest amount you may bid on a particular lot. Normally, bids must be at least one bidding increment over the current bid, although podium, fax and mail bidders submit bids at various times without knowing the current bid and may be as little as one dollar over another bid. However, these increments only apply to the current bid. Bids greater than one increment over the current bid can be any whole dollar amount. It is possible under several circumstances for winning bids to be between increments, sometimes only $1 above the previous increment.

CONDUCTING THE AUCTION:

11. Notice of the consignor's liberty to place reserve bids on his lots in the auction is hereby made in accordance with Article 2 of the Texas Uniform Commercial Code. A reserve is an amount below which the lot will not sell. THE CONSIGNOR OF PROPERTY MAY PLACE WRITTEN RESERVE BIDS ON HIS LOTS IN ADVANCE OF THE AUCTION. ON LOTS SUBJECT TO A RESERVE, IF THE LOT DOES NOT MEET THE RESERVE THE CONSIGNOR MAY PAY A REDUCED COMMISSION ON THOSE LOTS. Reserves are generally posted online about 3 days prior to the auction closing on Internet-Only auctions, and 7 days prior to the auction on Signature auctions. IF THERE IS AN UNMET RESERVE BID POSTED ON A LOT, THE CURRENT BID DISPLAYED ONLINE WILL AUTOMATICALLY BE SET AT ONE INCREMENT BELOW THE RESERVE BID. The Auctioneer will not knowingly accept (and reserves the right to reject) live telephone or floor bids from consignors. Any successful bid placed by a consignor on his consigned lot on the auction floor or by telephone during the live session, or after the reserves for an auction have been posted, will be considered an unqualified bid, and in such instances the consignor agrees to pay full Buyer's Premium and Seller's Commissions on the lot(s) even if (s)he buys them back.
12. The highest qualified Bidder shall be the buyer. In the event of any dispute between floor Bidders at a Signature Sale, the Auctioneer may at his sole discretion put the lot up for auction again. The Auctioneer's decision shall be final and binding upon all Bidders.
13. The Auctioneer reserves the right to refuse to honor any bid or to limit the amount of any bid which, in his sole discretion, is not submitted in "Good Faith," or is not supported by satisfactory credit, numismatic references, or otherwise. A bid is considered not made in "Good Faith" when an insolvent or irresponsible person, or a person under the age of eighteen makes it. Regardless of the disclosure of his identity, any bid by a consignor or his agent on a lot consigned by him is deemed to be made in "Good Faith".
14. All items are to be purchased per lot as numerically indicated and no lots will be broken. The Auctioneer reserves the right to withdraw, prior to the close, any lot or lots from the auction. Bids will be accepted in whole dollar amounts only.
15. No "buy" or "unlimited" bids will be accepted. Bidders will be awarded lots at approximately the increment of the next highest bid. No additional commission is charged for executing bids other than the Buyer's Premium applied to all successful bids. Off-increment bids may be accepted by the Auctioneer at Signature auctions.
16. Estimates will be given upon written request. It is recommended that Bidders approach or exceed the estimates in order to increase the chances of bidding successfully.
17. Auctioneer reserves the right to rescind the sale in the event of nonpayment, breach of a warranty, disputed ownership, auctioneer's clerical error or omission in exercising bids and reserves, or otherwise.
18. Outage Policy: Auctioneer occasionally experiences Internet and/or Server outages during which Bidders cannot participate or place bids. If such outage occurs, we may at our discretion extend bidding for the auction up to 24 hours. At our discretion, Auctioneer may consider two outages that occur very closely to one another to be one outage when extending such auction. This policy applies only to widespread outages and not to isolated problems that occur in various parts of the country from time to time.
19. Scheduled Downtime: Auctioneer periodically schedules system downtime for maintenance and other purposes; this scheduled downtime is not covered by the Outage Policy.
20. The Auctioneer or its affiliates may consign items to be sold in the auction sale, and may bid on those items or any other items in the sale. The Auctioneer or affiliates expressly reserve the right to modify any such reserve bids on these items or any others at any time prior to the live auction or the online closing based upon data made known to the Auctioneer or its affiliate.
21. The Auctioneer may extend advances, guarantees, or loans to certain consignors, and may extend financing or other credits at varying rates to certain Bidders in the auction.

PAYMENT:

22. All sales are strictly for cash in United States dollars. Cash includes: U.S. currency, bank wire, cashier checks, travelers checks, and bank money orders, all subject to reporting requirements. Credit Card (Visa or Master Card only) payments may be accepted up to $10,000 from non-dealers at the sole discretion of the auctioneer, subject to the following limitations: a) sales are only to the cardholder, b) purchases are shipped to the cardholder's registered and verified address, c) Auctioneer may preapprove the cardholder's credit line, d) a credit card transaction may not be used in conjunction with any other financing or extended terms offered by the Auctioneer, and must transact immediately upon invoice presentation, e) rights of return are governed by these Terms and Conditions, which supersede those conditions promulgated by the card issuer, f) floor Bidders must present their card. Personal or corporate checks may be subject to clearing before delivery of the purchases.
23. Payment is due upon closing of the auction session, or upon presentment of an invoice. The Auctioneer reserves the right to void a sale if payment in full of the invoice is not received within 7 days after the close of the auction.
24. Lots delivered in the States of Texas, California, or other states where the auction may be held, are subject to all applicable state and local taxes, unless appropriate permits are on file with us. In the event that sales tax is not properly collected due to an expired, inaccurate, inappropriate tax certificate or declaration or any other reason, bidder agrees to pay Auctioneer the actual amount of tax due. Lots from different auctions may not be aggregated for sales tax purposes.
25. In the event that a Bidder's payment is dishonored upon presentment(s), Bidder shall pay the maximum statutory processing fee set by applicable state law.
26. If the Auctioneer invoice(s) submitted by the Auctioneer is not paid in full when due, the unpaid balance will bear interest at the highest rate permitted by law from the date of invoice until paid. If the Auctioneer refers the invoice(s) to an attorney for collection, the buyer agrees to pay attorney's fees, court costs, and other collection costs incurred by the Auctioneer. If Auctioneer assigns collection to its in-house legal staff, such attorney's time expended on the matter shall be compensated at a rate comparable to the hourly rate of independent attorneys.
27. In the event a successful Bidder fails to pay all amounts due, the Auctioneer reserves the right to resell the merchandise, and such Bidder agrees to pay for the reasonable costs of resale, including a 10% seller's commission, and also to pay any difference between the resale price and the price of the previously successful bid.
28. The Auctioneer reserves the right to require payment in full in good funds before delivery of the merchandise to the buyer.
29. The Auctioneer shall have a lien against the merchandise purchased by the buyer to secure payment of the auction invoice. Auctioneer is further granted a lien and the right to retain possession of any other property of the buyer then held by the Auctioneer or its affiliates to secure payment of any auction invoice or any other amounts due the Auctioneer from the buyer. With respect to these lien rights, the Auctioneer shall have all the rights of a secured creditor under Article 9 of the Texas Uniform Commercial Code. In addition, with respect to payment of the auction invoice(s), the buyer waives any and all rights of offset he might otherwise have against the Auctioneer and the consignor of the merchandise included on the invoice.
30. If a Bidder owes Auctioneer or its affiliates on any account, the Auctioneer and its affiliates shall have the right to offset such unpaid account by any credit balance due Bidder, and it may secure by possessory lien any unpaid amount by any of the Bidder's property in their possession.
31. Title shall not pass to the successful Bidder until all invoices are paid in full. It is the responsibility of the buyer to provide adequate insurance coverage for the items once they have been delivered.

RETURN POLICY:

A. MEMORABILIA

32A. A MEMORABILIA lot (Autographs, Sports Collectibles, or Music, Entertainment, Political, Americana and/or Pop Culture memorabilia) when the lot is accompanied by a Certificate of Authenticity, or its equivalent, from an independent third party authentication provider, has no right of return. Under extremely limited circumstances, not including authenticity (e.g. gross cataloging error), a purchaser, who did not bid from the floor, may request Auctioneer to void a sale. Such request for evaluation must be made in writing detailing the alleged gross error, and submission of the lot to the Auctioneer must be pre-approved by the Auctioneer. A bidder must notify the appropriate department head (check the inside front cover of the catalog or our website for a listing of department heads) in writing of the purchaser's request and such notice must be mailed within three (3) days of the mail bidder's receipt of the lot. Any lot that is to be evaluated for return must be received in our offices with 30 days. AFTER THAT 30 DAY PERIOD, NO LOT MAY BE RETURNED FOR ANY REASONS. Lots returned must be in the same condition as when sold and must include the Certificate of Authenticity, if any. No lots purchased by floor bidders may be returned (including those bidders acting as agents for others). Late remittance for purchases may be considered just cause to revoke all return privileges.

B. COINS, CURRENCY, COMICS AND SPORTSCARDS

32B. COINS, CURRENCY, COMICS AND SPORTSCARDS Signature Sales: The auction is not on approval. No certified material may be returned because of possible differences of opinion with respect to the grade offered by any third-party organization, dealer, or service. There are absolutely no exceptions to this policy. Under extremely limited circumstances, (e.g. gross cataloging error) a purchaser, who did not bid from the floor, may request Auctioneer to void a sale. Such request for evaluation must be made in writing detailing the alleged gross error, and submission of the lot to the Auctioneer must be pre-approved by the Auctioneer. A bidder must notify Ron Brackemyre, (ext. 312) in writing of the bidder's request and such notice must be mailed within three (3) days of the mail bidder's receipt of the lot. Any lot that is to be evaluated must be in our offices within 30 days. Grading or method of manufacture do not qualify for this evaluation process nor do such complaints constitute a basis to challenge the authenticity of a lot. AFTER THAT 30-DAY PERIOD, NO LOTS MAY BE RETURNED FOR REASONS OTHER THAN AUTHENTICITY. Lots returned must be housed intact in the original holder. No lots purchased by floor Bidders may be returned (including those Bidders acting as agents for others). Late remittance for purchases may be considered just cause to revoke all return privileges.

33. Exclusively Internet, CurrencyAuction.com, Amazing Comics Auctions™ and Bullet auctions: THREE (3) DAY RETURN POLICY. All lots (Exception: Third party graded notes are not returnable for any

reason whatsoever) paid for within seven days of the auction closing are sold with a three (3) day return privilege. You may return lots under the following conditions: Within three days of receipt of the lot, you must first notify Auctioneer by contacting Customer Service by phone (1-800-872-6467) or e-mail (Bid@HeritageGalleries.com), and immediately mail the lot(s) fully insured to the attention of Returns, Heritage, 3500 Maple Avenue, 17th Floor, Dallas TX 75219-3941. Lots must be housed intact in their original holder and condition. You are responsible for the insured, safe delivery of any lots. A non-negotiable return fee of 5% of the purchase price ($10 per lot minimum) will be deducted from the refund for each returned lot or billed directly. Postage and handling fees are not refunded. After the three-day period (from receipt), no items may be returned for any reason. Late remittance for purchases revokes all Return-Restock privileges.

34. All Bidders who have inspected the lots prior to the auction will not be granted any return privileges, except for reasons of authenticity.

DELIVERY:

35. Postage, handling and insurance charges will be added to invoices. Please either refer to Auctioneer's web site HeritageGalleries.com for the latest charges or call Auctioneer.

COMPLETE SHIPPING AND HANDLING CHARGES:

36. Auctioneer is unable to combine purchases from other auctions or Heritage Rare Coin Galleries into one package for shipping purposes. Successful overseas Bidders shall provide written shipping instructions, including specified customs declarations, to the Auctioneer for any lots to be delivered outside of the United States.
37. All shipping charges will be borne by the successful Bidder. Any risk of loss during shipment will be borne by the buyer following Auctioneer's delivery to the designated common carrier.
38. Regardless of domestic or foreign shipment, risk of loss shall be borne by the buyer following Auctioneer's delivery to a shipper.
39. Any claims for undelivered packages must be made within 30 days of shipment by the auctioneer.
40. In the event an item is damaged either through handling or in transit, the Auctioneer's maximum liability shall be the amount of the successful bid including the Buyer's Premium.

CATALOGING:

41. The descriptions provided in any catalog are intended solely for the use of those Bidders who do not have the opportunity to view the lots prior to bidding.
42. Any description of the lots contained in this auction is for the sole purpose of identifying the items.
43. In the event of an attribution error, the Auctioneer may, at the Auctioneer's sole discretion, correct the error on the Internet, or, if discovered at a later date, to refund the buyer's money without further obligation. Under no circumstances shall the obligation of the Auctioneer to any Bidder be in excess of the purchase price for any lot in dispute.

WARRANTIES AND DISCLAIMERS:

44. NO WARRANTY, WHETHER EXPRESSED OR IMPLIED, IS MADE WITH RESPECT TO ANY DESCRIPTION CONTAINED IN THIS AUCTION. Any description of the items contained in this auction is for the sole purpose of identifying the items, and no description of items has been made part of the basis of the bargain or has created any express warranty that the goods would conform to any description made by the Auctioneer.
45. Auctioneer is selling only such right or title to the items being sold as Auctioneer may have by virtue of consignment agreements on the date of auction and disclaims any warranty of title to the coins.
46. Auctioneer disclaims any warranty of merchantability or fitness for any particular purposes.
47. Auctioneer disclaims all liability for damages, consequential or otherwise, arising out of or in connection with the sale of any property by Auctioneer to Bidder. No third party may rely on any benefit of these Terms and Conditions and any rights, if any, established hereunder are personal to the Bidder and may not be assigned. Any statement made by the Auctioneer is a statement of opinion and does not constitute a warranty or representation. Any employee of Auctioneer may not alter these Terms and Conditions, and, unless signed by a principal of Auctioneer, any alteration is null and void.
48A. COINS, CURRENCY, COMICS AND SPORTSCARDS – Coins sold referencing a third-party grading service ("Certified Coins") are sold "as is" without any express or implied warranty, except for a guarantee by Auctioneer that the Certified Coins are genuine. Certain warranties may be available from the grading services and the Bidder is referred to the following services for details of any such warranties: ANACS, P.O. Box 182141, Columbus, Ohio 43218-2141; Numismatic Guaranty Corporation (NGC), P.O. Box 4776, Sarasota, FL 34230; Professional Coin Grading Service (PCGS), PO Box 9458, Newport Beach, CA 92658 and ICG, 7901 East Belleview Ave., Suite 50, Englewood, CO 80111. Comic books sold referencing a third-party grading service ("Certified Comics") are sold "as is" without any express or implied warranty, except for a guarantee by Auctioneer that the Certified Comics are genuine. Certain warranties may be available from the grading services and the Bidder is referred to the following services for details of any such warranties: Comics Guaranty Corporation (CGC), P.O. Box 4738, Sarasota, FL 34230. Sportscards sold referencing a third-party grading service ("Certified Sportscards") are sold "as is" without any express or implied warranty, except for a guarantee by Auctioneer that the Certified Sportscards are genuine. Certain warranties may be available from the grading services and the Bidder is referred to the following services for details of any such warranties: Professional Sports Authenticator (PSA), P.O. Box 6180 Newport Beach, CA 92658; Sportscard Guaranty LLC (SGC) P.O. Box 6919 Parsippany, NJ 07054-6919; Global Authentication (GAI), P.O. Box 57042 Irvine, Ca. 92619; Beckett Grading Service (BGS), 15850 Dallas Parkway, Dallas TX 75248. Currency sold referencing a third-party grading service ("Certified Currency") are sold "as is" without any express or implied warranty, except for a guarantee by Auctioneer that the Certified Currency are genuine. Certain warranties may be available from the grading services and the Bidder is referred to the following services for details of any such warranties: Currency Grading & Authentication (CGA), PO Box 418, Three Bridges, NJ 08887.
48B. MEMORABILIA – Auctioneer does not warrant authenticity of a memorabilia lot (Autographs, Sports Collectibles, or Music, Entertainment, Political, Americana and/or Pop Culture memorabilia), when the lot is accompanied by a Certificate of Authenticity, or its equivalent, from an independent third party authentication provider. Bidder shall solely rely upon warranties of the authentication provider issuing the Certificate or opinion. For information as to such authentication provider's warranties the bidder is directed to: SCD Authentic, 4034 West National Ave., Milwaukee, WI 53215 (800) 345-3168; JO Sports, Inc., P.O. Box 607 Brookhaven, NY 11719 (631) 286-0970; PSA/DNA; 130 Brookshire Lane, Orwigsburg, Pa. 17961; Mike Gutierrez Autographs, 8150 Raintree Drive Suite A, Scottsdale, AZ. 85260; or as otherwise noted on the Certificate.
49. All non-certified coins and comics and currency are guaranteed genuine, but are not guaranteed as to grade, since grading is a matter of opinion. Grading is an art, not a science, and therefore the opinion rendered by the Auctioneer or any third party grading service may not agree with the opinion of others (including trained experts), and the same expert may not grade the same coin with the same grade at two different times. Auctioneer has graded the non-certified items, in the Auctioneer's opinion, to their current interpretation of the American Numismatic Association's standards as of the date the catalog was prepared. There is no guarantee or warranty implied or expressed that the grading standards utilized by the Auctioneer will meet the standards of ANACS, NGC, PCGS, ICG, CGC, CGA or any other grading service at any time in the future.
50. Auctioneer offers no opinion as to the validity of a grade assigned by any third-party grading service. Since we cannot examine C.G.A. encapsulated notes or Comics Guaranty Corporation (CGC) encapsulated comics, they are sold "as is" without our grading opinion, and may not be returned for any reason. Auctioneer shall not be liable for any patent or latent defect or controversy pertaining to or arising from any encapsulated collectible. In any such instance, purchaser's remedy, if any, shall be solely against the certification service certifying the collectible.
51. Due to changing grading standards over time and to possible mishandling of items by subsequent owners, the Auctioneer reserves the right to grade items differently than shown on certificates from any grading service that accompany the items. For the same reasons as stated above, the Auctioneer reserves the right to grade items differently than the grades shown in the catalog should such items be reconsigned to any future auction.
52. Although consensus grading is employed by most grading services, it should be noted as aforesaid that grading is not an exact science. In fact, it is entirely possible that if a lot was broken out of a plastic holder and was resubmitted to another grading service or even the same service, the lot could come back a different grade. Certification does not guarantee protection against the normal risks associated with potentially volatile markets.
53. The degree of liquidity for certified coins and collectibles will vary according to general market conditions and the particular lot involved. For some lots there may be no active market at all at certain points in time.

RELEASE:

54. In consideration of participation in the auction and the placing of a bid, a Bidder expressly releases Auctioneer, its affiliates, the Consignor, or Owner of the Lot from any and all claims, cause of action, chose of action, whether at law or equity or any arbitration or mediation rights existing under the rules of any professional society or affiliation based upon the assigned grade or a derivative theory, breach of warranty express or implied, representation or other matter set forth within these Terms and Conditions of Auction or otherwise, except as specifically declared herein; e.g., authenticity, typographical error, etc., and as to those matters, the rights and privileges conferred therein are strictly construed and is the exclusive remedy. Purchaser by non-compliance to its express terms of a granted remedy, shall waive any claim against Auctioneer.

DISPUTE RESOLUTION AND ARBITRATION PROVISION:

55. By placing a bid or otherwise participating in the auction, such person or entity accepts these Terms and Conditions of Auction, and specifically agrees to the alternative dispute resolution provided herein. Arbitration replaces the right to go to court, including the right to a jury trial.
56A. COINS & CURRENCY; If any disputes arise regarding payment, authenticity, grading or any other matter pertaining to the auction, the Bidder or a participant in the auction and/or the Auctioneer agree that the dispute shall be submitted, if otherwise mutually unresolved, to binding arbitration in accordance with the rules of the Professional Numismatists Guild (PNG) or American Arbitration Association (A.A.A.). The A.a.a. arbitration shall be conducted under the provisions of the Federal Arbitration Act with locale in Dallas, Texas. If an election is not made within ten (10) days of an unresolved dispute, Auctioneer may elect either PNG or A.A.A. Arbitration. Any claim made by a Bidder has to be presented within one (1) year or it is barred. An award granted in arbitration is enforceable in any court. No claims of any kind (except for reasons of authenticity) can be considered after the settlements have been made with the consignors. Any dispute after the settlement date is strictly between the Bidder and consignor without involvement or responsibility of the Auctioneer.
56B. ALL OTHER AUCTIONS; If any dispute arises regarding payment, authenticity, grading, description, provenance or any other material pertaining to the auction, the Bidder or the participant in the auction and/or the Auctioneer agree that the dispute shall be submitted, if otherwise mutually unresolved, to unbinding arbitration in accordance with the commercial rules of the American Arbitration Association (A.A.A.). The A.A.A. arbitration shall be conducted under the provisions of the Federal Arbitration Act with locale in Dallas, Texas. The prevailing party may be awarded his reasonable attorney's fees and costs. An arbitrator's award is enforceable in any court of competent jurisdiction. Any claim made by a Bidder has to be presented within one (1) year or it is barred. Any claim as to provenance or authenticity must be first transmitted to Auctioneer by credible and definitive evidence and there is no assurance such presentment that Auctioneer will validate the claim. Authentication is not an exact science and other contrary opinions may not be recognized by Auctioneer. Auctioneer in no event shall be responsible for consequential and incidental damages and the value of any item is determined by its high bid, which is Auctioneer's maximum liability. Provenance and authenticity are not guaranteed by the Auctioneer, but rather are guaranteed by the consignor. Any action or claim shall include the consignor with Auctioneer acting as interpleador or nominal party. While every effort is made to determine provenance and authenticity, it is up to the Bidder to arrive at that conclusion prior to bidding.
57. In consideration of his participation in or application for the auction, a person or entity (whether the successful Bidder, a Bidder, a purchaser and/or other Auction participant or registrant) agrees, that all disputes in any way relating to, arising under, connected with, or incidental to these Terms and Conditions and his purchases or default in payment thereof shall be arbitrated pursuant to the arbitration provision. In the event that any matter including actions to compel arbitration, construe the agreement, actions in aid or arbitration or otherwise needs to be litigated, such litigation shall be exclusively in the Courts of the State of Texas, in Dallas County, Texas, and if necessary the corresponding appellate courts. The successful Bidder, purchaser, or Auction participant also expressly submits himself to the personal jurisdiction of the State of Texas.

MISCELLANEOUS:

58. Agreements between Bidders and consignors to effectuate a non-sale of an item at auction, inhibit bidding on a consigned item to enter into a private sale agreement for an item, or to utilize the Auctioneer's auction to obtain sales for non-selling consigned items subsequent to the auction are strictly prohibited. If a subsequent sale of a previously consigned item occurs in violation of this provision, Auctioneer reserves the right to charge Bidder the applicable Buyer's Premium and consignor a Seller's Commission as determined for each auction venue and by the terms of the seller's agreement.

59. Acceptance of these terms and conditions qualifies Bidder as a Heritage customer who has consented to be contacted by Heritage in the future. In conformity with "do-not-call" regulations promulgated by the Federal or State regulatory agencies, participation by the Bidder is affirmative consent to being contacted at the phone number shown in his application and this consent shall remain in effect until it is revoked in writing. Heritage may from time to time contact Bidder concerning sale, purchase and auction opportunities available through Heritage and its affiliates and subsidiaries.

60. Storage of purchased coins: Purchasers are advised that certain types of plastic may react with the coin's metal and may cause damage to the coins. Caution should be used to avoid storage of coins in materials that are not inert.

STATE NOTICES:

61. Notice as to an Auction Sale in California. Auctioneer has in compliance with Title 2.95 of the California Civil Code as amended October 11, 1993 Sec. 1812.600, posted with the California Secretary of State its bonds for it and its employees and the auction is being conducted in compliance with Sec. 2338 of the Commercial Code and Sec. 535 of the Penal Code.

Rev. 1/25/05

Choose Your Bidding Method

Mail Bidding At Auction

Mail bidding at auction is fun and easy and only requires a few simple steps.

1. Look through the catalog, and determine the lots of interest.
2. Research their market value by checking price lists and other price guidelines.
3. Fill out your bid sheet, entering your maximum bid on each lot using your price research and your desire to own the lot.
4. Verify your bids!
5. Mail Early. Preference is given to the first bids received in case of a tie. When bidding by mail, you frequently purchase lots at less than your maximum bid.

Bidding is opened at the published increment above the second highest mail or Internet bid; we act on your behalf as the highest mail bidder. If bidding proceeds, we act as your agent, bidding in increments over the previous bid. This process is continued until you are awarded the lot or you are outbid.

An example of this procedure: You submit a bid of $100, and the second highest mail bid is at $50. Bidding starts at $51 on your behalf. If no other bids are submitted, you purchase the lot for $51. If other bids are placed, we bid for you in the posted increments until we reach your maximum bid of $100. If bidding passes your maximum: if you are bidding through the Internet, we will contact you by e-mail; if you bid by mail, we take no other action. Bidding continues until the highest bidder wins.

Auction #614

Interactive Internet™ Bidding

You can now bid with Heritage's exclusive Interactive Internet™ program, available only at our web site: www.heritagegalleries.com. It's fun, and it's easy!

1. Register on-line at http://www.heritagegalleries.com/common/register.php.
2. View the full-color photography of every single lot in the on-line catalog!
3. Construct your own personal catalog for preview.
4. View the current opening bids on lots you want; review prices realized archive.
5. Bid and receive immediate notification if you are the top bidder; later, if someone else bids higher, you will be notified automatically by e-mail.
6. The Interactive Internet program opens the lot on the floor at one increment over the second highest bid. As the high bidder, your secret maximum bid will compete for you during the floor auction, and it is possible that you may be outbid on the floor after internet bidding closes. Bid early, as the earliest bid wins in the event of a tie bid.
7. After the sale, you will be notified of your success.

It's that easy!

Telephone Bidding

To participate by telephone, please make arrangements at least one week before the sale date by calling our Customer Service Department at 1-800-872-6467.

We strongly recommend that you place preliminary bids by mail, Fax, or Internet, even if you intend to participate by telephone. On many occasions this dual approach has helped reduce disappointments due to telephone problems, unexpected travel, late night sessions and time zone differences, etc. We will make sure that you do not bid against yourself.

Condition Reports

Bidders may be interested in specific information not included in the catalog description of an item. Upon written request Heritage will, time permitted, as a service to our clients, attempt to provide additional information on any lot in this sale for the guidance and convenience of the bidder. Heritage may not be able to respond to all requests. Please note Condition Reports are written opinions of the sale catalogers describing the condition of property noting their opinions of damage or restoration of an item. Condition Reports are not to be relied on as statements of fact, representations, warranties or our assumption of any liability of any kind. Condition Reports do not extend the Limited Warranties provided in the catalog. Regardless of the issuance of a Condition Report, all bidders are reminded that each lot is sold "As Is". It is the bidder's responsibility to either personally evaluate each lot or have a knowledgeable consultant inspect the lot on the bidder's behalf. A reference to specific condition issues does not imply the lot is free from defects or the absence of other condition issues such as but not limited to age, wear, damage, restoration, alterations, or imperfections created during the making of the object.

1. **Name, Address, City, State, Zip**

   Your address is needed to mail your purchases. We need your telephone number to communicate any problems or changes that may affect your bids.

2. **References**

   If you have not established credit with us from previous auctions, you must send a 25% deposit, or list dealers with whom you have credit established.

3. **Lot Numbers and Bids**

   List all lots you desire to purchase. On the reverse are additional columns, you may also use another sheet. Under "Amount" enter the maximum you would pay for that lot (whole dollar amounts only). We will purchase the lot(s) for you as much below your bids as possible.

4. **Total Bid Sheet**

   Add up all bids and list that total in the appropriate box.

5. **Sign Your Bid Sheet**

   By signing the bid sheet, you have agreed to abide by the Terms of Sale listed in the auction catalog.

6. **Fax Your Bid Sheet**

   When time is short submit a Mail Bid Sheet on our exclusive Fax Hotline. There's no faster method to get your bids to us instantly. Simply use the **Heritage Fax Hotline number 214-443-8425**.

   When you send us your original after faxing, mark it "Confirmation of Fax" (preferably in red!)

MAIL/FAX BID SHEET

HERITAGE *Galleries & Auctioneers*

Heritage Galleries & Auctioneers
1-800-872-6467
3500 Maple Avenue
Dallas, TX 75219-3941
(All information must be completed.)

HG&A Auction
Submit Your Bids By Fax
FAX HOTLINE: 214-443-8425

NAME: WILLIAM STARK   CUSTOMER # (if known): _____
ADDRESS: 4739 - B BRADFORD DRIVE
CITY/STATE/ZIP: DALLAS, TX 75219
DAYTIME PHONE: (214) 555-8109   EVENING PHONE: (214) 528-3500
YOUR E-MAIL ADDRESS: _____
(E-MAIL bids MUST be sent to Bid@HeritageGalleries.com) Would you like a FAX or e-mail confirming receipt of your bids? If so, please print your FAX # or e-mail address here: _____
REFERENCES: New bidders who are unknown to us must furnish satisfactory trade references or a credit card in advance of the sale date.

Dealer References (City, State)
DESIGNS BY DAVID
SMITH'S FINE PAINTINGS

(Bid in whole dollar amounts only.) You are authorized to release payment history information to other dealers and auctioneers so that I may establish proper credit in the industry. (Line out this statement if you do not authorize release).

LOT NO.	AMOUNT	LOT NO.	AMOUNT	LOT NO.	AMOUNT	LOT NO.	AMOUNT
143	200	3210	325				
221	75						
1621	125						
2416	625						

PLEASE COMPLETE THIS INFORMATION:

1. IF NECESSARY, PLEASE INCREASE MY BIDS BY:
   ☑ 10% ☐ 20% ☐ 30% ☐ 50%
   Lots will be purchased as much below bids as possible.

2. ☐ I HAVE BOUGHT ANTIQUES/ART FROM YOU BEFORE (references are listed above)

William Stark
(Signature required) Please make a copy of your bid sheet for your records.

On all successful bids, I agree to pay an additional twenty percent (20%) Buyer's Premium and all mailing and shipping charges. I have read and agree to all of the Terms and Conditions of Sale: inclusive of paying interest at the lesser of 1.5% per month (18% per annum) or the maximum contract interest rate under applicable state law from the date of sale (if the account is not timely paid), and the submission of disputes to arbitration.

REV. 4/26/04

SUBTOTAL: 1475
TOTAL from other side: _____
TOTAL BID: 1475

SEE OTHER SIDE

The official prices realized list that accompanies our auction catalogs is reserved for bidders and consignors only. We are happy to mail one to others upon receipt of $1.00. Written requests should be directed to Kathy Eilers.

Dorothy *"Dot"* Talbert

Born in Port Lavaca, Texas in 1920, Dorothy "Dot" Talbert has been a well known and highly respected antiques and art glass dealer for over thirty years.

Dot began as a collector of Early American pattern glass, although her interests in and knowledge about art glass grew over the years until it became her passion. Mrs. R. A. McMurray, a friend and mentor, opened her extensive art glass collection to Dot, and together they poured over books and closely examined each piece, lovingly appreciating the workmanship and artistry involved in producing it. Over the years, Dot built an impressive library for research as her interests and collections changed.

As a new dealer in 1971, Dot set out on the antiques show circuit where she made many dear friends of both dealers and customers alike. In 1976, she opened *Show and Tell Antiques* in an historic mansion in Waco, Texas. The imposing three-story brick Mission-style home was built in 1909 by Robert Lazenby, proprietor of Waco's historic Circle "A" Ginger Ale Company and one of the original developers of the flavoring syrup used in Dr. Pepper. The stately rooms of the mansion have provided a charming setting for many pieces of fine furniture, paintings, and silver, though glass has always been the focus of *Show and Tell Antiques* and Dot's special love. Since Dot retired, the shop continues under the management of her son, Milton Talbert, Jr.

Dot has said many times that she has enjoyed the privilege of being the custodian of many magnificent treasures over the course of her career. Now she says it is time for others to have the joy and pleasure of owning these exquisite works of art.

SESSION ONE

Public-Internet Auction #614

Sunday, March 20, 2005, 10:00 AM, Lots 30001-30426

Dallas, Texas

A 19.5% Buyer's Premium Will Be Added To All Lots

Visit HeritageGalleries.com to view scalable images and bid online.

30001

30002

30001
A CONTINENTAL PORCELAIN PLATTER
B. Block & Co., c.1900

The central image depicts two females in classical dress by water, holding water lilies, cobalt surround with gilt and enamel beading, stamped underside with a beehive mark
13in. diamete
Estimate: 200-400

30002
A PAIR OF CONTINENTAL PORCELAIN FIGURINES
Royal Dux, c.1900

The Asian-styled male and female figures, both individually supported by an oval stepped platform decorated with flowers and gilt trim, the male figure holds a lantern in his right hand, the female holds a fan, both decorated in pale pink and white with flowers, blue sash on male and obi on female, gilt accents overall, the male has a pink porcelain stamp to the underside *Royal Dux Bohemia*, both stamped underside *Royal Dux Czechoslovakia*
20in. high (Total: 2 Items)
Estimate: 300-500

30003

30003
FOUR CONTINENTAL PORCELAIN PLATES
Minton, c.1909

Including a matching set of four Nineteenth-Century Minton desert plates with cerulean blue and gilt banding surrounding the center reserve depicting Highland landscapes with figures, impressed mark underside
9.2in. diameter (Total: 4 Items)
Estimate: 200-400

30004

30004
A FRENCH ORMOLU MOUNTED PORCELAIN VASE
Sèvres, c.1900

The pedestaled vase enameled in pink with gilt and enamel design featuring a woman in a forest scene in Art Nouveau style, floral and gilt design throughout, the vase with bronze handles, rim and pedestal, unsigned
10.1in. high
Estimate: 200-400

30006

30006
A GERMAN PORCELAIN COMPOTE
Von Schierholtz's Porcelain Manufactory, c.1907

The tri-footed to a lattice stemmed scroll pattern stem with a double handled low open work bowl with multicolored floral pattern to the interior, applied pink roses and green leaves to the exterior of the stem and bowl, gilt highlights to the foot, stem, handles and rim, stamped underside
6in. high
Estimate: 100-300

30005

30005
TWO FRENCH PORCELAIN ITEMS
Limoges, c.1890

Including a Theodore Havilland oval double-handled dish with gilded and scalloped rim over delicate rib and floral border in pink and blue centering a small wreath; *together with* a Tresseman & Vogt circular, double-handled bowl with gilded rim, pierced handles and a geometric green border, each piece with *Limoges/France* mark
The largest: 10.5in. diameter (Total: 2 Items)
Estimate: 100-150

30007

30007
TWO ENGLISH AND ONE GERMAN PORCELAIN SERVING PLATTERS
Various makers, c.1890

Comprising an Edge Malkin & Co. ivory ground oval platter with a brown transfer pattern of flowers and leaves; an English flow blue oval white ground platter with a blue pattern of grapes, flowers and scroll, gilt highlights near the rim; and a Villeroy and Boch Mettlach rectangular blue transfer pattern of flowers and ribbon with scroll borders, all stamped underside
The widest: 17.2in. (Total: 3 Items)
Estimate: 200-400

30008

A GERMAN PORCELAIN WHIMSY
Meissen, c.1960

Modeled as a miniature Asian slipper, the white porcelain body embellished with underglaze blue decoration heightened with iron-red, green, yellow, and puce overglaze, the collapsed rim of the slipper and the underglaze blue with gilt highlights, the sand-colored underside with underglaze blue crossed swords Meissen mark
2.1in. high
Estimate: 300-400

30009

FIVE GERMAN PORCELAIN RAMEKINS WITH UNDERLINER
Richard Klemm, Dresden, production 1886-1916

The round white body of each piece scattered with polychrome enamel flowers and bordered in gilt, each piece with blue overglaze mark with crowned *RK*, script *Dresden* and block letter *GERMANY*
1.5in. high (Total: 10 Items)
Estimate: 250-350

30010

A CONTINENTAL PORCELAIN BOWL
KPM, c.1930

The low lattice bowl with rope detail around the foot, decorated with pink roses and leaves to the center, gilt detail to the rim, stamped underside *KPM*
7.5in. diameter
Estimate: 100-200

30011

AN ASSORTED GROUP OF CERAMIC TABLEWARE
Various makers, various dates

The group includes two sets of eight teacups with matching saucers, one stamped Johnson Bros. and the other Staffordshire; eleven octagon-shaped plates stamped Rosenthal Bavaria; ten matching blue and white plates decorated with rabbits, stamped *Copeland Late Spode*; four matching blue and white plates decorated with a harbour scene, the 'Old Salem' pattern, stamped *Copeland Spode England*, and five unmatched plates of various sizes, all stamped underside
The largest: 10.5in. diameter (Total: 62 Items)
Estimate: 50-100

30012

TWO ENGLISH BONE CHINA FIGURINES
Royal Doulton and Royal Worcester, c.1980

Including 'Day Dreams' depicting a seated female with bouquet of red and yellow roses, *together with* 'First Dance' depicting a standing female in white with a maroon shawl, 'Day Dreams' with green *Royal Doulton* mark on underside, 'First Dance' with black *Royal Worcester* mark on underside
The tallest: 7.25in. (Total: 2 Items)
Estimate: 300-500

30013
A CONTINENTAL PORCELAIN VASE
Philip Rosenthal & Co., c.1898

The gilt foot ovoid form to a cylindrical collared neck with a flared rim with gilt loop handles, decorated in light green high-glazed ground with a center panel depicting a classical lady in a pink dress, gilt detail to the neck, central panel and reverse, stamped underside
10.4in. high
Estimate: 100-300

30015
COLLECTION OF BRITISH FLOW BLUE SEMI-PORCELAIN ITEMS
Bishop & Stonier, c.1890

Comprising a footed, covered tureen of flattened oval shape and a diner plate in the 'Sussex' pattern, the underside of the tureen basin and of the plate with underglaze blue mark *covered tureen*
6in. high (Total: 3 Items)
Estimate: 150-250

30016
TWO GERMAN PORCELAIN FIGURINES AND AN AMERICAN FIGURINE
Various makers, c.1920

Comprising two German figurines, a seated male and female in Eighteenth Century dress, both in yellow; an American female figurine of Scarlett in a pink dress with green accents, gilt muff and hat detail, the American figurine stamped underside *Florence Ceramics*
6.2in. high and 9in. high respectively (Total: 3 Items)
Estimate: 200-300

30014
SIX FLOW BLUE PORCELAIN ITEMS
Various makers, various dates

Comprising a Japanese 'blue willow' dinner plate; a Minton toothbrush holder depicting a pastoral setting with architecture; an Imari blue and white cup; a Japanese 'blue willow' saucer, an English 'blue willow' saucer, and an American 'blue willow' saucer; most stamped underside
The dinner plate: 9.7in. diameter (Total: 6 Items)
Estimate: 200-400

30017
FIVE AMERICAN PORCELAIN PIECES
Coxon Belleek, c.1926-1930

Including a square plate, an oval vegetable dish, an oval underliner, and two luncheon plates, each with cream ground hand-colored with multi-colored floral decoration, all pieces with black underglaze *Coxon Belleek* mark and with pattern number *D-1004-G* in gold, and each piece with an American retailer name in black underglaze
The widest: 10in. (Total: 5 Items)
Estimate: 200-250

30018
SIX BRITISH PORCELAIN BOWLS
Clementson Bros., c.1891

The six matching bowls in the Delft transfer pattern depicting stylized flowers and border to the inside of the bowl and the rim, stamped underside
9.7in. diameter (Total: 6 Items)
Estimate: 400-600

30019
FIVE BLUE AND WHITE PORCELAIN SERVING PIECES
Various makers, c.1891

Comprising a lidded pitcher, cylindrical tapering body with short spout depicting Abbey ruins in a transfer pattern; a matching cup and saucer with a gilt scalloped rim and edge, blue transfer pattern of garlands and flowers; a low wide bowl in the 'Davenport' pattern of flow blue floral design, raised shell motif to the rim with gilt highlights; and a plate with a flow blue pattern of flowers with a raised scroll pattern to the edge, gilt highlights at the rim, all stamped underside
The tallest: 6.2in. high (Total: 6 Items)
Estimate: 150-250

30020
THREE BRITISH PORCELAIN SERVING PIECES
J. H. W. & Sons, c.1892

Comprising a large oval platter, a medium oval platter and a round dinner plate in the Belmont transfer pattern of flowers and scrolls, gilt rim, all stamped underside
The widest: 15.5in. (Total: 3 Items)
Estimate: 200-300

30021
TWO ENGLISH AND TWO SWEDISH PORCELAIN SERVING PIECES
Copeland and Garrett, Gustavsberg, various dates

Comprising a Copeland and Garrett mid-Nineteenth Century oval scalloped rim serving dish, white ground with a warm yellow overall color hand-painted with multi-colored flowers, raised scroll border in white and gold; a Copeland white ground shrimp dish decorated with multi-colored flowers and a green border with stylized flowers, shell-form handle with gold detail; two contemporary Gustavsgerg green bowls with silver inlay, with bands of silver radiating out from the center and a border band, the other depicts a fish with air bubbles and a scalloped inlaid rim, all stamped underside
The largest: 12.5in. long (Total: 4 Items)
Estimate: 200-300

30022
TWO BRITISH PORCELAIN TUREENS
Alfred Meakin Ltd., Johnson Bros., c.1891

The scallop foot oval-form dish with double handles, flat lid with central dome and handle, decorated in the 'Raleigh' pattern of flow blue with gilt flower details; a scallop foot low, oval dish with double handles, ribbed rim, decorated in the 'Princeton' pattern of flow blue design depicting flowers with gilt details, two flowers to the inside, the first stamped underside *Raleigh, Alfred Meakin Ltd, England, Royal Semi Porcelain*, the second stamped *Princeton, Johnson Bros, England*
12in. long and 11.6in. long respectively (Total: 3 Items)
Estimate: 100-150

30023
A GERMAN EARTHENWARE STEIN
Mettlach, c.1896

The domed foot swelling to a collared base under tapering cylindrical form with neckband beneath spouted rim, the double 'C' handle fitted with pewter hinged mount with shaped thumb lift and high domed cover, decorated with a drinking scene signed *Heinr. Schlitt.*, the underside with incised castle and *METTLACH/VB* mark, incised model number *2176* and impressed *GESCHÜTZT* mark and stamped *954 GESCHÜTZT*
16in. high
Estimate: 400-600

30025
A GERMAN EARTHENWARE STEIN
Villeroy & Boch, c.1890

The ivory ground cylindrical half-litre stein decorated with a blue and white architectural vignette flanked by two stylized designs, deep purple glaze surrounding, floral bouquets to the lower and upper borders, applied handle and pewter lid, signed underside *V & B M*.
8.2in. high
Estimate: 200-400

30024
A GERMAN EARTHENWARE STEIN AND A GLASS RÖMER
Villeroy & Boch, Mettlach and unknown maker, c.1900

The quarter-litre stein with disc foot and barrel-shaped body with bas-relief dancing figures against a sky-blue ground, applied handle, *together with* a hand-blown green glass römer with disc foot and tapered body decorated with bands of applied threading, three 'pulled' bear-figure hollow handles and a row of three hollow bear heads, stein with green underglaze stamped *Mettlach* stamp, impressed model number *2086*
The tallest: 10.5in. (Total: 2 Items)
Estimate: 200-300

30026
A CONTINENTAL BEER SERVICE
Merkelbach & Wick, c.1921

The matching stoneware set includes six half-litre steins and a three-litre serving jug in ivory and green depicting a crest with stylized rampant lions on either side and scrolling vines, domed pewter lids to all, stamped underside
The stein: 7.6in. high, The jug: 15.5in. high (Total: 7 Items)
Estimate: 300-500

30027

30029
AN AMERICAN PORCELAIN CHALICE
Willets Manufacturing Co., c.1900

The round base rising to a cylindrical stem and bulbous cup in a pale pink to deep burnt red ground decorated with gooseberries and leaves, gilding to interior and rim, artist signed *Ile Roy* stamped underside *Belleek Willets*
11.2in. high
Estimate: 100-300

30029

30027
A GERMAN STONEWARE STEIN
Mettlach, c.1890

The tapering cylindrical and textured gray body with an applied panel on the obverse portraying a man in blue cap with an open stein in his uplifted right hand, the corners of the panel punctuated with applied roundels to simulate nail heads, the reverse with applied banner with Gothic script 'Der nicht liebt, trinkt und singt,/Es nie zu wahrer Freude bringt' ('That which neither lives, drinks, nor sings,/Bring it not to true joy') beneath the handle fitted with hinged pewter mount, thumb lift and flat-domed lid, the underside with impressed *Mettlach* mark and form number *1617*
6.75in. high
Estimate: 400-600

30030

30030
TWO IRISH PORCELAIN PITCHERS
Belleek, c.1890

The first a Melvin pitcher decorated fluted bulbous body with shamrocks around the foot and chevron border to the midsection, harp-shaped handle and tri-cornered rim; the second an octagonal fluted Thorn pitcher, the three feet and handle in the style of a branch, yellow or cobb iridescent glaze to the interior, feet, handle and thorn pattern to the body, stamped in black underside
6.7in. high and 6.2in. high respectively (Total: 2 Items)
Estimate: 300-500

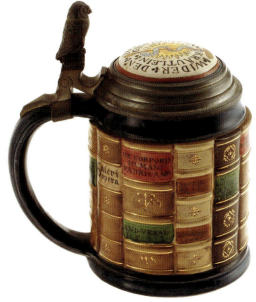

30028

30028
A GERMAN EARTHENWARE STEIN
Mettlach, c.1895

The half-litre cylindrical body simulating leather-bound book spines, the bold loop handle fitted with pewter hinged mount with owl-shaped thumb lift and ceramic-inset pewter cover with inscription 'WIDER DEN/KRAUTLEIN//TOD IST KEIN GEWACHSEN', the underside with impressed castle *Mettlach* mark, impressed model number *2001*
6.75in. high
Estimate: 200-400

30031
THREE GERMAN PORCELAIN ITEMS
R.S. Prussia, c.1890

Including a footed and double-handled shallow dish with raised poppy rim centering red and white rose decoration; a footed circular bowl with green, yellow and purple ground heightened with gilding, the center with red roses and white hydrangea; *together with* a quatre-foil footed bowl with shaped gilt rim over white rose and black berry border, the eight-lobed center with multi-colored poppy decoration, each with red *RS Prussia* mark
Each 10.75in. diameter (Total: 3 Items)
Estimate: 100-300

30033
FOUR GERMAN PORCELAIN ITEMS
R.S. Prussia, c.1890

Including an oblong double-handled green desert tray with pink rose decoration; a footed circular plate with pierced double handles and decorated with a bouquet of red roses with hydrangea; a footed circular plate with beaded and shaped rim and multi-colored poppy decoration; *together with* a small round bowl with scalloped rim and with multi-colored rose decoration, all pieces with *R.S. Prussia* mark
The widest: 12.5in (Total: 4 Items)
Estimate: 100-300

30032
A GERMAN PORCELAIN VASE
R.S. Prussia, c.1890

The footed and squared plinth under flared cylindrical body rising to a squared broad shoulder with double handles centering a short neck with shaped rim, the obverse decorated with four red poppies in a field, the reverse with a single poppy, the entire heightened with gilding, the underside with red *RS Prussian* mark
9in. high
Estimate: 100-200

30034
A GERMAN PORCELAIN PORTRAIT BOWL
R.S. Prussia, c.1890

The white circular form with shaped rim incorporating five repoussé iris, the five-petal central reserve with female in white toga-style attire holding a branch of apple blossoms, the underside with red *R.S. Prussia* mark
10in. diameter
Estimate: 300-600

30035
A COLLECTION OF GERMAN PORCELAIN ITEMS
R. S. Prussia and Royal Bayreuth, c.1890

Comprising R.S. Prussia matching pink rose decorated covered coffee pot, cup and saucer; a creamer and sugar with red poppy decoration; a quatre-foil covered creamer and sugar with wild-flower decoration; a medium-size covered tea pot with wild white rose decoration; a small covered tea pot with hydrangea decoration; four covered sugar bowls of various design; a large footed sugar bowl with white lily design; a creamer with rhododendron decoration; a single green cup; a double-handled desert plate; a covered syrup pitcher; a set of four berry bowls; *together with* a Royal Bayreuth footed green syrup pitcher and a green saucer, all pieces marked except for one covered sugar bowl
The tallest: 8.5in. (Total: 35 items)
Estimate: 400-500

30036
FOUR GERMAN PORCELAIN PIECES
R.S. Prussian, c.1890

Including a double-handled rectangular white cake tray with gilded beaded rim and decorated with a basket of roses, a pink double-handled elongated oval dish with bas-relief yellow flowers and poppies, a double-handled rectangular cake plate with gilt banding and eight swans, *together with* a green double-handled elongated oval dish with shaped rim and yellow rose decoration, the undersides of the rectangular basket of roses tray and the pink oval dish with red *RS Prussia* mark
The widest 12.25in. wide (Total: 4 Items)
Estimate: 200-300

30037
AN ASSORTMENT OF GERMAN PORCELAIN SERVING PIECES
Primarily R. S. Prussia, c.1890

Comprising a lidded teapot and matching cream and lidded sugar in pale green cabbage form with wavy handles decorated with pink roses; a serving bowl and four matching individual bowls in pale green with yellow flowers; a serving bowl and six matching individual bowls in blue with a tulip pattern; and a serving bowl with a champagne satin finish with large roses and swags, all stamped underside
The widest: 10.7in. (Total: 16 Items)
Estimate: 300-500

30038
TWO GERMAN PORCELAIN ITEMS
RS Prussia, c.1890

Including an oblong dish with water lily decoration, *together with* a round bowl with pink poppy decoration on a yellow and green ground, the underside of each with red *RS Prussia* mark
The tallest: 3in. high (Total: 2 Items)
Estimate: 300-400

30039
A CONTINENTAL PORCELAIN TEA SERVICE
R. S. Prussia, c.1880

Comprising a covered teapot, covered sugar and creamer, each with lobed body molded to resemble a green flower calyx and pink bud, the scrolled ribbon handle pierced and gilded, all pieces unmarked
The tallest: 7in. high (Total: 5 Items)
Estimate: 400-600

30040
AN ASSORTMENT OF GERMAN PORCELAIN ITEMS
Majority R. S. Prussia, c.1900

Comprising a chocolate pot with six matching footed cups, white ground decorated with small pink roses and a pale green border; a pair of fluted cups in blue to white decorated with roses; a creamer in white to green with dahlia and foliage; a four-footed creamer in white with peach highlights and pink roses; a scalloped rim plate depicting a winter scene; a swag and tassel footed cup decorated with roses; a lidded hair receiver in white and peach with pink roses and gold border to the lid; a yellow hat pin holder decorated with poppies; a stemmed and footed cup with buttresses in green with pink flowers; a white creamer with small green flowers and swags; a footed blue and white cup with pink roses and gold detail; white four-footed creamer with green and pink highlights; a tri-footed bowl with a blue interior and floral pattern to the center; a teapot and lid in pale green and pink with autumn foliage and spider webs, gilt handle; a six-sided lidded double-handle sugar dish in pale green with roses, majority stamped underside
The tallest: 10.5in. high (Total: 18 Items)
Estimate: 300-500

30041
TWO CONTINENTAL PORCELAIN BOWLS
R. S. Prussia, c.1880

Comprising a wide scalloped-edge bowl in a cream iridescent ground decorated with pink and white carnations, green accents behind the pattern, small gilt detailed scallops; a wide floral-form rim bowl in an iridescent cream rising to pale green ground decorated with pink carnations, white flowers with gilt bead stamen, both stamped underside
10in. diameter (Total: 2 Items)
Estimate: 200-300

30042
A PAIR OF FRENCH METAL-MOUNTED CAPPED SÈVRES URNS
attributed to Sèvres, c.1930

The torpedo-shaped capped white porcelain urns with footed, and concave-cornered square brass plinths supporting circular socles rising to elongated ovoid shaped urns with covers, the obverse of each with a gold enamel bordered reserve of figures and statues in landscape, each cover with brass pineapple finial, the underside of each urn with later black enamel paint and hand-painted, gold Sèvres mark, each of the hand-painted reserves with artist signature *Seurat*
25.5in. high (Total: 2 Items)
Estimate: 2,000-3,000

30043

30043
A CONTINENTAL CERAMIC CHARGER
Picasso, c.1953

The black ground incised with a night image of a house, tree, fence under a moon, blue incised stars to the rim with *8-12-53*, stamped underside *Edition Picasso*
16.5in diameter
Estimate: 400-600

30045

30045
AN AMERICAN POTTERY ART VASE
Van Briggle, c.1930

The bulbous to a cylindrical form vase in blue to green decorated with a stylized flower pattern, stamped underside *Van Briggle Color Spgs*
4.5in. high
Estimate: 50-150

30044

30044
AN AMERICAN POTTERY ART VASE
Weller, c.1915

The footed ovoid form with flaring green ribs beneath a horizontal band of bas-relief flowers heightened with polychrome, rising to an ivory neck with green rim, the interior with craquelure, the craquelure base unmarked
8.8in. high
Estimate: 100-300

30046

30046
A CONTINENTAL POTTERY CHALICE
Amphora Work, c.1925

The round foot rising to a ribbed panel of alternating green and white supporting a three handled cup decorated with three panels of gladiator faces, mottled pink and cobalt, stamped underside *Amphora Made in Czechoslovakia*
6.9in. high
Estimate: 100-300

30047

30047
AN AMERICAN BLUE 'WISTERIA' POTTERY VASE
Roseville, c.1937

The tapering cylindrical form centered between two triangular shaped handles, the blue and tan matte ground molded to depict trailing purple flowers and leaves, numbered underside
8.1in. high
Estimate: 400-600

30049

30049
AN AMERICAN SILVERTONE POTTERY VASE
Weller, c.1920

The round foot ovoid form with a short ruffled rim centered between two handles, decorated in a matte finish molded glaze of poppies and butterflies, stamped underside *Weller Ware*
11.7in. high
Estimate: 400-600

30048
A DECORATED PORCELAIN AMPHORA
Maker unknown, c.1920

The round foot bulbous form to a cylindrical neck decorated with a brown and tan mottled ground, incised design of a stylized parrot, multicolored flowers, leaves and shapes, blue and white border pattern to the body and neck, black rim, marked underside with *R*
17.5in. high
Estimate: 200-300

30048

30050

30050
TWO ENGLISH POTTERY PLATES
Moorcroft, c.1950

Including one large and one small circular plate with green and purple grapes, purple apples and three budgie on a hooker-green ground, the underside of the small plate with impressed block letter mark *MOORCROFT/MADE IN ENGLAND* and underglaze cipher *WM*, the larger plate with impressed block letter mark *MOORCROFT/MADE IN ENGLAND* and underglaze cipher *HM*
The largest 14in. diameter (Total: 2 Items)
Estimate: 500-800

30051

30051
A CONTINENTAL CERAMIC PLATE
Picasso, c.1947

The black ground plate depicts a white line drawing of a smiling face, red paint smudges to represent the cheeks, and four green 'leaves' to the plate edge, signed underside *Edition Picasso* and stamped *Madoura* and *D'apres Picasso*
9.4in. diameter
Estimate: 100-200

30052   30053

30052
THREE DANISH 'FLORA DANICA' BREAD AND BUTTER PLATES
Royal Copenhagen, mid-Twentieth Century

The Parnassia Kotzebuci Cham & Schldl. 'grass-of-parnassus' round plate *together with* a Ranunculus nivalis L.'buttercup' plate and a Draba hirta albicola Hartm. decorated plate all with pink ground pearl borders within gilt-edged serrated rims, model number 3552, stamped underglaze in green *Royal Copenhagen Denmark*
5.5in. diameter (Total: 3 Items)
Estimate: 300-500

30053
THREE DANISH 'FLORA DANICA' BREAD AND BUTTER PLATES
Royal Copenhagen, mid-Twentieth Century

Two Coptis Arifolia Salisl. 'three-leaf goldthread' decorated round plates and an Arctostaphylos Uva ursi Spr. 'bearberry' decorated plate with characteristic pink ground pearl borders within a gilt-edged serrated rim, model number 3552, stamped underglaze in green *Royal Copenhagen Denmark*
5.6in. diameter (Total: 3 Items)
Estimate: 300-500

30054

30054
A DANISH 'FLORA DANICA' FRUIT BOWL
Royal Copenhagen, mid-Twentieth Century

The Vaccinium Vitis idaea L. 'lingonberry' decorated interior oval form pierced basket, applied multicolored flowers to the exterior, characteristic pink ground pearl border within a gilt-edged serrated edge, centered between brown and green twig handles, model number 3536, stamped underglaze in green *Royal Copenhagen Denmark*, en suite with fruit basket stand

10in. long

Estimate: 2,800–3,200

30055
A DANISH 'FLORA DANICA' FRUIT BASKET STAND
Royal Copenhagen, mid-Twentieth Century

The Pyrola grandiflora Rad. 'arctic wintergreen' decorated oval form with a pierced gilt-edged serrated border, unglazed underside, model number 3537, stamped in green *Royal Copenhagen Denmark*, en suite with the Fruit Basket

10.5in. long

Estimate: 900–1,100

30055

30056

THREE DANISH 'FLORA DANICA' SAUCERS
Royal Copenhagen, mid-Twentieth Century

Comprising a low saucer decorated with the characteristic pink round pearl border within a gilt-edged serrated rim, model number 3597, stamped underglaze in green *Royal Copenhagen Denmark*
5.2in. diameter (Total: 3 Items)
Estimate: 300-500

30057

THREE DANISH 'FLORA DANICA' SAUCERS
Royal Copenhagen, mid-Twentieth Century

Comprising a low saucer decorated with the characteristic pink round pearl border within a gilt-edged serrated rim, model number 3597, stamped underglaze in green *Royal Copenhagen Denmark*
5.2in. diameter (Total: 3 Items)
Estimate: 300-500

30058

TWO DANISH 'FLORA DANICA' SALAD PLATES
Royal Copenhagen, mid-Twentieth Century

The first an Andromeda polifolia 'bog rosemary' decorated round plate with a pink ground pearl border within a gilt-edged serrated rim, model number 3573; the second a 'blackberry' decorated round plate with a green ground pearl border within a gilt-edged serrated rim, model number 3573, both stamped underglaze in green *Royal Copenhagen Denmark*
7.5in. diameter (Total: 2 Items)
Estimate: 500-600

30059

TWO DANISH 'FLORA DANICA' SALAD PLATES
Royal Copenhagen, mid-Twentieth Century

The first a Carex bi-color 'two-color sedge' decorated round plate with a pink ground pearl border within a gilt-edged serrated rim, model number 3573; the second a 'gooseberry' decorated round plate with a green ground pearl border within a gilt-edged serrated rim, model number 3573, both stamped underglaze in green *Royal Copenhagen Denmark*
7.5in. diameter (Total: 2 Items)
Estimate: 500-600

30060

TWO DANISH 'FLORA DANICA' SALAD PLATES
Royal Copenhagen, mid-Twentieth Century

The first a Botrychium Aernatum Sw. B europoeum 'grape fern' decorated round plate with a pink ground pearl border within a gilt-edged serrated rim, model number 3573; the second a 'red gooseberry' decorated round plate with a green ground pearl border within a gilt-edged serrated rim, model number 3573, both stamped underglaze in green *Royal Copenhagen Denmark*
7.5in. diameter (Total: 2 Items)
Estimate: 500-600

30061
A DANISH 'FLORA DANICA' LIDDED SUGAR BOWL
Royal Copenhagen, mid-Twentieth Century

The Potentilla procumbens Sibth. decorated large bowl *together with* the Cerastium glutinosum Fr. decorated lid, both with the characteristic pink ground pearl border within a gilt-edged smooth rim, the lid with a brown, green and ochre twig handle with multicolored flower terminals, model number 3582, both stamped underglaze in green *Royal Copenhagen Denmark*
5.7in. high x 6.1in. long
Estimate: 2,000-3,000

30062
A DANISH 'FLORA DANICA' LIDDED SUGAR BOWL
Royal Copenhagen, mid-Twentieth Century

The Geranium dissectum L. 'cut leaved geranium' decorated round lid *together with* the bowl, both with characteristic pink ground pearl borders within gilt-edged smooth rims, the bowl centered between two brown, green and ochre handles, the same style handle to the lid, model number 3502, stamped underglaze in green *Royal Copenhagen Denmark*
3.2in. high x 3.2in. diameter
Estimate: 600-800

30063
TWO DANISH 'FLORA DANICA' SALAD PLATES
Royal Copenhagen, mid-Twentieth Century

The Antennaria dioeca L. 'cat's foot' decorated salad plate *together with* the Trientalis europaea L. 'chickweed wintergreen' decorated salad plate both with characteristic pink ground pearl borders within a gilt-edged serrated rim, model number 3573, stamped underglaze in green *Royal Copenhagen Denmark*
7.2in. diameter (Total: 2 Items)
Estimate: 500-600

30064
TWO DANISH 'FLORA DANICA' SALAD PLATES
Royal Copenhagen, mid-Twentieth Century

Comprising a 'strawberry' decorated plate and a 'peach' decorated plate, both with characteristic green ground pearl borders within a gilt-edged serrated edge, model number 3573, stamped underglaze in green *Royal Copenhagen Denmark*
7.6in. diameter (Total: 2 Items)
Estimate: 500-600

30065
TWO DANISH 'FLORA DANICA' SALAD PLATES
Royal Copenhagen, mid-Twentieth Century

The first a Sedum annuum L. 'annual stonecrop' decorated round plate with a pink ground pearl border within a gilt-edged serrated rim, model number 3573; the second a 'cherry' decorated round plate with a green ground pearl border within a gilt-edged serrated rim, model number 3573, both stamped underglaze in green *Royal Copenhagen Denmark*
7.5in. diameter (Total: 2 Items)
Estimate: 500-600

30066
A DANISH 'FLORA DANICA' CREAM SOUP AND SAUCER
Royal Copenhagen, mid-Twentieth Century

Chrysosplenium oppositifolium L 'opposite-leaved Golden-saxifrage' decorated round double-handled bowl with characteristic pink ground pearl border within a gilt-edged rim, the saucer with serrated rim, model number 3612 on each piece, the underside of each stamped underglaze green *Royal Copenhagen Denmark*
The saucer 6.75in. diameter
Estimate: 400-600

30067
A DANISH 'FLORA DANICA' CREAM SOUP AND SAUCER
Royal Copenhagen, mid-Twentieth Century

Scutellaria hastifolia L. 'Norfolk skullcap' decorated round double-handled bowl with characteristic pink ground pearl border within a gilt-edged serrated rim, the saucer with serrated rim, model number 3612 on each piece, the underside of each stamped underglaze green *Royal Copenhagen Denmark*
The saucer 6.75in. diameter
Estimate: 400-600

30068
A DANISH 'FLORA DANICA' CREAM SOUP AND SAUCER
Royal Copenhagen, mid-Twentieth Century

Myosotis palustris with 'Boraginaceae' decorated round double-handled bowl with characteristic pink ground pearl border within a gilt-edged rim, the saucer with serrated rim, model number 3612 on each piece, the underside of each stamped underglaze green *Royal Copenhagen Denmark*
The saucer 6.75in. diameter
Estimate: 400-600

30069
A DANISH 'FLORA DANICA' RELISH DISH
Royal Copenhagen, mid-Twentieth Century

The Viola epipsila Ledeb. decorated oval dish with characteristic pink ground pearl border within a gilt-edged serrated rim, a green and brown twig handle with a yellow and blue flower terminal, model number 3540, stamped underglaze in green *Royal Copenhagen Denmark*
8.7in. long
Estimate: 700-900

30070
A DANISH 'FLORA DANICA' RELISH DISH
Royal Copenhagen, mid-Twentieth Century

The Antirrhinum Orontium L. 'lesser snapdragon' decorated oval dish with a pink ground pearl border within a gilt-edged serrated rim, green and brown twig handle with a yellow and blue flower terminal, model number 3540, stamped underglaze in green *Royal Copenhagen Denmark*
8.7in. long
Estimate: 500-700

30071
A DANISH 'FLORA DANICA' CREAM SOUP AND SAUCER
Royal Copenhagen, mid-Twentieth Century

Galium verum L. 'lady's bedstraw' decorated round double-handled bowl with characteristic pink ground pearl border within a gilt-edged rim, the saucer with serrated rim, model number 3612 on each piece, the underside of each stamped underglaze green *Royal Copenhagen Denmark*
The saucer 6.75in. diameter
Estimate: 400-600

30072
A DANISH 'FLORA DANICA' CREAM SOUP AND SAUCER
Royal Copenhagen, mid-Twentieth Century

Isnardia palustrio L. 'water purslane' decorated round double-handled bowl with characteristic pink ground pearl border within a gilt-edged rim, the saucer with serrated rim, model number 3612 on each piece, the underside of each stamped underglaze green *Royal Copenhagen Denmark*
9in. diameter
Estimate: 400-600

30073
A DANISH 'FLORA DANICA' CREAM SOUP AND SAUCER
Royal Copenhagen, mid-Twentieth century

Nasturtium palustre D.C. 'nasturtium' decorated round double-handled bowl with characteristic pink ground pearl border within a gilt-edged rim, the saucer with serrated rim, model number 3612 on each piece, the underside of each stamped underglaze green *Royal Copenhagen Denmark*
9in. diameter
Estimate: 400-600

30074
A DANISH 'FLORA DANICA' DINNER PLATE
Royal Copenhagen, mid-Twentieth Century

The Potentilla fruticosa L. 'shrubby cinquefoil' decorated round plate with a pink ground pearl border within a gilt-edged serrated rim, model number 3549, stamped underside in green *Royal Copenhagen Denmark*
10in. diameter
Estimate: 400-600

30075
A DANISH 'FLORA DANICA' DINNER PLATE
Royal Copenhagen, mid-Twentieth Century

The Rosa canina L. 'dog rose' decorated round plate with a pink ground pearl border within a gilt-edged serrated rim, model number 3549, stamped underglaze in green *Royal Copenhagen Denmark*
10in. diameter
Estimate: 400-600

30076
A DANISH 'FLORA DANICA' DINNER PLATE
Royal Copenhagen, mid-Twentieth Century

The Pyrola grandiflora Rad. 'arctic wintergreen' decorated round plate with a pink ground pearl border within a gilt-edged serrated rim, model number 3549, stamped underglaze in green *Royal Copenhagen Denmark*
10in. diameter
Estimate: 400-600

30076

30077
A DANISH 'FLORA DANICA' BOWL
Royal Copenhagen, mid-Twentieth Century

The Pyrola grandiflora Rad. 'arctic wintergreen' decorated round bowl with characteristic pink ground pearl border within a gilt-edged serrated rim, model number 3504, stamped underglaze green *Royal Copenhagen Denmark*
9in. diameter
Estimate: 800-1,000

30077

30078

30078
A DANISH 'FLORA DANICA' TRAY
Royal Copenhagen, mid-Twentieth Century

The Hieracium Pilosella L. 'dandelion' decorated round tray with a characteristic pink ground pearl border within a gilt-edged serrated rim, model number 3566, stamped underglaze in green *Royal Copenhagen Denmark*
9.7in. diameter
Estimate: 300-500

30080

30080
A DANISH 'FLORA DANICA' DINNER PLATE
Royal Copenhagen, mid-Twentieth Century

The Potentilla emaginata Pursh. decorated round plate with a pink ground pearl border within a gilt-edged serrated rim, model number 3549, stamped underglaze in green *Royal Copenhagen Denmark*
10in. diameter
Estimate: 400-600

30079

30079
A DANISH 'FLORA DANICA' DINNER PLATE
Royal Copenhagen, mid-Twentieth Century

The Sarothamnus scoparius Koch. 'broom' decorated round plate with a pink ground pearl border within a gilt-edged serrated rim, model number 3549, stamped underglaze in green *Royal Copenhagen Denmark*
10in. diameter
Estimate: 400-600

30081

30081
A DANISH 'FLORA DANICA' DINNER PLATE
Royal Copenhagen, mid-Twentieth Century

The Stachys annuus L. 'annual yellow woundwort' decorated with a pink ground pearl border within a gilt-edged serrated rim, model number 3549, stamped underglaze in green *Royal Copenhagen Denmark*
10in. diameter
Estimate: 400-600

30082

30082
A DANISH 'FLORA DANICA' TUREEN AND UNDERPLATE
Royal Copenhagen, mid-Twentieth Century

Comprising a tureen, lid and underplate, the Humulus Lupulus L. 'common hops' decorated oval underplate, the decoration to the trough, characteristic pink ground pearl border within a gilt-edged serrated rim, the underside unglazed, model number 3561; *together with* Trifolium hybridum L 'alsike clover' and Cichorium Intybus L. 'chicory' externally decorated oval tureen, pink ground pearl border within a gilt smooth edge, brown, green and ochre twig handle with multicolor flower terminals, model number 3560; with Lathyrus silvester B platyphyllus Rets. 'narrow-leaved everlasting pea' decorated domed lid with pink ground pearl border within a gilt-edged smooth rim, a brown, green and ochre twig handle with multicolored flower terminals, model number 3560, all stamped underglaze in green *Royal Copenhagen Denmark*
Overall: 11.3in. high x 16in. wide
Estimate: 10,000-12,000

30083

30083
A JAPANESE TAISHO PERIOD PORCELAIN VASE
Maker unknown, c.1915

The footed ovoid body rising to a collared neck with applied, pierced, gourd-shaped double handles extending up to a flared, ruffled rim, decorated with vivid overglaze enamels to depict two warriors and four women in a flowering garden setting with other men fishing in the mountainous landscape background, the neck with iron-red diapered decoration with circular reserves of flowers and Ka-mon, the entire with gilt highlights, the underside with six-character Japanese mark, the legible characters, 'Da Nippon' meaning Japan
30.5in. high
Estimate: 1,000-1,500

30084

30084
A JAPANESE MEIJI IMARI CHARGER
Maker unknown, 1910

The footed circular form with non-repeating brocade pattern in overglaze iron-red, white, yellow, green, aubergine, and gold on the obverse, the reverse with three underglaze blue designs and concentric circles centering the unglazed foot, the recessed bottom with spur mark, unmarked
18in. diameter
Estimate: 400-600

30085

30085
A JAPANESE TAISHO PERIOD KUTANI PORCELAIN BOXED TEA SERVICE
Maker unknown, c.1915

Comprising a fabric-upholstered hinged box, the lid opening to reveal a fitted interior with six cups and saucers, covered tea pot, sugar, and creamer, the obverse of each piece decorated with two women and child, the underside of each piece with a 'Da Nippon' (Japan) and 'Fu' (Good Fortune) character mark
The case: 5.5in. high, 18.5in. wide, 15in. deep (Total: 18 Items)
Estimate: 400-600

30086
A CHINESE CARVED WOOD FIGURE
Maker unknown, c.1900

Portraying the dual nature of Li Tie Gwai, one of the Eight Immortals, the carved face with inset green glass eyes near the bottom of the carving depicts Li's non-corporal traveling spirit, the standing figure with inset amber glass eyes depicts the elderly crippled beggar's body that Tie Gwai Li stole when his own body was misplaced, unsigned
20.5in. high
Estimate: 300-500

30088
A JAPANESE MEIJI IMARI CHARGER
Maker unknown, 1890

The shallow-footed circular form with triplicate brocade pattern in overglaze iron-red, green, aubergine, and gold surrounding a round central reserve in underglaze blue on the obverse, the reverse with underglaze blue floral wreath heightened with iron-red and underglaze blue concentric circles centering the unglazed foot, the recessed bottom with characteristic five spur marks, unmarked
18.5in. diameter
Estimate: 400-600

30087
A PAIR OF BRONZE FOO DOGS
Maker unknown, c.1900

The hollow cast in bronze seated foo dogs with heavily stylized curls to the mane and tail in a verdigris patina rubbed back at the high points to reveal the the bronze below, unsigned
15in. high (Total: 2 Items)
Estimate: 600-800

30089
A PORCELAIN DRAGONWARE TEA SERVICE
Maker unknown, c.1950

Comprising a teapot, creamer, lidded sugar bowl, four demitasse cups and saucers, two tea cups, six saucers, and six side plates decorated with a moriage dragon on an ivory to black ground, the demitasse cups have a lithophane of a geisha to the bottom of the cup, some stamped underside
Made in Japan
The tallest: 7in. (Total: 27 Items)
Estimate: 200-300

30090

30090
A CHINESE METAL AND ROSE QUARTZ BOX
Maker unknown, c.1920

The rectangular brass hinged and lidded box, highly decorated with a scroll and floral pattern, rose quartz panels to each side, a decorative diamond-shaped rose quartz set into a brass mount on the lid, unsigned
2.5in. high x 4.2in. long
Estimate: 200-400

30092

30092
A JAPANESE TAISHO CERAMIC TEA SERVICE
Maker unknown, c.1915

Comprising a covered tea pot, creamer, and sugar, six cups and saucers, and six dessert plates each with crackle glaze and decorated with figures and white dragons, the underside of the creamer with three gold characters, loosely translated 'fragrant mountain'
The tallest: 7.5in. high (Total: 24 Items)
Estimate: 200-300

30091

30091
A CHINESE SET OF EIGHT CARVED FIGURES
Maker unknown, c.1950

Depicting each of the Taoists Immortals, the hong-mu (blackwood) carvings with brass inlay, unmarked
The tallest: 11in. (Total: 8 Items)
Estimate: 400-600

30200

30093
A JAPANESE CABINET VASE
Maker unknown, c.1870

The tapering quatre-foil form with a short neck decorated in an alternating pattern of 'Thousand Crane' and 'Imperial Chrysanthemum', gilt surround with stylized chrysanthemums, fan-shaped stamp to underside
3.6in. high
Estimate: 300-400

30094

A JAPANESE PORCELAIN CHARGER
Maker unknown, early Twentieth Century

The charger is decorated in the 'Thousand Crane' pattern, an iron oxide red center medallion with a gilt Japanese symbol surrounded with multiple white cranes on a gilt ground, iron oxide red and gilt swirl pattern rim, Japanese symbols underside
15.7in. diameter
Estimate: 300-500

30095

A PAIR OF CHINESE PORCELAIN CHARGERS
Makers unknown, c.1942

The matching round chargers in a ground of Imperial yellow decorated with multicolored imperial dragons, a stylized floral and scroll border in pink and blue-green, stamped underside
14.5in. diameter (Total: 2 Items)
Estimate: 200-400

30096

A JAPANESE MEIJI CERAMIC TEA SERVICE
Maker unknown, c.1900

Comprising a covered tea pot, creamer, and sugar and four cups and saucers, each with crackle glaze and the Ka-mon of Shimazu and male figures with white dragon, the underside with three gold characters on brown rectangle, loosely translated 'fragrant mountain'
The tallest 6in. high (Total: 14 Items)
Estimate: 400-600

30097

A CHINESE PORCELAIN VASE
Maker unknown, early Qing Dynasty-Kangxi Period

The cylindrical form in celadon rising to a free flow sang de beouf glaze at the neck and shoulders, unsigned
11.9in. high
Estimate: 800-1,000

30098

A PAIR OF CLOISONNE CRANES
Makers unknown, c.1900

The hollow cranes, supported on a raised rectangular plinth, each holds a candlestick spike in its mouth, solid brass legs with a scale pattern, the beak and stem of the candlestick also in solid brass, the body, neck, head, tail, removable saddle and candlestick bobeche in blue ground cloisonne, unsigned
30.5in. high (Total: 2 Items)
Estimate: 500-700

30099
A PAIR OF CLOISONNE HENS
Makers unknown, c.1900

The bulbous tureen form hen in a blue ground with multicolored pattern, red comb, unsigned
10.5in. high (Total: 2 Items)
Estimate: 200-400

30100
A PAIR OF CHINESE FIGURAL COVERED BOXES/CANDLE HOLDERS
Makers unknown, c.1915

In the form of a recumbent ram, each with hinged lid that opens to rest on the figure's head and to form a candle holder, the exterior of each with blue ground with symmetrical all-over archaic elements—including birds—in white, yellow, iron-red, pink, green, and cobalt, the interior gilded, the unmarked underside with brass wire decoration and solid blue enamel
Closed: 6in. high, Open: 8.75in. high (Total: 2 Items)
Estimate: 400-600

30101
A CHINESE CLOISONNE PLATE
Maker unknown, late Qing Dynasty

The round blue ground plate decorated with peony blossoms and leaves, a grey bird, butterfly, and smaller red flowers, border pattern to the rim, reverse in blue, unsigned
9.6in. diameter
Estimate: 200-400

30102
A CHINESE CLOISONNE VASE
Maker unknown, late Qing Dynasty

The tapering cylindrical foot rising to a bulbous form with a long cylindrical neck and flared rim, cased in green enamel, exterior decoration in a ground of black and cerulean blue depicts multicolored birds, blossoms and stylized floral pattern, unsigned
9.5in. high
Estimate: 200-400

30103
A GROUP OF CLOISONNE ITEMS
Makers unknown, Twentieth Century

Comprising a vase with a tapering dome foot and bulbous body shouldering to a cylindrical neck and inverted rim, black ground decorated with stylized floral pattern and three mask shields; a rhinosaurus censor with a green ground decorated in a multicolored pattern, small saddle style lid with a brass finial; a animal form pricket in a blue ground decorated in a multicolored pattern, a blanket style lid towering to a brass needle candle holder; a turtle incense holder in a blue ground with a multicolored pattern, a small lid to the back with a brass finial; and a mystic dog in a blue ground with brass wire 'fur' pattern, lid to the center of the back, pale blue throat and undercarriage, all unsigned
The tallest: 8in. (Total: 5 Items)
Estimate: 200-400

30104
A CHINESE CLOISONNE DONKEY
Maker unknown, late Qing Dynasty

The lidded box in the form of a recumbent donkey, its feet folded underneath, in a blue ground with multicolored pattern, the saddle creating the lid, unsigned
7in. high
Estimate: 100-300

30105
A CHINESE CLOISONNE CHI LIN
Maker unknown, late Qing Dynasty

The cerulean and cobalt blue scale pattern to the body with a blue and red pattern on the head, solid brass horns, whiskers, dorsal mane, tail and hooves, unsigned
8in. high
Estimate: 100-300

30106
A CHINESE CLOISONNE CAMEL INKWELL
Maker unknown, late Qing Dynasty

The Bactrian camel form in a dark green ground with light green undercarriage and throat, the double hump forms the domed lids to the inkwell, unsigned
5.2in. high
Estimate: 200-400

30107
A GROUP OF CHINESE CLOISONNE ITEMS
Makers unknown, c.1900

Comprising a pair of bookends with a cloisonne central medallion in red; a white ground lidded jar; a pair of white lidded ovoid jars; a blue lidded jar decorated with white branches; a black cup with floral decoration; a red lidded urn with a yellow ground cartouche; a black ground vase decorated with flowers; a black ground tray with floral pattern; a dual-sided card case in blue; and a brass and enamel plate in blue, green and black, some items stamped underside *China*
The tallest: 6.2in. (Total: 12 Items)
Estimate: 200-400

30109
A JAPANESE MEIJI PERIOD CLOISONNE COVERED GINGER JAR
Maker unknown, c. 1880

The ovoid form with short neck and conforming domed lid with knob, the entire with copper-wire design filled with polychrome enamels, unmarked
4.75in. high
Estimate: 100-200

30108
A CHINESE CLOISONNE LIDDED CENSOR
Maker unknown, late Qing Dynasty

The tri-footed bulbous form double-handled censor with a domed lid and finial, decorated with a repeating foo dog pattern to the feet, handles and finial, the feet with coral cabochon eyes, the black ground body decorated with an imperial yellow dragon, green, blue and white floral motif to the underside, Greek key pattern to the rim, unsigned
8.8in. high
Estimate: 300-500

30110
A PAIR OF CHINESE CLOISONNE HORSES
Makers unknown, late Qing Dynasty

The lidded box in the style of a prancing horse, the front right leg raised, in a turquoise color ground, multicolor pattern overall, the saddle lid in a ground of terra cotta with a blue saddle blanket, the mane and saddle are removable, unsigned
9.5in. high (Total: 2 Items)
Estimate: 200-400

30111
A GROUP OF CLOISONNE ITEMS
Makers unknown, c.1900

Comprising a recumbent horse form pricket in turquoise ground with a multicolored design, re-movable saddle and 'smoke' form candle holder to the back; a pair of cranes in a blue ground with brass, legs and beak, multicolored design; a pair of prancing horses in a turquoise ground, blue, white and red saddles, each on a pierced wooden base; a pair of blue ground bears with a multi-colored design, each on a footed wooden base; a green ground pigeon with a multicolored pattern, light green foot, the neck and head form the lid; an oblong tray with a black ground depicting a dragon, a blue border to the edge, unsigned
The tallest: 10in. (Total: 9 Items)
Estimate: 600-800

30112
A PAIR OF CHINESE CLOISONNE RHINOSAURUS
Makers unknown, c.1925

The rhinosaurus are individually supported by an oval wooden base on four feet, the rhinosaurus in a burgundy ground with a multicolored design, lid to back, sticker to underside *Made in China*
6in. high (Total: 2 Items)
Estimate: 200-400

30113
A PAIR OF CHINESE CLOISONNE DUCKS
Makers unknown, late Qing Dynasty

The pair of ducks, one looking left, the other right, both in a blue ground with red, black and blue pattern, scale design to the legs, brass lotus blossom lid on the ducks back, holds lotus leaves in his beak, number stamp to underside
5.9in. high (Total: 2 Items)
Estimate: 200-400

30114
SIX CLOISONNE ITEMS
Makers unknown, c.1900

Including a bulbous form bowl with a short flared neck in mottled brown ground decorated with four shields of alternating dragon and bird pattern; a green and blue ground lidded tri-foot silver foil jar with ribbing to the body, decorated with butterflies and flowers; a bulbous tri-foot lidded jar in alternating swirl ground of blue, green and iridescent brown; two tri-footed compressed sphere lidded jars with a black ground underside and blue ground to top; a low round lidded jar in a black ground decorated with a square central medallion of butterflies to the lid, unsigned
The tallest: 3.8in. (Total: 10 Items)
Estimate: 400-600

30115
THREE CLOISONNE CENSERS
Makers unknown, c.1900

Comprising a duck form censer in a blue ground, the lid attached to the body by a chain; a goose form censer in a blue ground with a handle; and a resting goose form censer in blue ground, the wing forming the lid, unsigned
The tallest: 7.7in. (Total: 3 Items)
Estimate: 400-500

30116
A CHINESE CLOISONNE VASE
Maker unknown, late Qing Dynasty

The slightly flaring cylindrical form shouldering to a short flared rim in a mottled cobalt ground, six shield designs in a brown ground depicting birds and dragons, a horizontal architectural scene in a cerulean blue ground with mountains, and flowers, mottled deep green enamel interior to the neck, unsigned
11.9in. high
Estimate: 200-400

30117
A PAIR OF CHINESE CLOISONNE VASES
Makers unknown, late Qing Dynasty

The ovoid form with a cylindrical flaring neck cased in pale green, decorated with a black ground to the lower third, shield pattern with an alternating chatoyant green and red ground depicting dragon and birds, shoulder border pattern in a red ground with yellow and blue flowers, unsigned
6in. high (Total: 2 Items)
Estimate: 100-300

30118
SEVEN CLOISONNE TEAPOTS
Makers unknown, c.1900

Comprising a turquoise ground duck form teapot with multicolored wings and pattern; a black ground bulbous teapot decorated with chrysanthemums and peonies; a tri-foot black ground teapot decorated with alternating shields of green and blue with flowers and butterflies; a green ground teapot with multicolored floral discs; three green and cobalt ground teapots of various shapes decorated with a multicolored floral pattern, unsigned
The tallest: 5.6in. (Total: 14 Items)
Estimate: 500-700

30119
FOUR CHINESE QING DYNASTY CLOISONNE ITEMS
Makers unknown, c.1900

Including a pair of joss-stick holders in the form of dogs on custom-fitted wooden bases, a lift-top box in the shape of a swimming swan, and a covered wine pot in the shape of a duck, each piece with turquoise ground with yellow, green, iron-red, pink, green, and cobalt enameling, unmarked
The tallest: 9in. (Total: 4 items)
Estimate: 600-800

30120

A CLOISONNE PLATTER
Maker unknown, late Qing Dynasty

The round shallow platter with a central floral design of flowers and foliage on a black ground, surrounding multicolored and multidesign pattern, unsigned
11.9in. diameter
Estimate: 200-400

30122

TWO CLOISONNE GINGER JARS
Makers unknown, late Qing Dynasty

Comprising two lidded ginger jars, one with a black ground, the other with a blue ground, both depicting peony blossoms and rocks, unsigned
2.6in. high (Total: 4 Items)
Estimate: 50-100

30123

A GROUP OF CLOISONNE ITEMS
Makers unknown, c.1900

Comprising a round covered box, black ground with an imperial yellow dragon to the top; a round covered box in a black ground with an imperial yellow dragon to the side; a round covered box with a green ground and ornate pattern of flowers and butterflies; a black ovoid form vase decorated with circular images of a lotus flower and butterflies; an ovoid form vase in black and red decorated with a multicolored floral pattern; an ovoid form vase in a deep blue and green ground decorated with a floral pattern; a rectangular red ground tray decorated with multicolored flowers; and an organic shape tray in a black ground decorated with a multicolored floral pattern, one box signed *China*
The tallest: 5.1in. (Total: 11 Items)
Estimate: 400-600

30121

A PAIR OF CHINESE LATE QING DYNASTY CLOISONNE VASES
Makers unknown, c.1900

Each of the copper-wired ovoid bodies, the blue fish-scale socle spreading to a water (*sui*) motif beneath confronting Imperial yellow dragons and flaming pearls against a cloud-design black ground, the shoulder and neck with bands of (*ru yi*), flowers, and leaf banding, unsigned
9.5in. high (Total: 2 Items)
Estimate: 400-600

30124
A CHINESE CLOISONNE BOWL
Maker unknown, c.1980

The circular brass foot beneath flaring side everting to a scalloped rim, the entire with coffee-colored ground with all-over floral decoration in black, caramel, and royal blue, unsigned
9in. diameter
Estimate: 50-100

30125
A CHINESE CLOISONNE OIL LAMP
Maker unknown, c.1920

The undulating form depicting a dragon with upturned gilt metal head, the separate blue-scaled body with red, pink and white flames emitting from its leg joints, gilt metal spine ridge, elbows, feet, and tail, the brass tubular connector of the head with impressed with number *40*, no maker's marked found
4.5in. high
Estimate: 300-600

30126
AN AMERICAN TABLE LAMP WITH REVERSE-PAINTED GLASS SHADE
probably Handel, c.1925

The French style copper-patinated metal standard on oval foot rising to urn-shaped pillar with fleur de lis design, surmounted with domed oval olive-green 'chipped-ice' glass shade with a reverse-painted female figure silhouetted against a wooded horizon on obverse and reverse, unsigned
14in. high
Estimate: 100-300

30127
A METAL AND GLASS GLOBE LAMP
Muller Frere Luneville, c.1905

The Art Deco style lamp with a wrought iron octagonal flat foot on ball feet, geometric stem supporting a molded etched glass globe of stylized birds and flowers, globe signed on the side
9.7in. high
Estimate: 200-400

30128
A FRENCH ART DECO MANTEL CLOCK
Maker unknown, c.1930

Portraying fighting cockerels, the marble and onyx backed plinth repeating the curved and angular fan-shape lines of the silver dial with stylized Arabic numerals, the movement striking on the hour on bell, the white metal figures with cold paint decoration in dark green and red heightened with gold and silver, unmarked
19in. high
Estimate: 4,000-5,000

30129
AN AMERICAN OIL LAMP BASE
Maker unknown, c.1880

The mold-blown oil lamp supported by a domed foot decorated with a scroll pattern rising to a cylindrical stem and hollow bulbous reservoir, metal threaded insert, unsigned
9.5in. high
Estimate: 50-100

30130
A FRENCH BRONZE FIGURINE
Louis Kley (French, 1833-1911), c.1880

Based on a Sèvres pattern, a young girl pours water from a jar, raised on circular stepped plinth, signed beneath the figure's left foot *Mon. KLEY d'apres SÈVRES*
7in. high
Estimate: 600-800

30131
A SATIN GLASS AND BRASS LAMP
Maker unknown, c.1900

The brass stepped cylindrical base supporting a ovoid form with a cylindrical neck glass vase in ivory to robin's egg blue, brass cap to top, clear hollow glass finial, unsigned
32in. high
Estimate: 200-300

30133
AN ENGLISH SILVER AND GLASS CONDIMENT SET
Hutton & Sons, c.1904

The matching Arts and Crafts style condiment set including a pepper shaker, a salt cellar, and a mustard pot all with sterling mounts and glass inserts, all raised on small flared feet, the mustard pot inscribed 'Officer's U.S.S. Unimak' to the top of the lid, sterling hallmarks and makers mark underside
The tallest: 2.4in (Total: 3 Items)
Estimate: 250-450

30132
A FRENCH GLASS LAMP
Daum Nancy, c.1890

The disc foot rising to knobbed flaring mottled brown body, decorated with a snowy and wooded landscape, the underside signed *Daum Nancy* with *Cross of Lorraine* with later shade
9in. high lamp base only
Estimate: 100-200

30134
PAIR OF SCULPTED PHOTOGRAPHS
Maker unknown, c.1902

Portraying Edward VII (1841 - 1910), King of England from 1902-10, and his wife, Queen Alexandra (1844-1925), the embossed images based on the official coronation photographs taken of the royal couple in 1901 mounted in later mats and frames, the reverse with label of framer: Artsource of El Paso, Texas
The frame 5.25in. square (Total: 2 Items)
Estimate: 100-300

30135
THREE CONTINENTAL WATERCOLOR ON IVORY MINIATURE PORTRAITS
Artists unknown, c.1750

Including an oval depiction of a blue-eyed young woman in white cap, the reverse with the subject's platted hair, under glass in silver bezel-mounted locket; an oval portrait of a blue-eyed young woman wearing blue dress with lace collar, under glass in gold-plated locket with metal back *together with* an oval depiction of a white-haired gentleman, probably Prussian, with gold military medal, under glass; the female's portrait unsigned, the gentleman's portrait with script signature in red *St.*
The largest: 4in. long (Total: 3 Items)
Estimate: 900-1,200

30137
A FRENCH METAL VASE
Vincent, c.1900

The spelter vase with a tri-corner organic style foot supports a bulbous form with a cylindrical neck to a flared rim decorated in an Art Nouveau style of flowers and leaves in relief overall, a flowering branch style handle, all in a green patina, a putti in a brown patina applied to the side, signed on side *Vincent*
13.9in. high
Estimate: 100-300

30136
A CONTINENTAL ART GLASS LAMP
Maker unknown, c.1925

The brass framework of the two-part lamp comprises four raised feet flaring to a simple brass ring with an attached brass and beaded handle, the brass framework supports multiple strands of gradating small to larger faceted clear glass beads, the 'lid' of the basket is decorated with multiple glass strawberries, plums, apples, gooseberries and blackberries, stamped underside *Czechoslovakian*
9.5in. high
Estimate: 300-500

30138
A FRENCH BRONZE BUST
Emmanuel Villanis (1858 - 1914), c.1900

Depicting 'Saida' the female figure wears a headscarf and necklace, raised on rouge marble plinth, signature on reverse side, figure's left shoulder, foundry mark on socle *SOCIETE DES BRONZES DE PARIS*
8.75in. high
Estimate: 400-600

30139
AN AMERICAN LEADED GLASS AND BRONZE LAMP
Duffner & Kimberly, c.1910

The round base in the style of a tree trunk with roots in the original patina of oxide green rubbed to dark brown; the shade decorated in the style of alternating pink and white waterlilies, the ground color primarily in mottled blues, unsigned
Base: 30.2in. high Shade: 21.5in. diameter
Estimate: 3,000-4,000

30140
AN AMERICAN GILT BRONZE 'ZODIAC' DESK SET
Tiffany Studios, 1910

Comprising a pair of blotter ends, a two-cavity paper rack, a stamp box, a letter opener, a large inkwell, a pen tray, a paper clip, and a notebook cover, the design of each with Celtic strapping and roundel of zodiac symbols, the underside of each piece with impressed mark in block letters *TIFFANY STUDIOS/NEW YORK*
The tallest: 6.25in. (Total: 9 Items)
Estimate: 2,000-3,000

30141
AN AMERICAN BRASS OIL LAMP AND GLASS SHADE
Bridgeport Brass Co., c.1890

The electrified brass oil lamp with a pierced base to a twisted stamped stem supporting a cartouche and floral decorated lamp and fittings; the white bulbous shade with a cylindrical neck to a flared and ruffled rim, cased in pink, enamel decoration depicts flowers and leaves primarily in pink, green and yellow, clear glass hurricane, the lamp stamped *The New Rochester*
27.5in. high
Estimate: 400-600

30142
A FRENCH ART DECO FIGURAL GROUPING
Ivan René Rochard, c.1925

The white metal figures of greyhounds mounted on a black onyx plinth faced in white onyx, signed lower right corner of marble
17.5in high
An associate of the Salon des Beaux Arts Francais, Rochard won the salon bronze medal in 1941.
Estimate: 2,000-3,000

30143
A CONTINENTAL GLASS AND METAL LAMP
attributed to Loetz, c.1900

The cast metal lamp base in an Art Nouveau style supporting a six-sided, geometric-form yellow cased glass shade with a pulled feather pattern in iridescent green and ivory, the base is stamped underside *R. B. Co.*
15.2in high
Estimate: 300-500

30144
A VIENNESE BRONZE LAMP
Bergman, c.1890

The plinth supports a cold-painted bedouin scene of a male and female by a well, underneath a canopy of palm trees hung with an islamic style lamp, the entire lamp lights at the well, the hanging lamp and underneath the palm tree, stamped on the reverse
25in. high
Estimate: 2,000-3,000

30145
A TWENTY-EIGHT PIECE SET OF CONTINENTAL GLASS STEMWARE
Kosta, c.1930

The matching set comprising six white wine glasses, ten champagne glasses, six cordials and six liqueur glasses, all on an octagonal faceted foot and stem to a simple bowl, unsigned
The tallest: 4.9in. high (Total: 28 Items)
Estimate: 50-100

30146
EIGHT GLASS TUMBLERS
Kosta, c.1950

The slightly flaring cylindrical form with a heavy glass foot containing an internal controlled air bubble, unmarked
3.6in. high (Total: 8 Items)
Estimate: 25-50

30147
FOURTEEN GLASS TUMBLERS
Kosta, c.1950

The cylindrical form with short panels to the lower quarter, one glass has a *Kosta* sticker, unsigned
2.9in. high (Total: 14 Items)
Estimate: 25-50

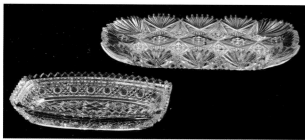

30148
TWO AMERICAN CUT GLASS TRAYS
Makers unknown, c.1900

Comprising a rectangular tray with fan form straight sides and sloping ends, indented corners, decorated with hobstars and crosshatching; a rectangular relish tray with a notched rim, decorated with hobstars, unsigned
14.7in long and 9.9in. long respectively (Total: 2 Items)
Estimate: 200-400

30149
AN AMERICAN CUT GLASS VASE, CARAFE AND BOWL
Various makers, c.1900

Comprising a Higgins and Seiter Florentine pattern vase, round foot to a trumpet form with notched and peaked rim; a Hawkes carafe with fans and hobstars; and a bowl decorated with hobstars, fans and crosshatching, carafe stamped underside
The tallest: 14.3in. high (Total: 3 Items)
Estimate: 200-400

30150
A CUT GLASS PITCHER AND ICE TUB
Makers unknown, c.1900

Comprising a tapering cylindrical form of hobstars, diamonds and circles, notched and scalloped rim, clear applied handle; and a bulbous form double-handle ice tub cut with hobstars, cane, notched prism and fans, notched scallop rim, unsigned
11in. high and 3in. high respectively (Total: 2 Items)
Estimate: 200-400

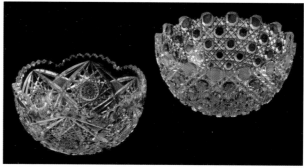

30151
TWO AMERICAN BRILLIANT CUT GLASS BOWLS
Makers unknown, c.1890

Including a Russian cut glass bowl *together with* a hobstars pattern bowl, unsigned
4.25in. high (Total: 2 Items)
Estimate: 400-800

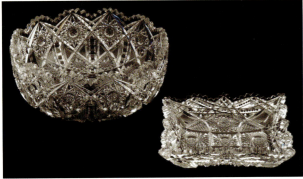

30152
AN AMERICAN CUT GLASS BOWL AND DISH
Makers unknown, c.1900

Comprising a straight-sided heavily cut bowl with a notched and scalloped rim, pattern depicts hobnails, crosshatch and stars; the square, low dish with flared sides to a notched and scalloped rim cut with hobstars, diamonds, crosshatching, unsigned
9in. diameter and 6.7in. wide respectively (Total: 2 Items)
Estimate: 200-400

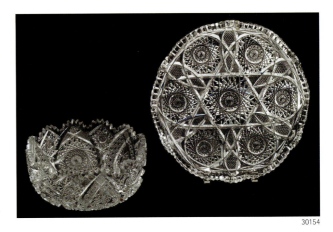

30154
AN AMERICAN CUT GLASS BOWL AND TRAY
Makers unknown, c.1900

Comprising a straight-sided heavily cut, notched and scalloped-rim bowl decorated with hobstars, crosshatching, 'Diamond and Button' pattern; a round tray with straight sides and notched and scalloped rim decorated with hobstars and diamond pattern, unsigned
8.8in. diameter and 12in. diameter respectively (Total: 2 Items)
Estimate: 300-500

30155
AN AMERICAN CUT GLASS BOWL AND ICE TUB
Makers unknown, c.1900

Comprising a heavy bulbous form bowl with vertical cuts to the lower half, a horizontal waist cut, and a sunburst pattern and stars to the upper half, scalloped and notched rim; the double handle ice tub with vertical cuts, diamond pattern and notched and scalloped rim, unsigned
9in. diameter and 7.5in. diameter respectively (Total: 2 Items)
Estimate: 200-400

30153
AN AMERICAN CUT GLASS CARAFE AND PITCHER
Makers unknown, c.1900

Comprising a bulbous form to a faceted and flared neck decorated with hobstars, fans and cross-hatching, zipper pattern to the neck; the tapering cylindrical form pitcher decorated with hobstars, diamond pattern and crosshatching, thumbprint design to handle, unmarked
7.5in. high and 10.5in. high respectively (Total: 2 Items)
Estimate: 200-400

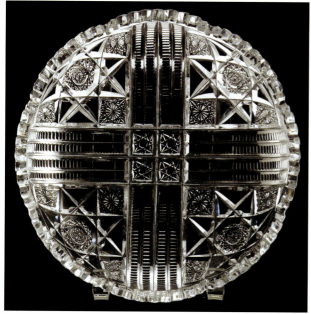

30156
AN AMERICAN BRILLIANT CUT GLASS BOWL
Hawkes, c.1920

The round low bowl with a scallop and notched rim decorated with a cut pattern of four hobstars divided by a wide four-band cross, stamped on the inside of the bowl
8in. diameter
Estimate: 100-300

30158
AN AMERICAN BRILLIANT CUT GLASS BOWL
Maker unknown, c.1900

The bulbous bowl, cut pattern of hobstars, fans, diamonds and buttons, scalloped and notched rim, unsigned
8in. diameter
Estimate: 50-150

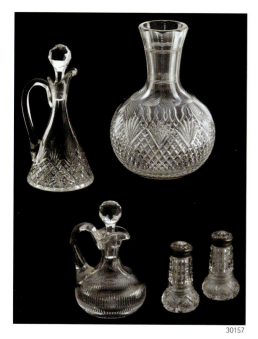

30157
A COLLECTION OF AMERICAN BRILLIANT CUT GLASS ITEMS
Various makers, c.1900

Including a globular carafe with 'Diamond Fan' pattern, probably by Higgins & Seiter, a cruet bottle with 'Diamond Fan' pattern, probably by Pitkins & Brooks, a cruet with fluted side and paneled neck, probably by Higgins & Seiter, *together with* a pair of salt and pepper shakers with hobstar decorated base tapering to a zippered neck and capped with sterling pierced covers, probably by Pitkins & Brooks, all glass unmarked
The tallest: 8.5in. (Total: 7 Items)
Estimate: 100-300

30159
A PAIR OF AMERICAN BRILLIANT CUT GLASS CANDLESTICKS
Hawkes, c.1920

The round foot with a star cut pattern to the underside supports a cylindrical column hollow form with a flared rim decorated with hobstars and thumbprints and vertical cuts, silverplate inserts, stamped on the top of foot
6in. high (Total: 2 Items)
Estimate: 75-200

30160
THREE AMERICAN BRILLIANT CUT GLASS ITEMS
Various makers, c.1900

Comprising an oval Libbey spoon dish with a star pattern to the foot, sides decorated with diamonds, hobstars and fans, a notched undulating rim; a round notched and scalloped rim nappy with a loop handle decorated with thumbprints, cut decoration depicts hobstars fans, and fine diamonds; a round low bowl with a notched and scalloped rim decorated pinwheel hobstar and fans; the Libbey spoon dish stamped on the inside
The largest: 9.6in wide (Total: 3 Items)
Estimate: 75-150

30161
AN AMERICAN BRILLIANT CUT GLASS BOWL
H. C. Fry Glass, c.1900

The notched and scalloped rim over six medium hobstars alternating with fine diamond panels over inverted fans centering a large hobstar in the bottom, acid-etched script *Fry* mark in the center of the bottom of the bowl
3.25in. high
Estimate: 200-300

30162
A SET OF EIGHT AMERICAN CUT AND ETCHED GLASS WHISKEYS
probably Higgins & Seiter, c.1920

Each with starburst basal design extending up the lower half of the cylindrical body, the upper half with grapevine motif, unmarked
3.1in. high (Total: 8 Items)
Estimate: 80-140

30163
FIVE CUT GLASS TUMBLERS
H. P. Sinclaire & Co., c.1920

The matching tumblers with a paneled lower quarter, a hobstar pattern and a floral vine border to the upper quarter, stamped underside
4in. high (Total: 5 Items)
Estimate: 75-150

30164
TWO AMERICAN BRILLIANT CUT GLASS BOWLS
Higgins & Seiter, c.1900

The pair of matching bowls in the 'Strawberry Diamond and Fan' pattern, unsigned
8.2in. diameter (Total: 2 Items)
Estimate: 100-300

30165
AN AMERICAN BRILLIANT CUT GLASS DRESSER SET
Hawkes, c.1920

Comprising an oval tray, a covered oval box, and a covered pomade jar, each piece with starburst centered by prism and hobstar panels, three pieces with Hawkes' trefoil ring enclosing a fleur de lis and two Hawkes acid-stamp mark on underside
3.25in. high (Total: 5 Items)
Estimate: 200-300

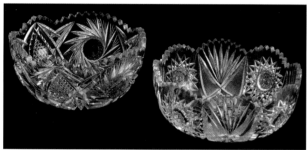

30166
TWO AMERICAN BRILLIANT CUT GLASS BOWLS
Makers unknown, c.1900

One with pinwheel-hobstar with diamond and button panels separated by zipper-cut prism, *together with* a hobstar and fan bowl with fine diamond panels, both bowls with notched and scalloped rims, unmarked
4in. high (Total: 2 Items)
Estimate: 100-300

30167
FOUR AMERICAN BRILLIANT CUT GLASS ITEMS
Hawkes, various makers, c.1900

Comprising a Hawkes cologne bottle, globular form with hobstars rising to a short cylindrical neck and a flared rim, faceted ball stopper; a flower cut cruet, tapering form with a flower pattern, applied handle with thumbprints and a faceted teardrop-shape stopper; a nappy cut to depict hobstars, crosshatching and fans, notched rim; and a rectangular relish dish with a hobstar center, buttons, crosshatching and fan at the rim, the cologne bottle stamped underside
The tallest: 9.3in. high (Total: 6 Items)
Estimate: 100-300

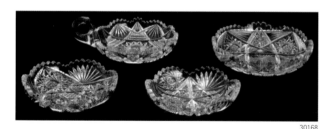

30168
FOUR AMERICAN BRILLIANT CUT GLASS ITEMS
Averbeck and others, c.1900

Including a nappie with hobstar, zippers and fans, an Averbeck 'Canton' pattern bon bon dish, a bon bon dish with fans and arches, a bon bon with central starburst double-zippers and hobstars
The largest: 7in. diameter (Total: 4 Items)
Estimate: 100-200

30169
AN AMERICAN CUT GLASS DISH
Maker unknown, c.1900

The shallow dish decorated with a central star pattern, hobnails and coinspots, notched and scalloped rim, unsigned
8in. diameter
Estimate: 100-300

30170
AN AMERICAN BRILLIANT CUT GLASS JEWEL BOX
Maker unknown, c.1900

The oval hinged and lidded jewel box cut with a double row of flutes to the lower half with a crosshatch pattern between the rows, the lid cut with fans, crosshatching and central hobstar, unsigned
5.6in. wide
Estimate: 75-150

30171
AN AMERICAN SILVER PLATE AND CUT GLASS SALAD SET
Gorham Co, and glass probably J.D. Bergen, c.1890

Comprising a serving spoon and fork, each with silverplated utensils attached to ovoid 'Button & Zipper' pattern cut glass handles, the backside of the silverplated utensils with impressed block letter *GORHAM CO* mark with anchor
11.25in. long (Total: 2 Items)
Estimate: 200-300

30173
AN AMERICAN GLASS LIDDED DRESSER BOX
C. F. Monroe Co., c.1890

The Wavecrest swirl and scroll mold lidded box in pale green ground with a brass hinged mount, enamel decoration depicts pink and blue daisy style flowers to the lower half and pink daisies with green leaves to the top, stamped underside *Wave Crest*
3.7in. high
Estimate: 200-300

30172
AN AMERICAN GLASS LIDDED DRESSER BOX
Wavecrest, c.1900

The pale blue swirl ribbed lower half with a hinged metal mount supporting a pale blue to ivory shell-form lid decorated with pink and brown flowers with enamel highlights, stamped underside *Wave Crest*
3in. high
Estimate: 200-400

30174
A DECORATED SATIN GLASS VASE
Maker unknown, c.1900

The cushion foot ovoid form to a stepped neck and cylindrical rim in pink satin irregular concentric diamond pattern decorated with a coralene design of a robin in a tree, ivory cased, unsigned
8.4in. high
Estimate: 200-300

30175

30175
AN ENAMELED GLASS VASE
possibly Stevens and Williams, c.1900

Of bulbous form, the collared cylindrical neck with a heavily ruffled rim, pale pink to deep pink decorated with enamel multicolored flowers, branches, dragonfly and butterfly, cased in ivory, gilt detail to foot and rim, unsigned
9in. high
Estimate: 200-300

30176

30176
A CONTINENTAL IRIDESCENT GLASS DESERT SERVICE
probably Lobmeyer, c.1910

Comprising a three-piece place setting for four, each of the twelve iridescent clear pieces with quatre-foil body etched with all-over star pattern, the obverse with an oval reserve centering the monogram C, the rim with gilding
3.6in. high (Total: 12 Items)
Estimate: 300-500

30177
AN ETCHED AND ENAMELED CRUET
Maker unknown, c.1930

The blue acid finish bulbous form cruet with a long cylindrical neck and flared rim decorated with enamel flowers, gilt detail to the shoulder and rim, tear-drop shaped stopper, unsigned
8.4in. high
Estimate: 100-300

30177

30178

30178
TWO BLUE BULB VASES AND A DIAMOND QUILT VASE
Makers unknown, c.1900

Comprising a blue purple ribbed bulbous form short neck to a flared rim bulb vase; a cobalt blue bulb vase ribbed bulbous form to a cylindrical neck and flared rim; a mold-blown blue bulbous ovoid form vase in a graduated diamond quilt pattern rising to a cylindrical neck and flared rim, unsigned
The tallest: 7.5in. high (Total: 3 Items)
Estimate: 100-300

30179
AN ENAMEL AND GILT DECORATED GLASS VASE
Maker unknown, c.1900

The short foot cylindrical form shouldered vase with a slender cylindrical neck to a flared rim in pink to ivory to pale yellow, enamel decoration depicts a gilt bird and scrolls, small white flowers on vines surround, gilt foot, collar and rim, numbers to underside
10.1in. high
Estimate: 100-300

30179

30181

30181
AN AMERICAN GLASS LIDDED DRESSER BOX
C. F. Monroe Co., c.1890

The Wavecrest swirl mold lidded box with a brass hinged mount, the pale yellow glass ground has enamel decoration depicting pink and white flowers with pale brown and green leaves, unsigned
4in. high
Estimate: 100-300

30180

30180
AN AMERICAN WINE RINSE AND SIX MASONIC CORDIALS
Makers unknown, c.1890

Comprising a cylindrical form wine rinse with fluted panels to the lower half; six Masonic American brilliant cut cordials on a faceted ball foot to a trumpet form with panels to the lower half, etched Masonic symbols to the upper half, unsigned
4.3in. high and 3.2in. high respectively (Total: 7 Items)
Estimate: 100-200

30182

30182
AN AMERICAN GLASS LIDDED DRESSER BOX
Wavecrest, c.1900

The oval ivory to pale blue box with a metal hinged mount supporting an oval pale blue to ivory lid decorated with pink, blue and green flowers with enamel highlights, raised scroll work to both the box and the lid, stamped underside *Wave Crest*
3in. high
Estimate: 200-400

30183

THREE AMERICAN MOLD-BLOWN GLASS BOTTLES AND A WHIMSY
South Jersey Glass, Nineteenth Century

Comprising a pinched cylindrical amber 125ml apothecary bottle with a short neck and flared rim; an amber round flattened flask-style bottle with a short neck in a diamond pattern; an amber flattened ovoid form with a short neck depicting General Taylor; and an amber blown glass hat-form whimsy, the apothecary bottle and the diamond pattern bottle are stamped in mold
The tallest: 8in. high (Total: 4 Items)
Estimate: 100-300

30185

A GLASS AND SILVER VASE
Maker unknown, c.1925

The ovoid form with a short flaring neck decorated in iridescent mottled blue-green Papillon pattern with sterling silver overlay to the front and rim, the glass unsigned, the silver stamped *Sterling* to the rim
3.6in. high
Estimate: 200-400

30184

TWO AMETHYST GLASS DECANTERS
Makers unknown, c.1915

Comprising a bulbous form decanter with a cylindrical neck and a tri-fold rim, teardrop-form stopper; and a six-panel rounded shoulder decanter, slightly flaring neck with a ball stopper, both unsigned
11.8in. high and 14in. high respectively (Total: 4 Items)
Estimate: 100-200

30186

AN AMERICAN PRESSED GLASS DECANTER AND SIX CORDIAL GLASSES
Cambridge Glassware, c.1910

Comprising a matching set in the 'Mount Vernon' pattern, the decanter a bulbous form in a diamond pattern to paneled shoulders and triple-collared neck with a flaring rim, hollow octagonal facet stopper; the cordials with a square foot to a diamond-knobbed stem, diamond pattern to the lower half of the bowl and simple upper half, unsigned
12in. high and 5in. high respectively (Total: 8 Items)
Estimate: 100-200

30187
TWO ENGLISH WINE GLASSES AND AN AMERICAN GLASS BOWL AND WINE GLASS
Makers unknown, c.1825

Comprising two green wine glasses on a round foot cylindrical hollow stem and bulbous bowl, one in a crackle pattern; a green American glass cylindrical foot bowl to a flaring and ruffled rim; and a green wine glass with a round foot partially hollow double bulb stem to a slightly flaring cylindrical bowl, unsigned
The tallest: 8in. (Total: 4 Items)
Estimate: 200-400

30189
AN AMERICAN GLASS VASE
Wavecrest, c.1900

The bottom of the white glass stick bottle fitted with footed gilt-metal mount, the obverse and reverse with conforming reserve of flowers, the sides painted pastel pink, rising to gilt-metal collar, the underside with red *Wave Crest* mark
8in. high
Estimate: 200-400

30188
AN AMERICAN GLASS AND BRONZE PAPERWEIGHT
Wavecrest, c.1900

The ribbed domed glass in ivory to pale pink decorated with a flowers and twigs, enamel highlights, supported by four bronze stylized leaf feet threaded to a fairy finial playing cymbals, unsigned
4.2in. high
Estimate: 200-400

30190
THREE SOUTH JERSEY AQUA GREEN GLASS ITEMS
Makers unknown, Nineteenth Century

Including a stick decanter with swirl body, a hyacinth bulb pot of tapered cylindrical form, *together with* bulbous cabinet vase with ruffled rim, the underside of each piece with uplifted and cut pontil, all pieces unmarked
9.25in. high (Total: 3 Items)
Estimate: 100-200

30191
A SATIN GLASS EPERGNE WITH SILVERPLATED MOUNTS
Maker unknown, c.1900

The silverplate foot decorated with beading and a floral pattern rising to a threaded platform to support the low satin glass bowl in white to a blue heavily ruffled rim, the second level of the silver mount has a swirl ribbed foot, cylindrical form to a filigree rim into which fits the ivory glass trumpet form ruffled rim vase, cased in blue, the glass epergne and vase are decorated in enamel depicting birds, leaves and flowers, unsigned
17in. high
Estimate: 300-500

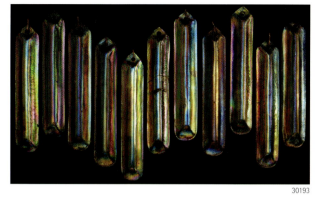

30193
ELEVEN AMERICAN ART NOUVEAU IRIDESCENT GOLD GLASS LUSTRE PRISMS
probably Quezal, c.1900

Each mold-blown baguette with faceted obverse and flat reverse, the pointed top pierced for hanging, each with green, blue, and magenta highlights, unsigned
9in. long (Total: 11 Items)
Estimate: 300-500

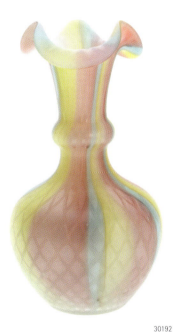

30192
A SATIN GLASS VASE
Maker unknown, c.1900

The bulbous form rising to a knobbed cylindrical neck with a tri-fold rim in a rainbow diamond quilt mother of pearl pattern, unsigned
6.2in. high
Estimate: 200-400

30194
COLLECTION OF AMERICAN GREEN GLASS ITEMS
Makers unknown, c.1880

Comprising a high-shouldered blown bottle with cut pontil, a mold-blown knob-stemmed cordial, and three mold-blown shot glasses, all unmarked
9.75in. high (Total: 5)
Estimate: 50-100

30195
FOUR AMERICAN PRESSED GLASS ITEMS
Various makers, c.1900

Comprising a Deleware pattern creamer, ivory ground with a cranberry stain to the raised pattern an rim; a Heisey souvenir custard goblet with a beaded swag to the bowl, rose pattern and Sun Prairie, Wis. to the front; a Heisey custard punch cup with a rose pattern to the side, gilt rim; and a green Georgia gem toothpick holder, paneled sides and beading to the neck and rim, unsigned
The tallest: 6.1in. (Total: 4 Items)
Estimate: 100-300

30197
AN AMERICAN GLASS LETTER HOLDER
Wavecrest, c.1900

The rectangular form with raised French-style cartouches painted with pink and white flowers, brass 'zipper' mount to lip rim, the underside with red *Wave Crest* mark
4.25in. high
Estimate: 300-500

30196
AN AMERICAN GLASS LIDDED DRESSER BOX
Wavecrest, c.1900

The flared bulbous form box in pale pink with two ivory ground cartouches, metal hinged mount supports a pink to ivory lid, the cartouches and center of the lid are decorated with blue and brown flowers with enamel highlights, raised relief flowers and scroll work to the box and lid, stamped underside *Wave Crest*
4.5in. high
Estimate: 300-500

30198
AN AMERICAN ART GLASS VASE
Steuben, c.1928

The flaring bulbous form in Green Jade over Alabaster depicting stylized blossoms on branches with clouds, engraved underside with the shape number *6078*
6.9in. high
Estimate: 800-1,000

30199
AN AMERICAN IRIDESCENT GOLD ART GLASS VASE
Lundberg Studios, Twentieth Century

The dome-footed body of elongated ovoid form with flared rim with magenta highlights, enhanced with green pulled-feather decoration in the 'Moiré Fern' pattern, the underside with short, cut pontil etched with signature, date and number: *Lundberg Studio 2000 041416*
11.75in. high
Estimate: 100-200

30199

30093

30200
AN AMERICAN ART GLASS VASE
Steuben, c.1905

The blue Aurene ribbed bulbous form with a cylindrical neck to a flared rim, stamped underside *Steuben*
4.9in. high
Estimate: 500-700

30201

30201
FIVE ITALIAN GLASS ITEMS
Murano, c.1960

Comprising a mirror black handkerchief vase with multicolored canes near the foot to represent flowers; a low flaring bowl with one third of the rim turned in, white ground with clear external casing, mottled and multicolored canes primarily in green to the inside, internal silver flakes; a low wide bowl with a scalloped rim in a white ground with multicolored canes in a mottled pattern with internal silver flakes; a clear low bowl with one quarter of the rim turn with a scroll, decorated with multicolored mottled canes with internal silver flakes; a low bowl with white ground and clear external ribbed casing, red interior casing with white canes to depict flowers, scalloped rim alternating between an upturned edge and straight edge, unsigned
The tallest: 9.5in high (Total: 5 Items)
Estimate: 200-400

30202

30202
AN AUSTRIAN IRIDESCENT GLASS SEASHELL
Loetz, c.1898

The footed shell form with applique seaweed rising form the foot on either side, patterned to resemble the surface of a shell, in iridescent gold with magenta highlights, engraved underside *Loetz Austria*
8.2in. high, 14.1in. long
Estimate: 800-1,000

30203

30204

30203
AN AMERICAN IRIDESCENT BLUE GLASS VASE
Maker unknown, c.1980

The molded cylindrical vase with flared and ruffled flora-form rim, unsigned
16in. high
Estimate: 100-200

30204
AN AMERICAN IRIDESCENT GOLD BLOWN GLASS VASE
Lundberg Studios, Twentieth Century

Entitled 'Moiré Fern', the dome-footed trumpet form with pulled-feather decoration to simulate watermarked fabric, the underside with cut pontil surrounded by script signature, date, and number *Lundberg Studios 1999 041414*
9.3in. high
Estimate: 100-300

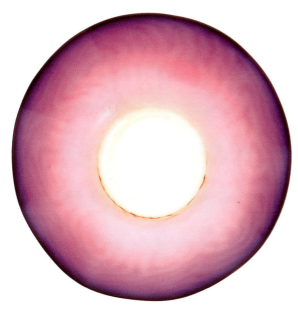

30205
AN AMERICAN ALEXANDRITE GLASS SAUCER
Libbey, c.1905

The flora-form with amber-yellow center graduating to magenta and then to the ultramarine blue rim, unmarked
5in. diameter
Estimate: 100-300

30207
AN AMERICAN ART GLASS VASE
Steuben, c.1925

The ivory ribbed double-gourd form rising to a flared and slightly scalloped rim, unsigned
5.9in. high
Estimate: 200-400

30206
SIX ITALIAN GLASS ITEMS
Murano, c.1960

Comprising a yellow cased glass low bowl with amber exterior bi-fold rim; a leaf shaped bowl with a green glass exterior and a mottled white and bronze interior, scalloped rim and pinched leaf stem handle; an amber to green bowl with a six petal flower shape foot to three square shape leaf forms, three slender curved handles coming together and curved back at the top; two amber interior to clear exterior controlled bubble trays with a shallow swirl pattern to the exterior, one slightly deeper than the other; and a clear leaping fish form figurine, the fish artist-signed to the underside and has a *Murano Made in Italy* sticker to the side
The tallest: 7.5in. (Total: 6 Items)
Estimate: 200-400

30208
AN AMERICAN GOLD CALCITE GLASS ROSE BOWL
Steuben, c.1925

The iridized lead glass globular body with vertical ribbing and shaped rim, the interior with Gold Aurene, unsigned
3.25in. high
Estimate: 300-600

30209
AN AMERICAN VASELINE GLASS FISH BOWL ON STAND
Maker unknown, c.1935

The black-painted geometrical metal stand with four curled prongs that secure the flattened spherical bowl with reverse rib motif, unmarked
40in. overall high (Total: 2 Items)
Estimate: 600-900

30211
AN AMERICAN IRIDESCENT GOLD ART GLASS VASE
Lundberg Studios, Twentieth Century

The green dome-footed body of elongated corset form with flared tri-lobed rim with magenta highlights enhanced with green pulled-feather decoration in the 'Moiré Fern' pattern, the underside with short, cut pontil etched with signature, date and number: *Lundberg Studio 2000 051060 081629*
13.25in. high
Estimate: 100-300

30210
A CONTINENTAL SILVER AND CUT GLASS SUGAR CASTER
Maker unknown, c.1900

The barrel form with starburst underside and three similar starbursts connected by scallops beneath a silver-collared rim with tension-fitted pierced cover, the silver rim with two Hungarian touch marks
5in. high
Estimate: 50-100

30212
THREE AMERICAN ART GLASS SERVING PIECES
Steuben, c.1934

Comprising a dome footed compote with four applied teardrop-style ornaments supporting a low, wide bowl; a bulbous nappy with a curled applied handle; and a tapering cylindrical pitcher with a double applied handle fusing into one at the top, all etched underside
The tallest: 10.5in. (Total: 3 Items)
Estimate: 300-500

30215
AN AMERICAN IRIDESCENT GOLD ART GLASS VASE
Lundberg Studios, Twentieth Century

The dome-footed body of elongated ovoid form with everted rim enhanced with green pulled-feather decoration in the 'Moiré Fern' pattern, the underside with short, cut pontil encircled with signature, date and number: *Lundberg Studio 1999 081629*
13.25in. high
Estimate: 100-300

30213
AN AMERICAN IRIDESCENT GOLD ART GLASS VASE
Lundberg Studios, Twentieth Century

The ovoid body with everted rim enhanced with 'Green Garland' pattern, the underside with short, cut pontil etched with signature, date and number: *Lundberg Studio 1999 0927266*
13.25in. high
Estimate: 100-200

30214
AN AUSTRIAN GLASS VASE
Loetz, c.1890

The green-gold ovoid form with iridescent peacock pulled-wave decoration, the underside with etched signature *Loetz/Austria*
8in. high
Estimate: 600-800

30216
THREE AMERICAN ART GLASS VASES
Lundberg Studios and others, Twentieth Century

Including a green-cased-in-clear trumpet vase with twelve orange rods radiating from the base of the green glass with clear applied foot, a blue-cased-in-clear-frosted glass trumpet vase with applied cobalt, *together with* a Lundberg cylindrical pink vase with concave sides decorated with green 'pulled feather' in the 'Moiré Fern' pattern, the interior with iridescent gold; the underside of the Lundberg 'Moiré Fern' vase with smooth pontil encircled with etched signature, date and number: *Lundberg Studios 1986 070915*
The tallest: 11.75in. high (Total: 3 Items)
Estimate: 400-600

30217
AN AMERICAN OPALESCENT ART GLASS PARFAIT
Tiffany & Co., c.1902

The round ivory opalescent foot supporting a cylindrical body with a flared rim decorated in clear to ivory to pastel blue ribs, engraved underside *L. C. T. Favrile*
5.1in. high
Estimate: 300-500

30217

30218
AN AMERICAN ART GLASS VASE
Steuben, c.1925

The round alabaster foot rising to a slender baluster form Rosaline vase, triangular paper label underside
11.9in. high
Estimate: 300-500

30218

30219
AN AMERICAN IRIDESCENT GOLD ART GLASS VASE
Lundberg Studios, Twentieth Century

The flared cylindrical body with everted rim, enhanced with 'Moiré Fern' pattern, the underside with etched pontil signature, date and number: *Lundberg Studio 2000 042678*
13.25in. high
Estimate: 200-300

30219

30220
AN AMERICAN ART GLASS VASE
Steuben, c.1905

The iridescent flaring bulbous form Blue Aurene vase with a short neck and flared rim, iridescent ultramarine blue with green and magenta flashes, engraved signature underside *Steuben Aurene*
10.5in. high
Estimate: 1,800-2,200

30220

30221
AN AMERICAN OPALESCENT ART GLASS SHERBERT
Tiffany & Co., c.1902

The round foot rising to a short clear stem supporting a ribbed bowl in pastel opalescent green with a flared rim, engraved underside *1281 L. C. T. Favrile*
3.5in. high
Estimate: 300-500

30221

30222
AN AMERICAN PEACH BLOW GLASS VASE
Hobbs, Brockunier & Co., c.1890

The Morgan Vase consisting of an amber gargoyle resin base and an ovoid form vase with a waisted cylindrical neck and flared rim in custard to ruby, cased in ivory, unsigned
10in. high
Estimate: 800-1,000

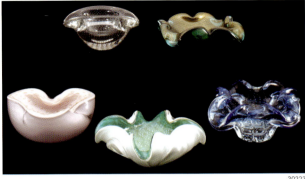

30223
FIVE ITALIAN GLASS TRAYS
probably Murano, c.1960

Including a controlled-bubble clear oval tray, a gold-suspended and controlled-bubble pink cased in clear trilobed tray, a controlled-bubble blue-cased-in-clear flora-form tray, a silver-suspended green-cased-in-white-cased-in-clear flora-form tray, *together with* a gold-suspended emerald green flora-form tray
The tallest: 2.5in. high (Total: 5 Items)
Estimate: 200-300

30224
AN AMERICAN ART GLASS VASE
Lundberg Studios, Twentieth Century

The white ovoid body with everted rim enhanced with green and blue pulled-feather decoration in the 'Moiré Fern' pattern, the underside with cut pontil, the underside of the foot rim with signature and date: *Lundberg Studios 1976*
13.25in. high
Estimate: 100-200

30225
AN AMERICAN ART GLASS COMPOTE
Tiffany & Co., c.1922

The round clear foot with an opalescent edge beneath a baluster form stem and low clear to opalescent plate decorated with green and blue morning glories, decorated prunts simulating drips to the underside of the plate, engraved underside *L. C. Tiffany Favrile 2099P*
2.4in. high x 7in. diameter
Estimate: 2,000-3,000

30226
AN AMERICAN ART GLASS LAMP
Steuben, c.1925

The gilt metal base supports a baluster form Gold Aurene over Mirror Black lamp, etched to depict gold poppies on a black ground, magenta flash to foot, brass lamp fittings, unsigned
27in. high
Estimate: 3,000-4,000

30227
A FRENCH OVERLAID AND ETCHED GLASS VASE
Emile Gallé, c.1900

The clear ovoid form with a cylindrical neck overlaid and etched to depict long stem flowers in pink and purple, signed in relief *Gallé*
7.6in. high
Estimate: 300-500

30228
AN ENGLISH SATIN AND ENAMEL GLASS VASE
Thomas Webb & Sons, c.1890

The ivory cased ovoid form to a ruffled rim in rose fish scale pattern with gilt floral pattern to the obverse and reverse with a butterfly on either side of the shoulder, gilt detail to the rim, enamel initials to the underside *G. S. F.*
7.4
Estimate: 900-1,100

30229

30229
AN ENGLISH TRIPLE-OVERLAID AND ETCHED GLASS CABINET VASE
Thomas Webb & Sons, c.1890

The bulbous form overlaid in cerulean-blue, white and amethyst and etched to depict undulating hibiscus branches with foliage, buds and flowers on the obverse, the reverse with a single bee, unmarked
1.6in. high
Estimate: 200-400

30230

30230
A FRENCH OVERLAID AND ETCHED GLASS VASE
Charles Schneider, c.1925

The cushion foot trumpet vase layered with mottled blue, white and purple, overlaid mottled purple geometric pattern to the foot and a stylized hanging flowers and border to the body and rim, raised signature to the side *Charder*, etched *Le Verre Francais* on the top of the foot and stamped *France* underside
5.9in. high
Estimate: 700-900

30231

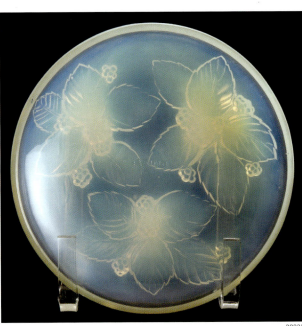

30231
AN ENGLISH OVERLAID AND ETCHED GLASS VASE
Thomas Webb & Sons, c.1900

The ovoid form with an everted rim in ruby ground overlaid with ivory and etched to depict trailing vines and border pattern, cased in ivory, unsigned
3.1in. high
Estimate: 200-300

30232
A FRENCH OPALESCENT GLASS BOWL
Sabino, c.1961

The tri-foot opalescent berry pattern low bowl, raised stamp to inside center
5.7in. diameter
Estimate: 100-200

30232

30233
A FRENCH OPALESCENT ART GLASS VASE
Sabino, c.1950

The ivory opalescent square foot supports a trumpet form vase depicting four rows of vertical fish in relief, stamped in mold on the side *Sabino Paris* and a paper label on underside *Made in France*
5.1in. high
Estimate: 100-300

30235
AN ENGLISH OVERLAID, ETCHED AND SILVER-MOUNTED GLASS CABINET VASE
Thomas Webb & Sons, c.1885

The frosted blue ground body overlaid in white and etched to depict oak branches with acorns, the sterling-rimmed collar with lion passant, leopard's head, Victoria duty mark, date mark of 1885-1886, and maker's mark *JWN* over *JTN*, glass unmarked
1.75in. high
Estimate: 500-800

30234
A FRENCH MOLD-BLOWN GLASS PLATE
René Lalique c.1940

The frosted to clear circular form with clear circular center surrounded by five graduated bands of pointed leaves enclosed by undulated rim, acid-etched stamp mark in block letters *R. LALIQUE/ FRANCE*
13.75in. diameter (Total: 1 Items)
Estimate: 100-300

30236
A FRENCH OPALESCENT MOLD-BLOWN 'DOMREMY' GLASS VASE
René Lalique, c.1926

The ovoid form with bas-relief depicting thistle plants and blooms, recessed block letter signature in mold *R. LALIQUE*
8.75in. high
Estimate: 300-500

30237
FOUR FRENCH OPALESCENT GLASS FIGURINES
Sabino, c.1950

Including two of 'Venus de Milo' and two of butterfly, each with paper maker's label
2.75in. high (Total: 4 Items)
Estimate: 100-300

30238
A FRENCH OVERLAID AND ETCHED GLASS VASE
Daum Nancy, c.1890

The square form vase overlaid and etched to depict mottled leaves in orange and reds, cased in mottled brown and yellow, raised signature on side *Daum Nancy* with the *Cross of Lorraine*
4.6in. high
Estimate: 300-500

30239
A FRENCH MOLDED GLASS BOX
René Lalique, c.1919

The cylindrical cover with frosted and tinted pattern 'Deux Pigeon', the conforming clear basin with extended foot, the side of the tinted cover with molded block letter signature *R. LALIQUE* and the underside of the clear basin with etched script *France*,
1.6in. high
Estimate: 800-1,200

30240
AN ENGLISH OVERLAID AND ETCHED GLASS BOWL
Thomas Webb & Sons, c.1890

The low bulbous bowl in clear etched finish overlaid in ivory to depict hanging vines and flowers, stamped underside *Thomas Webb & Sons. Cameo*
4.9in. diameter
Estimate: 300-500

30241
A FRENCH GLASS AND SILVER TANTALUS
Baccarat, c.1940

The three flattened sphere-form ribbed decanters, applied handles and spout with a ball stopper are supported in a silver rectangular geometric form three-stall holder with a mirrored foot, three caps attached to a single elevating bar lock down on the corresponding glass stoppers, the decanters stamped underside *Baccarat France*
8.1in. high x 13in. long (Total: 4 Items)
Estimate: 5,000-7,000

30243

A FRENCH OVERLAID AND ETCHED GLASS STICK VASE
Emile Gallé, c.1900

The oblong bulbous subtle double-gourd stick vase in orange to clear etched finished ground with a pattern of leaves and cherries in red, cameo signature to the reverse with a star preceding the signature *Gallé*
10in. high
Estimate: 800–1,200

30242

A FRENCH OVERLAID AND ETCHED GLASS VASE
Daum Nancy, c.1900

The bulbous to stick form vase in cobalt to mottled white ground overlaid and etched to depict green leaves and violets, signed on side *Daum Nancy*
8.2in. high
Estimate: 2,000–4,000

30244

THREE CRYSTAL EAGLES
Various makers, c.1980

Comprising a Baccarat eagle on rocks, wings held out and his head turned to the right; a Steuben eagle in profile with spread wings; and a geometric styled eagle, wings spread and looking toward his right, the Baccarat eagle stamped underside and signed on the side, the Steuben eagle signed underside
The tallest: 6.8in. (Total: 3 Items)
Estimate: 50–150

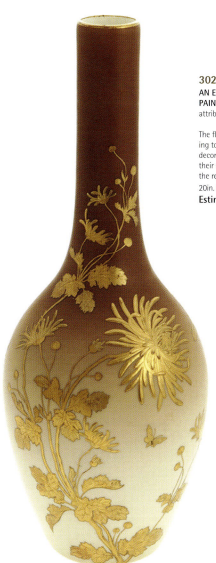

30245
AN ENGLISH CASED SATIN GLASS PAINTED ENAMEL VASE
attributed to Thomas Webb & Sons, c.1880

The flaring bulbous form in pale tan tapering to a cylindrical neck in brown, obverse decoration depicting gilt chrysanthemums on their stem, seven insects of various sizes to the reverse, gilt highlight to rim, unsigned
20in. high
Estimate: 1,200–1,500

30246
A FRENCH ART DECO STYLE GLASS VASE
Muller Frere Luneville, c.1905

The Art Deco style molded etched glass globular form vase with four raised vertical ribbed sections, three horizontal ribs to the lower half, layered triangular pattern to the upper half, stamped in mold on the side of the foot *Muller Frere Luneville*
6.2in. high
Estimate: 100–300

30247
A FRENCH ENAMEL DECORATED TUMBLER
Emile Gallé, c.1890

The paneled tumbler with polychrome enamel decoration, on the obverse a male figure and on the reverse his identification: *Le Marquis de Carabas,* a character from Charles Perrault's 'Puss in Boots' (*Le Maistre Chat,* or *le Chat Botté*), the underside of tumbler with black enamel signature *E. Gallé/Nancy*
4.3in. high
Estimate: 500–800

30248
A FRENCH OVERLAID AND ETCHED GLASS OIL BURNER
St. Louis Cristuax d'Art, c.1930

The ovoid body with cranberry-cut-to-clear geometric decoration, the neck with yellow metal collar and cover, opening to reveal a wick, the underside with diamond-enclosed mark *St. Louis Cristaux d'Art*
7in. high
Estimate: 600–900

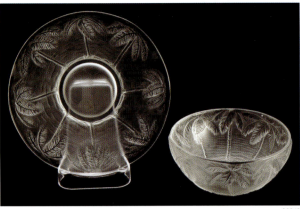

30249
A FRENCH MOLD-BLOWN GLASS BOWL AND UNDERLINER
René Lalique, c.1930

The frosted glass ensemble molded with palm tree and sea wave motif, the underside of each piece with diamond-etched script signature *Lalique/France*
bowl 2.125in. high, underliner 6.5in. (Total: 2 Items)
Estimate: 100-300

30250
A FRENCH GLASS BOWL
René Lalique, c.1925

The frosted and clear glass bowl with a design of stylized wheat, engraved underside *Lalique France*
9.8in. diameter
Estimate: 300-500

30251
A FRENCH OVERLAID AND ETCHED GLASS VASE
Emile Gallé, c.1890

The oval frosted pink form rising to a 'pinched' rim, overlaid in olive-green and brown and etched to depict a wooded landscape with lake, with cameo signature *Gallé*
6.4in. high
Estimate: 1,400-1,800

30252
A FRENCH OVERLAID AND ETCHED GLASS VASE
Emile Gallé, c.1890

The coupe form step foot in burnt orange with flashes of blue rising to a wide bulbous bowl in clear to a pale pink scalloped rim, decorated with burnt orange blossoms on branches, internal etched decoration of pale pink blossoms, raised signature to side *Gallé*
4.6in. high, 6.5in. diameter
Estimate: 1,500-2,000

30253

30253
AN ENGLISH OVERLAID AND ETCHED GLASS VASE
Stevens & Williams, c.1860

The ruby ground bulbous form to a cylindrical neck overlaid and etched in ivory to depict three panels of fox hunting scenes, stylized flowers between the panels, etched signature underside *J. Millward No. 12*
12.in. high

Illustrated in 'English Cameo Glass' by Ray and Lee Grover, page 164, illustration no. 131
Estimate: 3,000-5,000

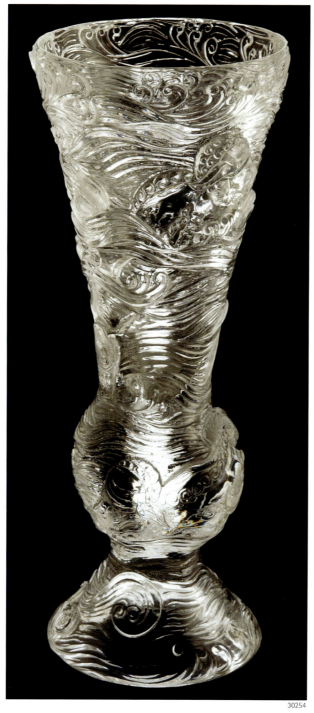

30254
AN ENGLISH ROCK CRYSTAL VASE
Thomas Webb & Sons, c.1900

The inverted trumpet form foot supporting a ball to trumpet form body deeply engraved and polished to depict stylized fish in waves, stamped underside *Thos. Webb & Sons.*
8.5in. high
Estimate: 3,000-5,000

The Dot Talbert Collection

30255

30255
A CONTINENTAL FIGURAL GROUP ON A SHELL STAND
Royal Dux, c.1890

The footed base supports a half shell with rose garland, the figural couple in Victorian dress stand on a tree trunk positioned behind the shell, pink triangle ceramic fired-on stamp
11.6in. high
Estimate: 200-400

30256

30256
FIVE CABINET PLATES
Various makers, various production dates

Including a Twentieth Century English Royal Doulton charger entitled 'Hampton Court'; an early Twentieth Century German shaped plate with yellow rose decoration; a German cabinet plate depicting reapers in the field; a mid-Nineteenth Century French Sèvres Chateau de St. Cloud hard paste portrait plate of Madame de Lavalliere, signed *Debrie, together with* an early Twentieth Century English portrait plate of a fisherman smoking a pipe, the 'Hampton Court' charger with green underglaze *Royal Doulton* mark, the German yellow rose plate with green overglaze mark *E.S. Germany*, the reapers plate with underglaze blue pseudo-beehive mark, the French portrait plate with underglaze blue *Sèvres* mark and with underglaze red *St. Cloud* mark, the English portrait plate unmarked
The largest: 13.5in. diameter (Total: 5 Items)
Estimate: 300-400

30257
A FRENCH CHAMPLEVE-MOUNTED PORCELAIN VASE
Maker unknown, c.1890

The foot comprising a circular brass disc supporting a green onyx socle and champleve-decorated brass stem, the pastel pink porcelain body of elongated ovoid form, the obverse with oblong reserve of two musical putti framed in raised gilt decoration, the reverse with trophy of musical instruments, surmounted by champleve-decorated neck with brass rim, the obverse reserve signed *Collot*
9.75in. high
Estimate: 100-300

30257

30258

30258
TWO ENGLISH CERAMIC TOBY MUGS
Royal Doulton, c1970, Rockingham, c.1890

The 'Yachtsman' depicts a simplistic style bust of a man wearing a black cap and a sailboat handle, signed with Royal Doulton stamp; the second mug depicts an stylized face of a man in brown and green glaze with handle in back, unsigned
7.7in. high and 8in. high respectively (Total: 2 Items)
Estimate: 200-300

30259

30259
FOUR ASIAN CHAMPLEVE ITEMS
Makers unknown, c.1920

Comprising a wall-mounted Holy Water dispenser of hexagonal form with conforming hinged lid; a cigarette urn; a double-handled ovoid vase with white onyx plinth; a covered match box, each unmarked
The tallest: 6.25in. (Total: 4 Items)
Estimate: 300-500

30260

30260
A FRENCH MOLD-BLOWN OPALESCENT GLASS PLATE
Sabino, 'Henri IIII', c.1970

The center depicting the conjoined busts of Henri IV of France, wearing the ribbon and cross of the Order of the Holy Ghost, and his Queen, Marie de Medici, and intaglio inscription 'HENR. IIII. R. CHRIST.' (Henry the Fourth, Most Christian King) MARIA. AVGVSTA'. (Empress Marie), surrounded by six demi-lune reserves of stylized flowers and leaves, diamond-point inscription *Edition limitée 1970/Sabino/France*
8.25in. diameter
Estimate: 200-400

30261

30261
AN ENGLISH METAL AND LITHOPHANE TEAPOT WARMER
English, c.1890

The footed metal warmer with four-panel porcelain lithophane depicting harbor scenes, each panel titled 'Thousand Isles', glass insert and pierced metal lid, signed *Brocken* on one lithophane
4.4in. high
Estimate: 100-200

30262

30262
TWO CONTINENTAL PARIANWARE ITEMS
Makers unknown, c.1900

The first, a footed ovoid pitcher with bas-relief figural decoration and with glazed interior, unsigned; the second, a German miniature bisque bust of Dante, stamped underside *Germany*
The bust: 7in. high (Total: 2 Items)
Estimate: 100-200

30263
THREE HAND-PAINTED CERAMIC ITEMS
Nippon and F. Thomas Porcelain Factory, c.1910

Comprising two Nippon hatpin holders; a plate with landscape decoration; a German plate with double handles and decorated with red poppies; *together with* a green bowl with red and yellow roses, each piece with respective maker's mark
The hatpin holders: 4.25in. high (Total: 5 Items)
Estimate: 200-400

30264
A FRENCH WHITE METAL FIGURE
Ernest Rancoulet, c.1900

The copper-patinated figure of a peasant maiden carrying a basket with flowers, wine over her shoulder and a baton in her left hand, standing on a circular stepped plinth, modeled signature on lower hem of skirt *Rancoulet*
18.5in. high
Estimate: 200-400

30265
A FRENCH WHITE METAL FIGURE
Ernest Rancoulet, c.1900

The copper-patinated figure of a peasant maiden carrying water and standing on a circular stepped plinth, modeled signature on lover hem of skirt *Rancoulet*
18in. high
Estimate: 200-300

30266
FOUR CONTINENTAL PORCELAIN BLACKAMOOR FIGURINES
Rosenthal, c.1956

Each dressed in servant attire carrying various serving dishes with food, each signed underglaze with the *Rosenthal* stamp
each 7.5in. high (Total: 4 Items)
Estimate: 400-600

30267
AN ITALIAN CONTROLLED-BUBBLE GLASS BOWL
Maker unknown, c.1930

The clear, five-lobed and flared foot supporting the golden-citrine flower-formed bowl enhanced with suspended silver, each of the five petals curling inward to form a shaped and undulating rim, unsigned
2.25in. high, 7in. diameter
Estimate: 100-200

30269
FOUR FRENCH BISQUE FIGURINES
Makers unknown, c.1930

The first pair a Victorian couple in white porcelain with peach-colored attire and raised gilt pattern; the second couple primarily attired in pink and white, both holding flowers, each unsigned 10.7in. high and 11.7in. high respectively (Total: 4 items)
Estimate: 100-200

30268
A FRENCH MOLD-BLOWN OPALESCENT GLASS PLATE
Sabino, 'Grand Prix', c.1971

The center depicting Hercules, surrounded by six demilune reserves of stylized flowers and leaves; diamond-point inscription *Edition limitée 1971/Sabino/France*
8.25in. diameter
Estimate: 200-400

30270
A PAIR OF CHAMPLEVE ENAMEL CANDLESTICKS
Maker unknown, c.1890

Bronze with inlaid multi-colored enamel, removable bobeche and wax pans, cast rococo bases, unsigned
5.8in. high (Total: 2 Items)
Estimate: 100-300

30271
A GERMAN PORCELAIN FIGURINE
W. Goebel, c.1914

The ivory bisque oval plinth supports a female figure in peasant attire pouring milk in front of a dog cart containing milk jugs, pulled by two dogs, the title of the piece in relief to the front of the plinth *La L'aitiere flamande*, stamped underside
7.5in. high
Estimate: 200-400

30272
AN ASSORTED LOT OF CERAMIC AND GLASS ITEMS
Various makers, various dates

Comprising a Royal Bonn vase, stamped underside; three matching Limoges nut dishes, stamped underside; a Davenport plate, impressed underside; an Alleptons Gaudy Welsh pattern creamer, stamped underside; a cobalt glass pitcher with applied handle, unsigned
The tallest: 9.1in. high (Total: 7 Items)
Estimate: 100-300

30273
A LARGE GLASS PAPERWEIGHT
Maker unknown, Twentieth Century

With white and red internal flowers and air bubbles for the stamens, unsigned
6.5in. diameter
Estimate: 100-300

30274
AN AMERICAN SILVER ARTS AND CRAFTS STYLE SWEET MEAT BASKET
Tiffany Studios, c.1915

Round pedestal foot supporting a flaring bowl with elaborate floral cut-out decoration, threaded rim and handle, Old English *B.F.* monogram in center, marked underside
5.7in. across, 5.5in. across
Estimate: 100-300

30275
TWO ENGLISH PORCELAIN TOBY MUG CREAMERS
Royal Doulton, c.1946

Comprising one creamer formed as an older man with a white cravat and brown hat titled 'Old Charley'; the second formed as a man winking with a fish handle titled 'The Poacher', both stamped underglaze with the Royal Doulton mark
3.4in. high and 3.7in. high respectively (Total: 2 items)
Estimate: 100-150

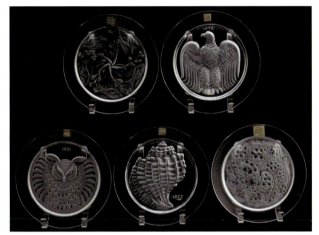

30276
FIVE FRENCH ETCHED ANNUAL COMMEMORATIVE PLATES
René Lalique, Twentieth Century

Comprising five different images, 1967 fish ballet, 1971 owl, 1972 shell, 1974 silver pennies, and 1976 Bi-Centennial eagle, all images etched on reverse, each plate etched *Lalique France* and with its own box
8.5in. diameter (Total: 5 Items)
Estimate: 200-300

30277
A GERMAN DORE BRONZE AND IVORY SCULPTURE
Else Fürst, c.1911

The early Twentieth Century bronze inset with carved ivory, set upon a marble base, depicts a woman in Edwardian dress playing a guitar, Gladenbeck Foundry, Berlin, signed on edge, *Else Fürst, 1911*
7.8in. high
Estimate: 700-1,000

30278

30278
FOUR FRENCH PATE D' VERRE PLATES
Daum Nancy, c.1970

Comprising four different colored designs depicting mythological scenes of the four seasons, raised signature on each *Daum ED*
10.4in. diameter (Total: 4 Items)
Estimate: 700-1,000

30280

30280
AN AMERICAN CERAMIC PITCHER AND BASIN
Warwick China Co., c.1895

The footed round basin and the ovoid pitcher with transfer decoration of springs of purple flowers on the interior and exterior surfaces and with sponged gold rims, both pieces with underglaze black mark *WARWICK CHINA*
12.5in. high (Total: 2 Items)
Estimate: 300-400

30281

30281
FOUR AMERICAN PAPERWEIGHT GLASS OBJECTS
Joe St. Clair, c.1970

Comprising a chamber stick, a scent bottle, a figural bird paperweight, all yellow and clear, *together with* a green and clear scent bottle, impressed signature in pontil
The tallest: 5.3in. high (Total: 6 Items)
Estimate: 100-300

30279

30279
A COLLECTION OF WEST GERMAN EARTHENWARE ITEMS
Hümmel, late Twentieth Century

Comprising a 'Culprits 44A' lamp; 'Little Scholar' and 'School Girl' figures; '1977 FIRST EDITION ANNUAL BELL'; two '1979/9th ANNUAL PLATES' in original box, and one '1980/10th ANNUAL PLATE' in original box; both figures with underglaze black 'full bee' mark, lamp with underglaze blue 'full bee' mark, bell and all three plates with underglaze blue 'new bee' mark
The lamp base without shade: 12.25in. high (Total: 7 Items)
Estimate: 500-700

30282
A GERMAN PORCELAIN FIGURINE
Unger, Schneider & Hutchenreuther, c.1880

The ivory bisque female figure in classical dress holding an urn and chalice, stamped in porcelain
11in. high
Estimate: 100-200

30284
TWO ENGLISH PORCELAIN PLATES
Royal Doulton, c.1977

The limited edition artist-signed boat scenes, one depicting a harbour scene titled 'Sailing with the Tide', the other a ship at sea titled 'Running Free', signed under glaze and in the design *Stobart*, with presentation boxes
10in. diameter (Total: 2 Items)
Estimate: 150-200

30283
AN ENGLISH PORCELAIN FIGURINE
Royal Doulton, c.1930

The porcelain figural group, mother and child seated at a harpsichord, a man playing a woodwind instrument, all in 18th Century dress; the bone china lady 'Autumn Breezes' depicts a young woman in Victorian attire with wind swept clothing, stamped underside
The tallest: 7.5in. (Total: 2 Items)
Estimate: 150-200

30285
AN ENGLISH 'BEACHCOMBER' CERAMIC FIGURINE
Royal Doulton, c.1972

The octagonal base supporting a male figure seated upon a bag of shells and holding a shell in his right hand; green maker's mark *Beachcomber/HN2487*; incised number *43*
6.75in. high
Estimate: 100-300

30286

30286
THREE GERMAN PORCELAIN FIGURINES
Various makers, Twentieth Century

Each depicting a female dressed in floral-encrusted lace attire; the tallest figure with underglaze *M V* of *Muller & Co.* and with *Dresden Dec./Germany* on the underside; the seated figure with underglaze *Furstenberg* maker's mark on the underside; the small standing figure with impressed cipher of *Scheibe-Alsbach Porcelain Manufactory VEB* on the underside
The tallest: 4.5in. high (Total: 3 Items)

Estimate: 100-300

30287

30287
A BRITISH PEWTER ICE CREAM MOLD
Maker unknown, c.1868

The one-quart, three-part footed cylindrical form with a top depicting fruit in pewter, the threaded foot and lid are removable from the body revealing a fluted interior, stamped on the inside of the foot with the diamond hallmark of the British Empire
7in. high

Estimate: 100-300

30288

30288
FOUR AMERICAN GLASS PAPERWEIGHTS
Probably Joe St. Clair, c.1970

Including a controlled-bubble yellow flower on green ground, a segmented and controlled-bubble red apple, a segmented and controlled-bubble green pear, and a segmented and controlled-bubble yellow pear, all unmarked
The tallest: 6.5in. (Total: 4 Items)

Estimate: 100-200

30289

30289
THREE GERMAN PORCELAIN FIGURINES
Furstenberg and Oldest Volkstedt Porcelain Factory, c.early Twentieth Century

Comprising a small Furstenberg female dancer wearing a tiered lace dress with magenta bodice, a large Furstenberg figural grouping in Louis XV style with lady dressed in green-bodiced lace ensemble and seated before her French-style dressing table and mirror applying her make-up, *together with* an Oldest Volkstedt lady with posey; the small Furstenberg figure with 'crowned F' and 'Made in Germany' in underglaze blue on the underside, the large Furstenberg with 'crowned F' and 'Dresden' in underglaze black, and the Oldest Volkstedt with underglaze blue factory mark
The tallest: 7.5in. (Total: 3 items)

Estimate: 800-1,100

30290
THREE GERMAN PORCELAIN MUSICIAN FIGURINES
Meissen, c.1880

Comprising three monkeys playing musical instruments, each stamped with crossed swords underglaze
The tallest: 5in. high (Total: 3 Items)
Estimate: 200-300

30292
A CUT PAPER CROSS
Schereen-Schnitte, c.1900

The walnut and gold leaf frame with an ivory detailed paper cut-out cross and border on a brown velvet background, unsigned
18in. high x 15.3in. wide
Estimate: 100-150

30291
FOUR CONTINENTAL PORCELAIN FIGURINES
possibly Dresden, c.1920

Comprising a figural group on a gilt-trimmed base of a seated woman in a voluminous lace dress with applique flowers, a gentleman in a purple coat kissing her hand; the second a female in a multi-tiered dress of lace in pink and ivory; the third a ballerina; the fourth a seated woman in a lace skirt with applique flowers, various marks
Various sizes (Total: 4 items)
Estimate: 300-500

30293
A WOODEN GILT AND POLYCHROME DECORATED SANTOS FIGURE
Maker unknown, late Nineteenth Century

The platform base supports a figure of St. Theresa in blue-grey and gilt robes, unsigned
10.5in. high
Estimate: 600-800

30294
A GILT AND POLYCHROME DECORATED WOODEN SANTOS FIGURE
Maker unknown, c.1880

The carved wooden pedestal base supports the figure of St. Rogue in robes of brown and burgundy with gilding, a dog sits at his feet, unsigned
7in. high
Estimate: 200-400

30296
TWO ART NOUVEAU CERAMIC ITEMS
Makers unknown, c.1900

Comprising a double-handled ovoid vase with roundel of female head profile beneath swags of flowers; a covered dresser box with bas-relief of female head on obverse and glazed in pink, yellow, brown and green, each unsigned
The vase: 8.75in. high (Total: 3)
Estimate: 100-300

30295
A RUSSIAN ICON
Maker unknown, c.1850

The oil on board icon depicting the Virgin, Jesus and angels with a brass stylized overplate, unsigned
10.7in. high, 8.5in. wide
Estimate: 700-1,000

30297
AN ENGLISH MAJOLICA-STYLE STONEWARE VASE
Doulton Lambeth, c.1900

The heavily-potted ovoid form with raised decorative bands at foot, waist and shoulder, the short neck with flared and ruffled rim, unglazed underside with incised *DOULTON/LAMBETH/ENGLAND/148*, and with impressed letters *ha* and inscribed letters *AB*
6in. high
Estimate: 100-300

30298

30298
AN AMERICAN 'DONATELLO' POTTERY JARDINIERE
Roseville, c.1920

The ovoid form ribbed to the lower and upper edge in pale yellow and green with a scenic band depicting Donatello in sienna and cream, unsigned
6.6in. high
Estimate: 100-200

30300
AN AMERICAN 'MOSTIQUE' POTTERY VASE
Roseville, c.1915

Of the Arts and Crafts period, the tapering cylindrical body with flaring rim, decorated in green, yellow and blue design, marked underside *164*
8in. high
Estimate: 100-200

30300

30299

30299
TWO AMERICAN POTTERY VASES
Roseville, c.1945

The first a decorative pitcher mottled brown to mottled yellow ground with a relief design of a cactus and flower on both sides, glossy finish; the second a Freesia mold two-handled vase in shades of green with freesia in pale yellow and purple, satin finish, mold stamped underside
12.2in. high and 7.2in. high respectively (Total: 2 Items)
Estimate: 200-300

30301

30301
A PAIR OF AMERICAN BROWN 'FREESIA' POTTERY VASES
Roseville, c.1950

Each with disc foot swelling to amphora shaped body, angular double handles, the obverse with white and yellow raised freesia design and the reverse with white freesia, each with raised *Roseville* mark
8.5in. high (Total: 2 Items)
Estimate: 200-300

30303
AN AMERICAN 'APPLE BLOSSOM' POTTERY PLANTER
Roseville, c.1948

The pink rectangular planter with two branch form handles to the ends, raised mark and style number underside
11in. long
Estimate: 100-300

30302
A GROUP OF AMERICAN POTTERY ITEMS
Van Briggle, c.1910

Comprising an ivory Lorelei ovoid form vase depicting a female figure, her head and arm forming the rim; an elongated ovoid pitcher rising to a cylindrical tapering neck and handle in blue and green glaze; a pair of tulip form candlesticks in shades of blue and green, each incised underside
The tallest: 10.5in. high (Total: 4 Items)
Estimate: 100-300

30304
AN AMERICAN POTTERY LAMP
Van Briggle, c.1930

The footed bulbous form with ribbed tapering sides in shades of green and blue, original metal fittings and lamp shade in blue plastic with dried flowers, grasses and butterflies, incised signature underside
11.3in. high (Total: 2 Items)
Estimate: 200-400

30305
AN AMERICAN POTTERY VASE
Newcomb College style, c.1930

The two-handled baluster form in a mottled mid-brown to rust colored glaze decorated with a green ivy pattern near the rim, unsigned
10.5in. high
Estimate: 100-300

30306
A PAIR OF AMERICAN 'TEASEL' POTTERY CANDLESTICKS
Roseville, c.1938

The pink low candlesticks with a round foot supporting a candle cup flanked by raised decorative scroll handles, depicts a stylized plant with long, thin petals, marked underside
2in. high
Estimate: 100-200

30307

30307
AN AMERICAN POTTERY BOWL
Roseville, c.1924

The brown glazed form decorated with a band of stylized grapevine to the wide part of the body, marked underside
3.2in. high
Estimate: 100-300

30309

30309
AN AMERICAN POTTERY CORNISH VASE
Weller, c.1897

The bulbous form to a cylindrical neck in the Cornish pattern of matte mottled blue with two green leaves and a stylized hanging flower, two small scroll handles to the body, marked underside *C*
8.5in. high
Estimate: 600-800

30308

30308
TWO AMERICAN 'SNOWBERRY' POTTERY VASES
Roseville, c.1930

The first, with wedge-shaped plinth supporting a flattened body with angular handle; the second, with wedge-shaped plinth supporting a cornucopia body, each underside with molded *Roseville/U.S.A.*
The tallest: 7.25in. high (Total: 2 Items)
Estimate: 100-200

30310

30310
THREE AMERICAN 'ZEPHYR LILY' POTTERY ITEMS
Roseville, c.1930

Comprising a pair of candlestick holders *together with* a footed cylindrical double-handled vase with oval rim, each piece with molded *Roseville/U.S.A.* mark
The tallest: 9.25in. (Total: 3 Items)
Estimate: 200-300

30311

30311
AN AMERICAN POTTERY ART VASE
Weller, c.1930

The ovoid mottled blue glaze form, short tapering cylindrical neck, opposed spiral knob handles, decorated in the Cornish pattern of painted and embossed leaves and a branch in greens and browns with cherries in red and blue, signed underside
7.5in. high
Estimate: 800-1,200

30312

30312
AN AMERICAN GREEN 'PINE CONE' POTTERY CENTER BOWL
Roseville, c.1931

The elongated form in molded pine cone design with pine branch handles, raised mark underside
16.3in. long
Estimate: 200-400

30313

30313
TWO AMERICAN POTTERY VASES
Hull, c.1946

Both depicting a yellow magnolia over a mint green to pink ground in matte finish; the first, a vase with two handles low to the foot; the second, a cornucopia form with a stylized scroll handle, both marked underside
9.1in. high and 8.9in. high respectively (Total: 2 Items)
Estimate: 100-300

30314

30314
AN AMERICAN BLUE 'BUSHBERRY' POTTERY BASKET
Roseville, c.1950

The disc foot supporting an arrowhead-shaped body with asymmetrical twig handle, the obverse with single leaf design, the reverse with double leaf design, the underside with raised *Roseville* mark
8.5in. high
Estimate: 100-200

30315
AN AMERICAN POTTERY TRAY
Roseville, c.1940

The rectangular tray with off-set rectangular reserve with floral silhouette, the entire piece in Roseville pink glaze; standard raised *Roseville* mark
5in. long
Estimate: 100-200

30316
TWO AMERICAN GREEN 'PINE CONE' POTTERY BOWLS
Roseville, c.1931

Each bulbous form with a short slightly tapering neck and two branch handles to either side, marked underside
The largest: 4.2in. high, 6.5in. wide; the smaller: 3.2in. high, 5in. wide (Total: 2 Items)
Estimate: 100-300

30317
AN AMERICAN PINK 'PEONY' POTTERY BOWL
Roseville, c.1950

The shallow, textured body with double handles and shaped rim conforming to the yellow peony raised decoration on obverse and reverse, raised mark *Roseville/U.S.A.* on underside
3.5in. high
Estimate: 100-200

30318
AN AMERICAN POTTERY VASE AND PITCHER
Weller, c.1923

The vase in the Bonita pattern, the pitcher with oak leaves over a blue-green ground, both signed underside
4in. high and 8.6in. high respectively (Total: 2 Items)
Estimate: 100-300

30319
TWO PIECES OF AMERICAN POTTERY
Roseville and Weller, c.1940

Including a Roseville 'Thorn Apple' blue globular vase with double handles beneath the secondary rectangular vase openings, underside with molded *Roseville* mark; *together with* a Weller 'Dogwood' vase, the underside with impressed *Weller* mark,
The tallest: 5.5in. (Total: 2 Items)
Estimate: 100-200

30320
AN AMERICAN 'BLEEDING HEART' POTTERY VASE
Roseville, c.1940

The domed disc foot supports an elongated ovoid body with raised pink flower decoration on obverse and reverse, the high shoulders set with angular double handles beneath an hexagonal everted rim, raised *Roseville U.S.A.* mark on the underside
12.25in. high
Estimate: 100-200

30322
FOUR PIECES OF AMERICAN ART POTTERY
Roseville, c.1930

Comprising a 'Freesia' double-handle vase; a 'Water Lily' blue double-handle vase; a 'Magnolia' brown planter; a square 'Gardenia' brown vase, each piece with molded *Roseville/U.S.A.*
The tallest: 7.25in. (Total: 4 Items)
Estimate: 100-200

30323
AN AMERICAN ART POTTERY FIGURAL VASE
C. Romanelli, c.1941

The ivory oval foot rising to a tree trunk with a female nude leaning against it, three openings in the tree trunk, stamped underside
9.6in. high
Estimate: 100-200

30321
AN AMERICAN 'WHITE ROSE' POTTERY JUG
Roseville, c.1930

The deep cylindrical foot to an ovoid form with squared and spouted rim, the loop handle arching boldly from the vessel, the obverse and reverse with raised white rose spray design, the underside with molded *Roseville/U.S.A.* mark
7.5in. high
Estimate: 100-200

30324
AN AMERICAN 'GARDENIA' POTTERY HANGING BASKET
Roseville, c.1920

The pale green melon ribbed form with a slightly pointed underside rising to a corseted decoration depicting white gardenia and leaves over a band of burnt sienna, two handles by the rim, three pierced holes to the rim for hanging, raised stamp *USA* by handle
5.4in. high
Estimate: 100-200

30325
AN AMERICAN POTTERY EWER
Weller, c.1900

The flaring bulbous form in standard glaze of brown to green rising to a cylindrical neck and flared tri-fold rim in brown to black, large looping handle, the body decorated with yellow and burnt red flowers and leaves, stamped underside *Louwelsa Weller 577*
21.5in. high
Estimate: 200-400

30327
A GERMAN PORCELAIN CENTERPIECE
Schierholtz C.G. & Sons, c.1907

The base depicts a male angel draped in green fabric holding a cornucopia, the round basketweave bowl depicts multicolored flowers in the center, applied multicolored flowers and gilt detail overall, stamped underside
11.1in. high
Estimate: 300-500

30328
A CONTINENTAL PORCELAIN TEA SET
Maker unknown, c.1910

Comprising a globular covered tea pot, cream, open sugar bowl, three cups and saucers, each piece with ivory ground and panels of red and green heightened with heavy gilt decoration and with a round, artist-signed figural reserve on the obverse, each piece with green underglaze beehive mark on the underside, the teapot with gilt rose mark
The tallest: 4.8in. high (Total: 10 Items)
Estimate: 300-400

30326
A GERMAN PORCELAIN LIDDED URN
Mettlach, c.1880

The domed foot to a short collared stem supporting a large amphora form with a short neck and flared rim, two applied leaf form handles in green and gold, overall ground in brown tones with applied decoration to the obverse and reverse depicting two large Germanic eagles in black with a shield and wreath, gilt crown and ribbon, a female head of Justice wearing a blue blindfold below each handle, gilt scales behind and olive leaves below, a border decoration of the governmental state crests of Germany around the neck, a stepped finial decorated with a wreath of acorn leaves intertwined with a ribbon around the lid, stamped underside
17in. high
Estimate: 600-800

30329
A GROUP OF PORCELAIN ITEMS
Various makers, c.1900

Comprising a Royal Doulton teapot in yellow ochre with green leaf pattern; a KPM white ground plate with a peach and daisy pattern to the center, gilt rim; four demitasse cups and matching saucers in pale yellow with stylized brown flowers, gilt detail to rim and handle; two blue double handled vases with white herons to the front and gilt highlights overall; and a Goedewaagen blue pitcher decorated with a mottled pattern and a rope handle, all stamped underside
The tallest: 8.1in. high (Total: 14 Items)
Estimate: 200-400

30330
FIVE CONTINENTAL PORCELAIN PLATES
Dresden and Royal Austria, c.1883

Comprising four matching Czechoslovakian hand-painted plates in a pale yellow ground with rust colored flowers with green stems, gilt spider web to design and to rim, stamped underside *Royal Austria O. & A. G.*; together with a white porcelain ground divided into four alternating floral and figural patterns, central flower with radiating borders in gold matching the gold border to the rim, stamped underside
8.6in. diameter and 9in. diameter respectively (Total: 5 Items)
Estimate: 100-200

30331
A GERMAN CABINET PLATE
Langewiesen Factory, c.1895

The deep-footed circular form with bands of gilding, cerulean-blue, and ivory surrounding the central reserve rendered in polychrome enamels to depict the exploits of Odysseus and Nausikao, the central reserved signed *J. Arm‚ller*, the underside with overglaze cobalt blue pseudo-beehive mark and with overglaze red hand-scripted title, *ODYSSEUS AND NAUSIKAO*
10.6in. diameter
Estimate: 400-600

30332
A CONTINENTAL PORCELAIN PLATE
Langewiesen Factory, c.1900

The plate decorated with a central image depicting Odysseus and Telemachos surrounded by a gilt, pale yellow and cerulean blue band with additional gilt and white bead details, marked underside with a blue beehive
10.5in diameter
Estimate: 100-300

30333
A GROUP OF ENAMELED PORCELAIN AND GLASS OBJECTS
Sèvres, Limoges, Wavecrest

The first, a signed Sarlan Die Limoges enamel and foil over copper vase with fifteen multi-colored butterflies; the second, a Wavecrest multi-colored enamel dresser jar with gilt metal rim; the third, a Sèvres multi-colored enamel bud vase with gilt metal mount
The tallest: 6in. high (Total: 3 Items)
Estimate: 400-600

30335
AN ENGLISH STONEWARE URN
Doulton, c.1883

The wide foot tapering to a knopped stem supports a short bulbous base with a cylindrical body and small flared rim, faucet in the lower part of the body, low lid with knob handle, primarily in ironstone blue with ivory garland and birds overlay, impressed stamp underside
13.4in. high (Total: 3 Items)
Estimate: 300-500

30334
A FRENCH PORCELAIN TABLE LAMP
Sèvres, c.1950

The circular yellow metal plinth base under a bulbous porcelain body decorated with polychrome swags of flowers, gilding, and cobalt banding at the base and throat, the rim capped with yellow metal mount extending into a leaf-decorated standard *together with* a vintage, blue-banded silk shade, metal plinth stamped underside *France*
The lamp without bulb or shade 14.5in. high
Estimate: 300-500

30336
A FRENCH PORCELAIN DESSERT SERVICE
Lewis Strauss & Sons and Blakeman & Henderson Limoges, c.1905

Featuring a Blakeman & Henderson Limoges desert service comprising an oblong cake plate and six matching round plates, each piece with gilded shaped rim and transfer ware pink rose decoration; each with green underglaze *Limoges* stamp mark and with brown overglaze *Blakeman & Henderson* stamp mark, *together with* a Déposé Strauss Limoges square cake plate with scalloped and gilded border, pastel blue border and ivory ground with hand-painted and gilded bouquets of pink roses, blue *Limoges* and green *Déposé* stamp marks on unglazed underside; a Lewis Strauss round plate with shaped, beaded and gilded rim, the white ground with incised underglaze decoration and with hand-painted painted and gilded bouquets of pink roses, blue overglaze *Strauss* stamp mark and green underglaze *Limoges* mark
The largest 10.5in. square (Total: 9 Items)
Estimate: 200-300

30337
AN AMERICAN PORCELAIN AND SILVER OVERLAY TEA SET
Lennox, c.1900

The brown glaze with stylized Art Deco design lidded teapot with insert, lidded sugar dish and creamer, signed underglaze with the *Lennox* stamp
6.1in. high, 3.8in. high and 4in. high respectively (Total: 3 Items)
Estimate: 200-300

30338
THREE JAPANESE HAND-PAINTED PORCELAIN ITEMS
Nippon, Twentieth Century

A sugar and creamer with wild roses and gilt highlights, green mark, a hat pin holder with multi-colored flora and gilt accents, blue mark,
The tallest: 4.6in. (Total: 4 Items)
Estimate: 100-200

30339
A PAIR OF GERMAN PORCELAIN PLATES
Mitterteich, c.1940

Each footed and deep plate with circular reserve depicting mythological figures centered by alternating roundel reserves and gilt decorated panels, the underside with transfer and gilt mark *MITTERTEICH/Bavaria/Made in Germany*
10.7in. diameter (Total: 2 Items)
Estimate: 100-200

30340
THREE BRITISH PORCELAIN ITEMS
Wedgwood, late Eighteenth and Twentieth Century

Comprising a Twentieth Century vase depicting classical figures and garlands of grapes and leaves held by lion heads in ivory relief, stamped underside; a late Eighteenth Century plate depicting a female with a garland of flowers, three blossoms hovering, the border a garland of leaves and buds all in ivory relief, unsigned; a Twentieth Century black basalt cylindrical form lidded box, depicting classical figures and trees, the lid with leaves and a flower finial, stamped underside
4in. high, 6.1in. diameter; 3.5in. high respectively (Total: 3 Items)
Estimate: 300-500

30341
THREE BRITISH BLUE JASPERWARE CERAMIC ITEMS
Wedgwood, c.1970

Comprising a 1969 Christmas plate depicting Windsor Castle; a cylindrical beaker with flared rim and decorated with alternating mythological figures and trees; and a compote with fruiting grapevine wreath decoration at the foot and interior rim, each with impressed *WEDGWOOD/MADE IN/ENGLAND,* each piece with additional numerical and alphabetical impressed marks
The tallest: 3.8in. (Total: 3 Items)
Estimate: 200-500

30342
TWO PIECES OF CERAMICWARE
Wm. Guerin-Pouyat Elite and unknown, c.various dates

Comprising a French porcelain cabinet nappy of footed and elongated quatre-foil form with bas-relief floral design and with gilded split-handle surmounted with flower, the shallow bowl interior hand-painted with yellow roses, the exterior in celadon green, the rim gilded; *together with* an American footed and bulbous-shaped ceramic ewer with corn motif rendered in matte pink, green and gold; the nappy with underglaze green *William Guerin & Co. of Limoges* mark and with signature of artist *M.I. Lyon*; the ewer with impressed mark *Registered/3017/13F*
The tallest: 12.9in. (Total: 2 Items)
Estimate: 200-400

30343
A FRENCH PORCELAIN DIVIDED SERVING DISH
Maker unknown, c.1910

The double-shell form with a gilded crossed strap handle, rose decoration, glazed underside with incised *C* and gilt-painted numbers *5007/14 1*
4in. high
Estimate: 100-200

30344
A PAIR OF CONTINENTAL PORCELAIN LIDDED URNS
Vienna, c.1885

The two-handled, footed and stemmed urns with a tapering ovoid body rising to a short flared rim are supported by a square pedestal base, the primary background in burgundy also with bands of yellow and robin's egg blue, the body of the urns depict an artist-signed scene of three women with a putti in a pastoral setting, the reverse has a smaller image of a putti, stylized floral band to the center of the body, gilt floral details overall and solid gilt handles, rim and bands to urn, lid and base, stamped underside with beehive in blue
13.2in. high (Total: 4 Items)
Estimate: 500-700

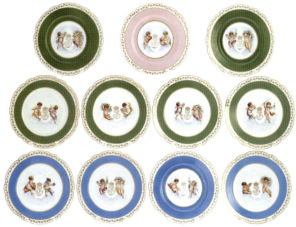

30345
ELEVEN CONTINENTAL PORCELAIN PLATES
Sèvres, c.1846

The white ground with wide colored band centering a pair of putti that flank a gilt 'double-Louis' crowned cipher, gilt leaf pattern to edge of plates, six plates with a green band, four blue and one pink, all with underglaze blue *Sèvres 1846* mark, four with underglaze red *Chateau des Tuileries* mark, and seven with underglaze red *Chateau de St. Cloud* mark, all eleven with artist signature *Debrie*
9.5in. diameter (Total: 11 Items)
Estimate: 600-900

30346

30346
A JAPANESE PORCELAIN HAND-PAINTED VASE
Nippon, c.1891

The four-sided ovoid form with a short tapering inverted neck, cobalt ground with four pastoral scenic panels primarily in green, gilt floral decoration and enamel beads to cobalt with gilt threading and beads to the foot and rim, stamped underside in blue
5.5in. high
Estimate: 50-150

30348

30348
A FRENCH PORCELAIN FIGURAL COMPOTE
Maker unknown, c.1900

The hard paste porcelain compote depicts a male and female in Victorian style dress on either side of a tree trunk, the base and stem are a stylized tree with a lattice ovoid bowl on top covered in grapevines and grapes, primarily in green with purple grapes, gilt thread and beading overall, unsigned
15.5in. high
Estimate: 400-600

30347

30347
THREE GERMAN PORCELAIN ITEMS
R.S. Prussia, c.1890

Including a matching demi-tasse cup and saucer with pink rose decoration and gilding, *together with* scalloped plate with beaded and gilded pink rim surrounding a fleur de lis scalloped border to the central reserve of white, pink and orange roses, the cup and the plate with overglaze red *RS Prussia* mark
The tallest: 3in. (Total: 3 Items)
Estimate: 100-200

30349

30349
TWO CONTINENTAL PORCELAIN CREAMERS AND SUGAR
Royal Bayreuth and unknown, c.1902

Comprising a matching cream and open sugar bowl in a rounded corner rectangular form with geometric handles, in black satin finish with a classical figural form to the sides in white, decorative Greek key border to the shoulder edged in gold, gilt rim, white ground interior, Royal Bayreuth stamp underside in blue; a second smaller ovoid form creamer in black satin finish depicting a Greek chariot scene on obverse and reverse in white, decorative Greek key border edged in gold near the foot, gilt detail to handle and rim, Grecian discus thrower stamp to underside
The tallest: 3.5in. high (Total: 3 Items)
Estimate: 50-150

30350

30352

30352
FIVE GERMAN PORCELAIN PLATES
Meissen, c.1880

Including four bread and butter plates, each with gilt rim and garlands of flowers centering a central bouquet of flowers, *together with* one condiment plate with raised gilt rococo and floral design, marked underside
The largest 8in. diameter (Total: 5 Items)
Estimate: 100-300

30350
TWO CONTINENTAL PORCELAIN BOWLS AND A SERVING DISH
R. S. Prussia, c.1880

The first, a wide decorative scalloped-rim bowl with a pale yellow ground and multicolored floral pattern to the interior, rim has a lemon yellow band and gilt highlights; the second, a wide impressed floral decoration rim bowl with a multicolored floral pattern to the interior, arch design to the sides with green and floral highlights; *together with* an oblong serving plate with two handles, floral relief decoration to the rim, pink and yellow poppy pattern, each stamped underside
10.7in. diameter, 10.1in. diameter and 13in. long respectively (Total: 3 Items)
Estimate: 300-500

30353
AN AUSTRIAN PORCELAIN LIDDED URN
Maker unknown, c.1900

The four-sided pedestal base supports a round domed foot rising to a short stem and tapering out to a baluster form body in a burgundy ground with an artist signed front panel depicting a mythological scene with Venus, a smaller panel to the reverse depicts a woman in Greco-Roman garb, decorative panel between the two in pink with gilt decoration overall, gilt border to the base, top of pedestal rim and two geometric handles, domed shaped tapering lid with a small finial, signed underside with beehive and *Austria*
17.8in. high
Estimate: 300-500

30353

30351

30351
A GERMAN ART NOUVEAU PAINTED ENAMEL VASE
Royal Bonn, c.1905

The baluster form vase tapers to a narrow neck with gilt decoration, one side with an autumnal landscape, the other with the bust of a woman with flowing hair, artist-signed *Franz Anton, Dingendorf*, marked underside
7.6in. high
Estimate: 300-500

30354
A GERMAN PORCELAIN BOWL AND CHARGER
Meissen, c.1947

The group consists of a low wide scallop rim bowl in white hard paste porcelain ground with a yellow background interior, a heavy relief pattern of swirled leaves in white and gold on the interior; the charger in white hard paste porcelain with a floral pattern to the center has a broad gilt scalloped border with additional gilt detail, marked underside with crossed swords in blue
11in. and 12.6in. diameter respectively (Total: 2 Items)
Estimate: 300-500

30355
THREE GERMAN PORCELAIN PLATES AND A SPOON
Meissen, c.1900

The group consists of dessert plates in a white ground with ribbing and raised floral pattern to two, basket weave pattern to third, multicolored floral design to center and gilt rim to all three; the spoon in a white ground with pink border to the back of the spoon, multicolored flowers also to back and top of handle, the bowl of the spoon depicts a couple in a pastoral setting, gold detail overall, signed with crossed swords
8.5in. diameter, spoon: 7.7in. long (Total: 4 Items)
Estimate: 300-500

30356
A JAPANESE PORCELAIN VASE
Nippon, c.1890

The Art Nouveau design with two handles, primarily in green with a band to the shoulders of pink flowers and green leaves, yellow ground to the handles and rim, gilt trim and beading to the foot, shoulders and neck, stamped underside with *Hand Painted Nippon*
6in. high (Total: 4 items)
Estimate: 50-150

30357
TWO BOWLS AND THREE CONTINENTAL PORCELAIN PLATES
Haviland, Meissen, c.1880

The two Haviland & Co. bowls in a white ground and cobalt glaze with elaborate gilt and silver floral pattern to the center and everted rim; the Charles Field Haviland side plate in a white ground with cobalt glaze and detailed gilt floral center and rim; the two Meissen plates in a cobalt glaze over a white ground in a ribbed swirl pattern and a raised gilt floral design to the center, all stamped underside
9.5in. diameter, 8.5in. diameter, 9.5in. diameter respectively (Total: 5 Items)
Estimate: 300-500

30358
A GERMAN CABINET PLATE
Langewiesen Factory, c.1895

The deep-footed circular form with bands of gilding, cerulean-blue, and ivory surrounding the central reserve rendered in polychrome enamels to depict the exploits of Odysseus and Hermes, the central reserved signed *H. Görner,* the underside with overglaze cobalt blue pseudo-beehive mark and with overglaze red hand-scripted title, *ODYSSEUS AND HERMES*
10.6in. diameter
Estimate: 400-600

30360
A FOURTEEN-PIECE FRENCH PORCELAIN CHOCOLATE SET
CH Field Haviland Limoges, c.1920

The set consists of six cups and saucers, chocolate pot and lid in rose design, maker's mark under glaze (Total: 14 Items)
Estimate: 300-400

30361
A GERMAN COMPOTE AND FOUR SAUCERS
Meissen, Twentieth Century

Comprising a compote on a stepped funnel foot supporting a round plate with an flared edge in a braided pattern, multicolor flowers to plate and base; gilt detail to rim and base; the saucers with a deep bowl in white ground with cobalt center pattern with a multicolored floral border and gilt details overall, stamped underside with crossed swords
The compote: 2.2in. high, 5.7in. diameter; The saucer: 6.6in. diameter (Total: 5 Items)
Estimate: 200-300

30359
TWO GERMAN PORCELAIN VASES, EN SUITE
R.S. Germany, c.1890

Each of cylindrical form, the salesman samples with a short collar and everted rim, the shaded green ground each depicting a woman garbed in Victorian attire, one vase stamped underglaze *RS Germany*
4in. high (Total: 2 Items)
Estimate: 200-400

30362
A GERMAN FIGURAL GILT AND ENAMEL VASE
Erdmann Schlegelmilch, Germany, c.1905

Oxblood, blue and purple glaze with raised gilt decoration, a large central panel with an Elizabethan scene, two women and a man with floral accents, marked underside
8in. high
Estimate: 100-300

30364
A JAPANESE PORCELAIN VASE
Nippon, c.1891

The ovoid form with two triangular gilt handles at the rim, satin finish hand painted scene depicts a moonlit pond with two swans, water lilies and reeds, gold beaded border to rim and base, stamped underside
8.5in. high
Estimate: 100-200

30363
SIX GERMAN PORCELAIN PLATES AND A CHARGER
Dresden, c.1918

The set includes six matching plates and a charger with an open pierced rim and scalloped edge, multicolored central floral design and floral pattern to rim, gilt details, stamped underside
The plates: 10in. diameter; The charger: 10.7in. diameter (Total: 7 Items)
Estimate: 300-500

30365
A FRENCH PORCELAIN CHOCOLATE SERVICE
Haviland & Co. Limoges, c.1900

Comprising a lidded chocolate pot, four cups and saucers in white porcelain with a floral pattern of carnations, gilt handles and gilt details to the foot of the pot and the rim, stamped underside
The pot: 9in. high (Total: 10 Items)
Estimate: 100-300

30366

30366
A PATE-SUR-PATE PORCELAIN VASE
Maker unknown, c.1890

The cushion foot supporting a flattened ovoid form with a cylindrical neck to flared rim, two decorative ring handles on either side of the neck, raw umber ground with an ivory pate-sur-pate image of a bird in her nest suspended in water reeds, stylized border decoration to neck, gilt rim and base, unsigned
8.2in. high
Estimate: 300-500

30367

30367
FIVE GERMAN PORCELAIN CUP AND SAUCER SETS
Meissen, c.1880

Comprising two sets with floral design and gilt pattern; a white and gilt set; a cobalt, floral and gilt set; and a blue and white set, each marked underglaze with crossed swords, the blue and white saucer set double struck
Various sizes (Total: 10 Items)
Estimate: 200-400

30368

30368
A BAVARIAN HAND PAINTED PORCELAIN VASE
Philip Rosenthal Co., c.1910

An egg-shaped vase with narrow flared rim, the obverse with a winged cherub playing a harp covered in rose garlands nestled upon a cloud, the reverse with multi-colored glaze, marked underside *B.C.H. 1900* and a maker's mark
7.8in. high
Estimate: 300-500

30369

30369
TWO FRENCH FRAMED PORCELAIN PLATES
Sèvres, c.1890

The design begins with a cerulean blue and gilt border, the first center image depicts two maidens in a classical background, artist signed *R. Herr*, the other image is of two maidens and a young man in a pastoral background, artist signed *Elly Wieden*
18in. x 18in. (Total: 2 Items)
Estimate: 300-500

30370

30370
AN ENGLISH PORCELAIN FLOW BLUE COVERED VEGETABLE DISH
Johnson Bros. c.1890

The white ground fully decorated in flow blue floral and leaf pattern with gilt scroll handles, signed under glaze *Peach Royal/ semi-porcelain/ Johnson Bros/ England*, inside lid has been restored
5.5in. high (Total: 2 Items)
Estimate: 150-250

30371

30371
AN ORIENTAL FLOW BLUE COVERED CHEESE DISH
Maker unknown, c.1860

Wedge-shaped top pierced with two holes and decorated with gold accents and pagoda-style buildings, rests on a conforming footed underplate, impressed underglaze mark on interior wall of cover, impressed marks and underglaze blue marks on underside of the cheese rest
Overall: 5in. high (Total: 2 Items)
Estimate: 200-400

30372

30372
THREE ORIENTAL FLOW BLUE PLATES
Maker unknown, c.1890

The group all depict the same pattern in flow blue, all signed underglaze *Hong Kong*
10.3in. dia (Total: 3 Items)
Estimate: 200-300

30373

30373
EIGHT ASSORTED FLOW BLUE PORCELAINS
Makers unknown, c.1910

Comprising a rectangular platter, two candle sticks, ring holder, hat pin holder, two covered jars, and a lid all in a floral and leaf design with gilt highlights, unmarked
Assorted sizes (Total: 10 Items)
Estimate: 400-600

30374

30374
A ENGLISH FLOW BLUE COVERED SAUCE TUREEN AND STAND
Wallis Cimson & Co., c.1880

Each piece with trademark under glaze, decoration with roses, gold highlights and rosettes within panels
5.5in. high (Total: 3 Items)
Estimate: 200-400

30375
AN ORIENTAL FLOW BLUE LIDDED SERVING DISH
Maker unknown, c.1890

The octagonal-shaped pedestal bowl with a white ground and flow blue oriental design with matching lid, signed underglaze *Hong Kong*,
6.7in. high (Total: 2 Items)
Estimate: 300-500

30375

30376
FIVE BRITISH PORCELAIN SAUCERS AND A PLATTER
Various makers, c.1890

Comprising five flow blue saucers of four different designs, two have gilt detailing; the oval scalloped and gilt rim serving plate in a flow blue pattern, all stamped with various maker marks
The saucers: 6in. diameter; The platter: 12in. wide (Total: 6 Items)
Estimate: 300-500

30377
AN ENGLISH PORCELAIN VASE
Minton, c.1909

The ovoid form with a short cylindrical neck in a blue and white pattern of prunus blossoms, stamped underside
7.4in. high
Estimate: 100-300

30378
THREE GERMAN PORCELAIN ITEMS
Meissen, c.1920

Comprising a square serving dish in a blue and white 'blue onion' pattern with gilt detail to the rim; a round straight-side bowl with a blue-on-white pattern of flowers and beetles, gilt edge rim and border to base; a shallow footed bowl with a stepped tapering edge to a scalloped rim, blue floral pattern with beetles, all marked underside with crossed swords
The largest: 9in. square (Total: 3 Items)
Estimate: 200-400

30379
AN ENGLISH FLOW BLUE COVERED SAUCE TUREEN
H. Charles Meigh, c.1840

The earthenware covered tureen with matching underplate, blue and white architectural and floral decoration, mark impressed under glaze
6in. high (Total: 3 Items)
Estimate: 300-500

30380
SIX FLOW BLUE PLATES
Various makers, c.1890

The group consisting of three architectural scenes, two maritime scenes and one historical scene, all marked under glaze
9.5in. to 10in. dia (Total: 6 Items)
Estimate: 200-300

30382
A BRITISH FLOW BLUE PORCELAIN JARDINIERE
Maker unknown, c.1920

The cushion foot bulbous form with a scalloped rim, blue and white pattern depicts flowers and leaves to the front and back, Greek key design to the neck, gold highlights overall, unsigned
9in. high
Estimate: 200-400

30381
AN ENGLISH IRONSTONE PLATTER
Johnson Bros, c.1913

The oval ivory ground platter with a 'Mongolia' pattern blue transfer ware scene to the center of two birds in a landscape, broad blue design border to the edge, stamped underside
14.5in. wide
Estimate: 200-400

30383
SEVEN BRITISH PORCELAIN SERVING PIECES
Various makers, c.1890

The group consists of two matching dinner plates, two matching dessert plates, two saucers and a gravy boat all in flow blue patterned stoneware, all stamped with various makers marks
Various sizes (Total: 7 Items)
Estimate: 300-500

30385
A COLLECTION OF GERMAN 'TOMATO AND APPLE' CERAMIC ITEMS
Royal Bayreuth, c.1910

Comprising two large, one medium and one small covered bowls, *together with* a creamer and a mustard pot with spoon, all with glazed undersides with maker's stamp
The tallest: 3.6in. (Total: 12 Items)
Estimate: 400-600

30384
A GERMAN 'POPPY' COFFEE POT
Royal Bayreuth, c.1900

The green leafy base and handle support a large blooming poppy, the detachable lid of two open poppy blossoms, stamped underside *Royal Bayreuth*
8.7in. high
Estimate: 600-800

30386
A GERMAN CERAMIC 'STRAWBERRY' CREAMER AND SUGAR
Royal Bayreuth, c.1910

Comprising a strawberry-shaped creamer with leaf-shaped rim and spout extending into a stem-shaped handle, *together with* a covered strawberry-shaped sugar bowl with sculptural stem knob; both stamped underside *Royal Bayreuth*
The tallest: 5in. (Total: 3 Items)
Estimate: 400-600

30387
SEVEN CONTINENTAL LEAF PLATES
Royal Bayreuth, c.1890

The group consists of four nappy plates, two berry plates and an under plate all in shades of green, two of the nappy plates have yellow flowers and one nappy plate has pink and yellow flowers at the edge, four stamped underglaze with the *Royal Bayreuth* mark, one stamped *Bavaria*
Various sizes (Total: 7 Items)
Estimate: 200-400

30388
TWO CONTINENTAL CERAMIC FIGURAL CREAMERS
Royal Bayreuth, c.1940

Including one matte-finish Mallard duck and one high-glaze Green Frog, each with overglaze blue maker's mark
The tallest: 3.8in. high (Total: 2 Items)
Estimate: 100-200

30389
A GERMAN PORCELAIN NAPPY
Royal Bayreuth, c.1902

The oval form wider at one end and a handle on the other depicting the form of a radish leaf and a radish, the root forming the handle, stamped underside *Royal Bayreuth*
7.6in. long
Estimate: 100-200

30390
A GERMAN PORCELAIN BOWL
Royal Bayreuth, c.1902

The four-footed low bulbous 'elk' bowl with an elk head at one end and antlers to the rim, in white to chestnut brown with black details to the head, stamped underside *Royal Bayreuth*
2.6in. high, 5.6in. long
Estimate: 100-200

30393
FIVE GERMAN 'TOMATO' CERAMIC ITEMS
Royal Bayreuth, c.1930

Including a shaped plate with raised turnip-leaf and tomato decoration, *together with* two pair of tomato-shaped salt and pepper shakers, the plate with overglaze blue maker's mark, salt and pepper shakers unmarked
The plate 7.5in. width (Total: 5 Items)
Estimate: 50-100

30391
A GERMAN PORCELAIN CREAMER
Royal Bayreuth, c.1957

The creamer in the form of a clown bending over in yellow with a white ruffled collar and green buttons, the head and hat forming the spout, stamped underside
4.4in. high
Estimate: 200-400

30394
THREE GERMAN CERAMIC CREAMERS
Royal Bayreuth, c.1925

Comprising a large poppy-shaped creamer, *together with* two tomato-shaped creamers of differing shapes; the poppy creamer unmarked; each of the tomato creamers stamped underside *Royal Bayreuth*
4.8in. high (Total: 3 items)
Estimate: 300-500

30392
THREE CONTINENTAL TOMATO PATTERN CERAMIC ITEMS
Royal Bayreuth, c.1902

Comprising a teapot, mustard jar, and sugar bowl, each of the lidded pieces molded and glazed to resemble stylized tomatoes, each stamped underside
The mustard: 3.8in. high (Total: 6 Items)
Estimate: 150-200

30395
A GERMAN PORCELAIN BOWL
Royal Bayreuth, c.1900

The pumpkin shaped body with a stylized foliage foot in green, body in red over a white ground, stamped underside with the *Royal Bayreuth* stamp
4in. high
Estimate: 200-300

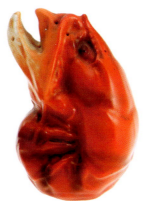

30396
A PAIR OF CONTINENTAL CERAMIC 'LOBSTER' SALT AND PEPPER SHAKERS
Royal Bayreuth, c.1940

Each of the teardrop forms depicting a lobster with curled tail and uplifted pincers, the head and pincer area of each pierced, both with overglaze blue maker's mark
The tallest: 3in. (Total: 2 Items)
Estimate: 100-200

30397
A CONTINENTAL 'LOBSTER' CREAMER AND SUGAR
Royal Bayreuth, c.1930

Comprising a globular pitcher with claw-shaped spout and green handle *together with* a covered sugar bowl, the oblong basin depicting a lobster tail, the conforming top the head and pincers; underside of creamer and basin with overglaze blue mark
The tallest: 4in. high (Total: 2 Items)
Estimate: 200-300

30398
TWO GERMAN PORCELAIN CREAMERS
Royal Bayreuth, c.1888

The sea shell design pair both in multicolor pattern on a white ground, signed underglaze with the *Royal Bayreuth* stamp
4.5in. high and 3.5in. high (Total: 2 Items)
Estimate: 200-300

30399
A GERMAN CERAMIC 'LOBSTER' CELERY DISH AND SINGLE-HANDLED BOWL
Royal Bayreuth, c.1920

The first, an oblong celery dish in the shape of a lobster; the second, a handled bowl also in the shape of a lobster; the celery dish with glazed green maker's mark, the other with glazed blue maker's mark
The celery: 2.75in. high, 13in. long, 5in. wide (Total: 2 Items)
Estimate: 100-200

30400

30400
A GERMAN 'ROSE TAPESTRY' CERAMIC BOX
Royal Bayreuth, c.1950

The round and textured base with conforming separate lid decorated with pink and yellow roses, stamped underside *Royal Bayreuth*
2in. high, 3.25in. diameter (Total: 2 Items)
Estimate: 200-500

30401

30401
A GERMAN 'ROSE TAPESTRY' COVERED BOX
Royal Bayreuth, c.1920

The textured shell-shaped base and conforming lid with yellow, pink, and white rose decoration and gilded rim, stamped underside *Royal Bayreuth* in blue
1.75 in. high (Total: 2 Items)
Estimate: 200-300

30402

30402
A GERMAN 'ROSE TAPESTRY' CREAM AND SUGAR
Royal Bayreuth, c.1902

The matching cream and sugar set on a molded foot with a bulbous form and short flared rim, muted green ground with small pink roses, applied handles in satin gilt, stamped underside *Royal Bayreuth*
2.5in. high (Total: 2 Items)
Estimate: 100-200

30403

30403
A GERMAN 'ROSE TAPESTRY' COVERED BOX
Royal Bayreuth, c.1910

The lozenge-shaped and textured form with conforming separate lid decorated with pink and yellow roses, stamped underside *Royal Bayreuth*
1.5in. high, 4.75in. long, 4in. wide (Total: 2 Items)
Estimate: 300-500

30404
A GERMAN 'ROSE TAPESTRY' VASE AND PLATE
Royal Bayreuth, c.1930

The ovoid-shaped cabinet vase with gilded rim decorated with pink and white roses; the textured plate with pink and white roses and a shaped, gilt-banded rim; both stamped underside *Royal Bayreuth*
The vase: 4.5in. high (Total: 2 Items)
Estimate: 300-600

30405
A GERMAN 'ROSE TAPESTRY' CREAMER
Royal Bayreuth, c.1902

The round foot rising to a cylindrical pinched form depicting pink roses and green leaves, satin finish gold handle, stamped underside *Royal Bayreuth*
3.3in. high
Estimate: 200-400

30406
A PAIR OF GERMAN 'ROSE TAPESTRY SHAKERS
Royal Bayreuth, c.1940

Comprising a salt and pepper, each spreading foot with a tapering cylindrical textured body rising to a pierced button top, decorated with pink, orange, and white roses, both stamped underside *Royal Bayreuth* (Total: 2 Items)
Estimate: 300-500

30407
THREE CONTINENTAL PORCELAIN TRAYS
Royal Bayreuth, c.1890

Each of rectangular form, the first decorated with pink and yellow roses; the second decorated with tan and pink roses; the third decorated in a white and pink floral spray design, all signed with the *Royal Bayreuth* stamp
The largest: 8in. high, 11.3in.wide (Total: 3 Items)
Estimate: 600-900

30408

A GERMAN 'ROSE TAPESTRY' VASE
Royal Bayreuth, c.1930

The rouleau-shaped and textured body with flared collar and gilt-banded rim, decorated with pink and yellow roses and stylized white flowers with yellow centers; stamped underside *Royal Bayreuth*
5.9in. high
Estimate: 400-600

30410

A GERMAN 'ROSE TAPESTRY' DISH
Royal Bayreuth, c.1902-1917

The leaf-shaped and textured body decorated with pink and yellow roses, the shaped rim with gilt banding, stamped underside *Royal Bayreuth*
1.5in. high
Estimate: 200-400

30409

A SET OF FIVE GERMAN 'ROSE TAPESTRY' PLATES
Royal Bayreuth, c.1919

Comprising five matching side plates in a pale green ground depicting orange roses to the center and pink roses around the edge, gilt detail to the edge, stamped underside *Royal Bayreuth*
6in. diameter (Total: 5 Items)
Estimate: 500-800

30411

A GERMAN 'ROSE TAPESTRY' VASE AND COVERED SUGAR BOWL
Royal Bayreuth, c.1930

The double handled cabinet vase with pink and orange roses and gilt rim; the double handled covered sugar bowl with pink, white and yellow roses, both stamped underside *Royal Bayreuth*
The taller: 3.8in. (Total: 3 items)
Estimate: 300-500

30412

30412
A GERMAN 'ROSE TAPESTRY' COVERED BOX
Royal Bayreuth, c.1940

The textured shell-shaped base and conforming lid with yellow and pink rose decoration and gilded rim, underside with overglaze blue *Royal Bayreuth* mark
1.75in. high (Total: 2)
Estimate: 200-300

30413

30413
A GERMAN 'ROSE TAPESTRY' DISH AND NAPPY
Royal Bayreuth, c.1930

The textured elliptical vanity dish with pink, white and yellow roses *together with* a clover-shaped nappy with pink, white and yellow roses, both stamped underside *Royal Bayreuth*
(Total: 2 Items)
Estimate: 200-400

30414

30414
A GERMAN CERAMIC 'ROSE TAPESTRY' PITCHER
Royal Bayreuth, c.1910

The textured cylindrical body with pinched-spout and decorated with red and pink roses and smaller yellow-centered flowers, the shaped handle and rim with gilding, glazed underside with blue maker's mark
6.75in. high
Estimate: 200-300

30415

30415
A GERMAN 'ROSE TAPESTRY' CABINET VASE
Royal Bayreuth, c.1920

The textured and footed ovoid form decorated with pink and yellow roses, gilt-banded rim, stamped underside
4.4in. high
Estimate: 100-300

30416
TWO GERMAN 'ROSE TAPESTRY' CREAMERS
Royal Bayreuth, c.1902

The first on a round base tapering to the body with a stepped in and then slightly flaring neck in subtle colors of pale green leaves, pink and orange to white roses, applied handle in a gilt satin finish; the second on a round foot and bulbous form with a pinched spout in brighter colors of green and large pink roses, applied handle in glossy gold, both stamped underside *Royal Bayreuth*
4.6in. high and 4in. high respectively (Total: 2 Items)
Estimate: 300-500

30417
A GERMAN 'ROSE TAPESTRY' HAIR RECEIVER
Royal Bayreuth, c.1925

Raised on three gilded feet, the textured and compressed cylindrical base with conforming separate lid with a hole in the center, decorated with dusty matter roses and pastel pink flowers with yellow centers, partial transfer stamp underside *Royal Bayreuth*
3in. high, 4.1in. diameter (Total: 2 Items)
Estimate: 200-400

30418
A GERMAN 'ROSE TAPESTRY' CHOCOLATE SERVICE
Royal Bayreuth, c.1920

Comprising a covered chocolate pot, four cups and saucers, each with textured body decorated with pink roses and heightened with gilding, each piece stamped underside
The tallest: 9in. (Total: 10 Items)
Estimate: 200-400

30419
AN IRISH 'HENSHALL TWIG' PORCELAIN BASKET
Belleek, c.1890

The ivory lace form rises from a rope style foot to a flared rim with a stylized branch handle and applique floral pattern along rim, fired on porcelain stamp underside
7.2in. high
Estimate: 600-900

30420
AN IRISH 'NEPTUNE' PORCELAIN TEA SERVICE
Belleek, c.1956

The set includes a lidded teapot with two shell feet and a tapering swirl shell-form body with an incurved rim, yellow opalescent handle, rim border and top of lid; six shell form cups with a yellow opalescent interior and handle; six saucers with yellow opalescent centers, all stamped underside in green
The teapot: 6in. high (Total: 8 Items)
Estimate: 200-400

30422
TWO IRISH HEART-SHAPED PORCELAIN BASKETS
Belleek, production 1921-1954

Each with basket-platt and heart-shaped center with flaring ribs rising to a conforming rim, the larger basket further enhanced with applied floral and foliage decoration; the smaller with impressed mark *Belleek/Co. Fermanagh/Ireland*, the larger with impressed mark *BELLEEK/IRELAND*
The largest: 2in. high (Total: 2 Items)
Estimate: 500-700

30421
AN IRISH 'ABERDEEN' PORCELAIN PITCHER
Belleek, c.1891

The ivory baluster form rises to a tapered neck and large flared spout with a stylized handle, applique blossoms over a fluted and medallion decorated body, stamped underglaze with Belleek mark in black ink
9.4in. high
Estimate: 300-500

30425
AN IRISH PORCELAIN CUP, SAUCER AND PLATE
Belleek; Willets Manufacturing Co., c.1926; 1879

Comprising an Irish Belleek plate in the shamrock pattern, ivory ground with three strands of shamrocks radiating from a center ring, stamped underside in black; a Willets Belleek cup and saucer set with a spiral pattern to the cup, purple and gold flowers border the rim of the cup and plate, scalloped rim, gilt handle, marked underside
The plate: 9.5in. diameter (Total: 3 Items)
Estimate: 100-200

30423
AN IRISH PORCELAIN PLATE
Belleek, c.1890

The hexagonal-shaped lace pattern with basket weave center and stylized twig handle, fired on porcelain signature
10.8in. diameter
Estimate: 300-500

30424
AN IRISH PORCELAIN VASE AND FIGURINE
Belleek, Twentieth Century

The round footed bulbous form tapering to a slender neck and flaring to a notched rim, 'thistle' pattern with two applied thistle flowers and leaves to each side, stamped in black; the figurine on a rectangular base depicts a leprechaun sitting on a mushroom with opalescent details, stamped underside *Belleek* in green
5.2in. high and 5.4in. high respectively (Total: 2 Items)
Estimate: 200-400

30426
AN IRISH 'ABERDEEN' PORCELAIN PITCHER
Belleek, c.1946

The ivory bulbous base rising to a slim collared neck and flaring to the spout and stylized handle, applied flowers to mid-section, stamped underglaze with Belleek mark in black ink
7.1in. high
Estimate: 300-500

End of Session One

SESSION TWO

Public-Internet Auction #614
Sunday, March 20, 2005, appr. 2:00 PM, Lots 30427-30977
Dallas, Texas

A 19.5% Buyer's Premium Will Be Added To All Lots

Visit HeritageGalleries.com to view scalable images and bid online.

30427
THREE AMERICAN LIDDED VASELINE GLASS JARS
Makers unknown, c.1900

The set includes three matching jars, two larger, one smaller, each with a round paneled foot rising to a short stem supporting an ovoid paneled body and collared rim, the round paneled lid rises to a faceted finial, unsigned
10.4in. high, 8.5in. high respectively (Total: 6 Items)
Estimate: 200-400

30428
A COLLECTION OF AMERICAN VASELINE GLASS ITEMS
Various makers, various dates

Including a figure of a perched pelican; a covered sugar bowl depicting in form and pattern a pineapple; a mid-Twentieth Century thick and heavy oblong bowl; a footed round compote with diamond-quilted bowl; an oblong dish with maple leaf decoration forming the bowl's sides and notched rim; an Adams & Co. 'Wildflower' pattern covered dish; three sherberts with crenelated rims; a Fenton opalescent ovoid pitcher with clear applied handle; a mid-Twentieth Century L.G. Wright opalescent 'Daisy and Button' pattern sugar bowl; a Northwood opalescent 'Alaska' pattern footed bowl; and a Fenton opalescent 'basket weave' shallow bowl with pierced rim; each unmarked
The tallest: 7.25in. (Total: 15 Items)
Estimate: 400-600

30429
AN AMERICAN ETCHED VASELINE GLASS COMPOTE
Pierpoint Corp., c.1890

The vaseline round disc foot with a clear controlled bubble stem supporting a low bowl with everted flange in vaseline with a grapevine pattern to the flange and foot, unsigned
6.5in. high, 12.1in. diameter
Estimate: 300-500

30430
SEVEN AMERICAN VASELINE GLASS ITEMS
Various makers, c.1890

Comprising a pair of candle sticks; a basket weave design goblet; a shaped serving bowl; a triangular shaped dish with handle; a cruet bottle with stopper; and a footed rectangular cake stand marked *Clarks Teaberry Gum* on the foot
Various sizes (Total: 7 Items)
Estimate: 400-600

30433
TWO OPALESCENT ITEMS AND VASELINE GLASS CAKE PLATE
Makers unknown, c.1900

Comprising a green pressed glass covered butter dish; a footed spiral pattern vase in pale yellow to opalescent white; a vaseline glass cake plate with a fleur de lis stem, unsigned
6.5in. high, 3in. high, 11in. diameter respectively (Total: 4 Items)
Estimate: 200-400

30431
FOUR AMERICAN VASELINE GLASS ITEMS
Makers unknown, c.1915

Comprising a pair of tri-footed candlesticks, a center bowl and a flower frog; the candlesticks rise from a wide base to a tapered neck and bulbous shaped top; the low bulbous bowl in an opalescent bright green with a wide flared rim; a round lipped flower frog with eleven openings, all unsigned
6.8in. high, 12.4in. diameter, 3.2in. diameter respectively (Total: 4)
Estimate: 200-300

30434
A PAIR OF AMERICAN VASELINE GLASS GOBLETS AND JUICER
Makers unknown, c.1860

The matching faceted goblets *together with* an unmatching faceted juicer,
The goblets: 6in. high, The juicer: 4.2in. high (Total: 3 Items)
Estimate: 100-150

30432
A COLLECTION OF AMERICAN VASELINE GLASS ITEMS
Makers unknown, c.1920

Comprising an iridescent center bowl with everted rim; a nesting chicken covered dish with basket-weave bottom; a four-mold stemmed rose bowl with 'beaded scale' pattern; a heart-shaped box with lipped cover; a controlled-bubble bowl with scalloped rim, all pieces unsigned
The tallest: 9in. (Total: 7 Items)
Estimate: 200-400

30435
SIX AMERICAN VASELINE GLASS ITEMS
Makers unknown, c.1915

Comprising a ruffled rim compote; two opalescent vaseline hobnail bowls with ruffled rims; a shallow bowl with an opalescent scalloped rim; a tri-footed shallow dish with an opalescent scalloped tri-fold rim; a toothpick holder in the form of an elephant head, unsigned
The compote: 6.8in. high 10in. diameter (Total: 6 Items)
Estimate: 200-400

30436
AN AMERICAN MOLD-BLOWN 'APPLE TREE' CARNIVAL GLASS PITCHER AND SIX TUMBLERS
Fenton, c.1905

The Marigold pitcher with flared and ruffled rim, a clear loop handle, *together with* six matching tumblers, unsigned
The tallest: 9.25in. (Total: 7 Items)
Estimate: 200-400

30437
A GROUP OF AMERICAN OPALESCENT MARIGOLD PRESSED GLASS ITEMS
Various makers, c.1900

Comprising a tumbler attributed to either Northwood or Dugan with a pattern of storks in rushes; a Northwood eight-facet carnival glass mug with singing birds, stamped in mold underside; two Fenton orange tree wine glasses
The tallest: 5.4in. high (Total: 4 Items)
Estimate: 100-300

30438
FOUR AMERICAN CARNIVAL GLASS DRINKING VESSELS
Northwood and Imperial Glass Co., c.1925

Comprising a Northwood 'Singing Bird' pattern green mug, the lower interior with maker's mark; an Imperial 'Grape' pattern purple cordial, unsigned; an Imperial purple toothpick holder, the lower interior with maker's mark; an Imperial Glass Co. 'Tiger Lilly' pattern 'Helios' green tumbler, unsigned
The tallest: 4.25in. high (Total: 4 Items)
Estimate: 200-300

30439
AN AMERICAN MARIGOLD 'OCTAGON' CARNIVAL GLASS CORDIAL SET
Imperial Glass Co., c.1930

Comprising a bulbous decanter with ovoid stopper and six footed cordial glasses, in the 'Octagon' pattern, all pieces with hobstar, strawberry diamonds and starburst designs, unsigned
The tallest: 10in. (Total: 8 Items)
Estimate: 100-300

30440
AN AMERICAN MARIGOLD 'CRACKLE' CARNIVAL GLASS WATER SET
Imperial, c.1930

Comprising a water pitcher with a faceted foot supporting a cylindrical body with an applied faceted handle, *together with* six faceted foot, trumpet-form tumblers, all with a craquelure pattern, unsigned
7.8in. high and 4.6in. high respectively (Total: 7 Items)
Estimate: 100-300

30442
AN AMERICAN 'IMPERIAL GRAPE' CARNIVAL GLASS CARAFE
Maker unknown, c.1909

The green iridescent cushion foot bulbous form rising to a ribbed and collared neck with a flared rim, heavy relief grapes and leaves to the body, beaded pattern to the collared neck, unsigned
8.5in. high
Estimate: 100-200

30441
AN AMERICAN CARNIVAL GLASS BOWL AND VASE
Northwood and maker unknown, c.1930

The opalescent heavy ruffled rim bowl with magenta and blue to the inside, floral design and horseshoe to the center with 'Good Luck' over; the opalescent vase primarily in deep red with a round base tapering to a flared scalloped asymmetrical rim, the bowl with the *Northwood* stamp underside
8.8in. diameter and 9.5in. high respectively (Total: 2 items)
Estimate: 200-300

30443
AN AMERICAN CARNIVAL GLASS 'IMPERIAL GRAPE' DECANTER AND TWO CORDIALS
Maker unknown, c.1930

The bulbous form tapering to a cylindrical ribbed and collared neck, flared rim and ribbed bulb stopper; two matching cordial glasses, unsigned
12in. high and 3.8in. high respectively (Total: 4 Items)
Estimate: 100-200

30444
AN AMERICAN 'MAPLE LEAF' CARNIVAL GLASS WATER SET
Dugan, c.1908

Comprising a pitcher and six tumblers, golden opalescent finish, unsigned
The pitcher: 8.8in. high (Total: 7 Items)
Estimate: 100-300

30445
A COLLECTION OF AMERICAN CARNIVAL GLASS
Various makers, c.1930

Comprising a single iridescent clear nappie of leaf form and thirteen pieces of marigold color including a footed goblet, two 'Grape and Lattice' pattern tumblers, one Dugan 'Stork & Rushes' pattern tumbler, one 'Water Lily and Cattails' pattern tumbler, one Imperial Glass 'Fashion' pattern punch cup, one Imperial Glass 'Imperial Grape' pattern punch cup, one Fenton 'Orange Tree' pattern sherbert, One 'Maple Leaf' pattern sherbert, one Northwood 'Acorn Burrs' pattern bowl, one 'Dragon Scales' bowl, one 'Acorn' pattern bowl, and one 'Button' pattern creamer, all pieces unmarked except the Northwood bowl
The tallest: 5.8in. high (Total: 14 Items)
Estimate: 200-300

30446
A FRENCH MOLD-BLOWN OPALESCENT GLASS BOWL
Sèvres, c.1970

The low, wide bowl depicting flower buds and leaves in milky opalescent relief, etched underside *Sèvres*, also signed in mold *Etling France 151*, a paper label affixed to interior
7.9in. wide
Estimate: 100-300

30447
A GROUP OF AMERICAN WHITE OPALESCENT GLASS ITEMS
Makers unknown, c.1900

Comprising a compote; a Northwood vase; a hobnail pattern vase; a threaded spool pattern raised bowl; a hobnail pattern rose bowl; a tri-footed bowl in a 'shell and wild rose' pattern with an opalescent pierced egg and dart rim; a tri-footed bowl in a 'leaf and bead' pattern; a pressed glass pitcher in a floral pattern; each unmarked
The tallest: 10.5in. high (Total: 8 Items)
Estimate: 100-300

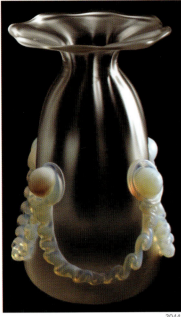

30448
A SATIN AND OPALESCENT GLASS VASE
Richardson Glass, c.1890

The four-sided tapering form flaring to a wide everted scalloped rim, clear satin finish with an opalescent garland, unsigned
5.1in. high
Estimate: 100-200

30449
A GROUP OF WHITE OPALESCENT GLASS BOWLS
Makers unknown, c.1900

Comprising a reeded tri-footed bowl with a large ruffled opalescent rim; a tri-footed bowl in a 'ruffles and rings' pattern with a tightly ruffled opalescent rim; a wide bowl in a jeweled heart pattern with a large ruffled and beaded opalescent rim; a palm pattern clear to opalescent ruffled rim bowl; a tri-footed bowl in a beaded cable pattern with a ruffled opalescent rim; a bowl in a 'spokes and wheels' pattern with a tri-lobed opalescent rim, all unsigned
The tallest: 4in. high (Total: 6 Items)
Estimate: 100-200

30450
SIX WHITE OPALESCENT GLASS ITEMS
Various makers, c.1900

Comprising a Northwood footed and stemmed low compote in the 'Pearls and Scales' pattern; a Jefferson Glass Co. creamer in the 'Iris and Meander' pattern; a deep bowl in the 'Roulette' pattern; a four-footed bowl in 'Beaded Drape' pattern; a Jefferson Glass Co. square-footed low bowl in 'Shell and Dots' pattern; a round ribbed foot supporting a ribbed 'Button Panel' pattern bowl; each unmarked
The tallest: 5in. (Total: 6 Items)
Estimate: 100-300

30451
SEVEN WHITE OPALESCENT GLASS ITEMS
Makers unknown, c.1900

Comprising three round footed bowls in the 'Argonaut' shell pattern in clear to opalescent; two low, wide bowls in the 'Many Loops' pattern; two round footed bowls in the 'Vintage' pattern depicting grapes and vines; each unsigned
The tallest: 3.7in. high (Total: 7 Items)
Estimate: 100-300

30452
THREE PIECES OF AMERICAN 'INTAGLIO' PATTERN GLASS
Northwood, c.1920

Comprising a large pitcher and a creamer and sugar, each piece with a quatre-foil domed foot and a short, beaded stem beneath a quatre-foil body, with raised floral and scrolling leaf decoration terminating in an opalescent white shaped rim, the pitcher and creamer with twisted opalescent white handle, unmarked
The tallest: 8.25in. high (Total: 3 Items)
Estimate: 100-200

30453

AN AMERICAN OIL LAMP
Maker unknown, c.1900

The white metal pierced circular base with four feet extending to a shaped standard fitted with alabaster beneath a pierced white metal top fitted with a replacement globular white glass shade freely painted with white and red roses on the obverse, and with a two buds and single rose on the reverse, electrified, the standard unsigned, the glass shade with signature on the reverse *Amber Woodlee*
27.5in. high (Total: 3 Items)
Estimate: 200-300

30453

30455

30455

A SET OF TWELVE BOHEMIAN RUBY CUT GLASS GOBLETS
Maker unknown, c.1880

The matching set each with a round domed foot, disc collar and conical body decorated with alternating designs of elaborate cartouche and deer in the woods, unsigned
6.1in. high (Total: 12 Items)
Estimate: 600-800

30454

30454

A SET OF ELEVEN BOHEMIAN RUBY CUT GLASS GOBLETS
Maker unknown, c.1900

The matching set each with a round domed foot, disc collar and conical body decorated with alternating designs of elaborate cartouche and deer in the woods, unsigned
5.1in. high (Total: 11 Items)
Estimate: 500-800

30456

30456

AN AMERICAN 'FISH AND DOLPHIN' CHOCOLATE GLASS BOX
Greentown (Indiana Tumbler and Goblet Co.), design by Jacob Rosenthal, production 1900-1903

The cornucopia-shaped body depicting a scaled and open-mouthed dolphin with fish surmounted oval cover, the entire rendered in mottled brown slag glass, unmarked
3in. high
Estimate: 600-900

30457

30457
A BOHEMIAN MALACHITE GLASS VASE
Riedel Glassworks, c.1940

The molded octagonal base rising to a baluster form vessel designed with six nude females in high bas-relief dancing around a flowering tree, the mold designed by Curt Schlevogt in the 1930s, original foil *Ingrid* label used by Riedel for production of this vase
5in. high
Estimate: 200-400

30459

30459
A PAIR OF ENGLISH ENAMELED AND GILDED GLASS CLARET JUGS
Maker unknown, c.1910

Each of the green, flattened globular bodies with long neck terminating in a tri-corner rim with applied clear reeded handles and clear hollow stoppers, the obverse of each with white enamel lilies of the valley and gilt leaf decoration, cut pontil, unsigned, with painted orange numbers *7* and *30* respectively
The tallest: 11in. high (Total: 4 Items)
Estimate: 700-900

30458

30458
A VENETIAN GLASS CUP AND TRAY
Maker unknown, c.1900

The demitasse in blue and white swirl pattern with a beige rim; the tri-fold footed tray in lace and internal gold design, unsigned
2in. high and 6in. wide respectively (Total: 2 Items)
Estimate: 200-300

30460

30460
A VICTORIAN GLASS SYLLABUB BARREL AND PLATE
Maker unknown, c.1880

The cobalt lidded barrel-form container with matching charger accented with gold, unsigned
13in. high (Total: 3 Items)
Estimate: 200-400

30461
A PAIR OF WINE GOBLETS AND A GLASS CRUET
St. Louis, West Virginia Glass Co., c.1900

The matching chartreuse St. Louis goblets, baluster facet stem, gilt detail to the foot and bowl, etched garland pattern to the bowl; a clear to green bulbous form cruet decorated in medallion sprig pattern, cylindrical neck with flared rim, applied handle in clear with a faceted stopper, unsigned
6.6in. high and 7in. high respectively (Total: 4 Items)
Estimate: 200-400

30462
FOUR VENETIAN GLASS BASKETS
Various makers, c.1915

Comprising a pale pink coralene finish, clear handle and yellow applique leaves on either side of handle; a pink quilt pattern with a ruffle rim and clear handle; a yellow ribbed pattern with flared rim and applique flower and leaf; and a shallow red with blue rim, clear handle and applique flower and leaf, all unsigned
Various sizes (Total: 4 Items)
Estimate: 150-250

30463
AN AMERICAN PRESSED GLASS PLANTER AND CENTERPIECE
Cambridge, c.1920

The frosted molded pink Tiffin planter depicts classical figures, swan stamped in mold with *Cambridge* mark
Various sizes (Total: 2 Items)
Estimate: 200-300

30464
EIGHT OPALESCENT GLASS TUMBLERS
Various makers, c.1890

Comprising four coin spot pattern, two clear with white, one blue and one cranberry; the other four have a fern pattern in blue, cranberry, yellow and white, all unsigned
The tallest: 4in. (Total: 8 Items)
Estimate: 150-200

30465
A SET OF AMERICAN CROESUS IMPERIAL GREEN PRESSED GLASS ITEMS
Riverside Glass Works, c.1910

Comprising a tri-footed covered butter dish; a tri-footed ovoid form spooner with a slightly flared scalloped rim; four cylindrical tumblers, unsigned
The tallest: 5.5in. (Total: 7 Items)
Estimate: 200-400

30466

30466
A COLLECTION OF SPATTER GLASS AND COIN SPOT PATTERN ITEMS
Makers unknown, c.1900

Comprising a spatter ware tumbler with white and yellow ground heightened with cranberry and copper; a cranberry and opalescent white tumbler with inverted clear coin spot pattern; a cranberry tumbler with inverted opalescent white coin spot pattern; a Fenton purple tumbler with opalescent white coin spot pattern; *together with* a blue finger bowl with inverted opalescent white coin spot pattern, each unmarked
4in. high (Total: 5 Items)
Estimate: 100-200

30467

30467
AN AMERICAN ART GLASS SUGAR BOWL
New England Glass Co., c.1890

The green opaque bulbous form with a flared rim, applied handles, deep mottled pattern along rim, unsigned
3.7in. high
Estimate: 600-900

30468

30468
A SET OF TEN RUBY CUT GLASS TUMBLERS
Maker unknown, c.1900

The lower third of the tumbler in a design of button arches, ruby flashed to the top two thirds, unsigned
3.8in. high (Total: 10 Items)
Estimate: 200-400

30469

30469
FIVE BOHEMIAN GOBLETS AND DECANTER
Makers unknown, Twentieth Century

Comprising two green goblets, two cobalt goblets, and a yellow goblet all in various patterns with faceted stems; the decanter a cut glass green to clear round base supporting a bulbous form rising to a tapered neck and flared rim, clear stopper, all unsigned
The decanter: 14.2in. high; the goblets: various sizes (Total: 7 Items)
Estimate: 600-800

30470

30470
SIX COLORED GLASS TUMBLERS AND A BULB VASE
Makers unknown, c.1920

Comprising a satin chartreuse conical form bulb vase with a flared rim; a yellow satin swirl pattern tumbler cased in white; a chartreuse to opalescent coin spot tumbler; a pink to pale pink enameled tumbler depicting a floral design; an amethyst Northwood leaf medallion faceted tumbler; a cranberry faceted tumbler with enamel floral decoration; and a cranberry coin spot tumbler with silver floral enameling, all unsigned
The bud vase: 6.1in. high (Total: 7 Items)
Estimate: 200-400

30471
FOUR HOBNAIL GOBLETS
Various makers, c.1930

Comprising one dark green hobnail cordial and three 'Thousand Eye' waters in lime green, watermelon green, aqua blue, unsigned
4in. high and 6in. high respectively (Total: 4 Items)
Estimate: 100-150

30473
TEN AMERICAN GLASS DRINKING VESSELS
Various makers, c.1930

The group consists of five pressed tumblers, three enameled tumblers, two enameled goblets and one molded goblet in a cabbage leaf pattern, all in blue, unsigned
Various sizes (Total: 10 Items)
Estimate: 300-500

30472
A SPANGLED VASE AND ROSE BOWL
Makers unknown, c.1890

The vase, a 'Jack-in-the-Pulpit' form in mottled white, yellow and deep red on a clear body with silver mica flecks; the rose bowl, mottled clear and white to a cerulean blue eight-crimped rim with silver mica flecks, both unsigned
5.8in. high and 3.7in. high respectively (Total: 2 Items)
Estimate: 150-200

30474
THREE AMERICAN PRESSED GLASS ITEMS
Makers unknown, c.1915

Comprising a low bowl in blue hobnail and fan pattern; a compote with a six-pointed ruffled rim; a footed pitcher in blue 'diamond and button' pattern; each unsigned
The tallest: 6.4in. high (Total: 3 Items)
Estimate: 100-150

30475
FIVE ENAMEL DECORATED GLASS DRINKING VESSELS
Makers unknown, c.1890

All in the style of Mary Gregory, comprising a footed to bulbous and fluted cylindrical form in olive green depicting a young girl holding a flower; a clear bulbous footed tumbler depicting a boy; a pink cylindrical tumbler depicting a boy with a net; a green bulbous footed form with an applied handle depicting a boy; and a clear tapering tumbler depicting a boy, unsigned
The tallest: 6.2in. (Total: 5 Items)
Estimate: 200-400

30476

30478
AN AMERICAN ETCHED AND ENAMELED GLASS GOBLET
St. Louis, c.1910

Cut green to clear crystal with a faceted stem and smooth base, gilt enamel threading to rim and base, 6.6in. high
Estimate: 150-200

30478

30476
AN AMERICAN PATTERN GLASS PITCHER AND TUMBLER
Northwood, c.1890

The tri-footed base supports a 'Geneva' pattern with a custard ground and matching pattern tumbler, the pitcher enameled with green and red decoration over the pattern, the tumbler has green and gold enameling over decoration
8.5in. high and 3.5in. high respectively
Estimate: 200-300

30477

30477
THREE AMERICAN OPALESCENT GLASS ITEMS
Northwood, c.1897

All three in the 'Alaska' pattern, comprising a blue square-footed dish with a milky ruffled border and domed lid; *together with* a blue round, scalloped milky-edged sugar and creamer, unsigned
The tallest: 6in. (Total: 4 Items)
Estimate: 300-500

30479

30479
A CUSTARD GLASS PITCHER AND CUP
Makers unknown, c.1890

Comprising a 'Creased Scroll' pitcher with a small red floral pattern and stylized green fronds; a 'Delaware' cup with a green etched floral pattern, each unsigned
9in. high and 3.8in. high respectively (Total: 2 Items)
Estimate: 100-200

30480
FOUR CONTINENTAL ENAMELLED GLASS VASES
Various makers, c.1890

The four vessels are all enameled with various floral motifs, two amethyst and two green, all unsigned,
8in. to 10in. high (Total: 4 Items)
Estimate: 200-300

30481
AN AMERICAN SPATTER GLASS GAVEL
Maker unknown, c.1910

The black ground with multi-color white, yellow, orange and red spatter
7in. long
Estimate: 100-300

30482
FOUR AMERICAN CUSTARD GLASS TUMBLERS AND THREE AMETHYST GLASS TUMBLERS
Various makers, c.1905

Comprising a Fenton custard glass in the 'Cherry and Scale' pattern; a Georgia gem pattern custard glass; two ring band pattern souvenir custard tumblers, one decorated with a sepia-toned photograph of 'Balance Rock,' the other with the text *Souvenir of Waukegan Ill.*; two enameled amethyst tumblers; and a cranberry cut-to-clear tumbler, each unsigned
The tallest: 3.9in. high (Total: 7 Items)
Estimate: 100-200

30483
A GROUP OF ENAMELED GLASS ITEMS
Various makers, c.1900

Comprising a matching pair of green glass vases in the style of Mary Gregory one with a male figure, the other a female; a Mary Gregory style wine glass; a Mary Gregory style vaseline glass bud vase; a green faceted tumbler; and a cobalt blue cylindrical lidded box with enamel decoration
The tallest: 7.5in. (Total: 7 Items)
Estimate: 200-300

30484
TEN AMERICAN BLUE AND OPALESCENT GLASS SERVING PIECES
Various makers, c.1890

Comprising a Geo. Davidson & Co. clear blue to opalescent footed ribbed bowl with a scalloped rim; a Fenton 'Water Lily and Cattails' pattern spooner, footed and double handled bright blue to an opalescent scalloped rim; a Jefferson Glass Co. 'Sea Spray' pattern footed nappy in clear blue to an opalescent scalloped rim; two 'Old Man Winter' pattern blue glass baskets with blue clear to opalescent twist handles, one basket more cerulean blue, the other more greenish blue; an English hobnail shallow dish with a ruffled and scalloped opalescent rim; a cylindrical clear blue and opalescent swirl pattern vase with a ruffled opalescent rim; a wildflower pattern footed goblet with a diamond pattern to the rim; a blue glass lidded dish in the form of an iron on a trivet with a twist handle, raised on three feet, diamond pattern to the underside and lid; a deep blue glass butler with a ridge-pattern to the underside, unmarked
The tallest: 5.5in. high (Total: 11 Items)
Estimate: 200-400

30485
TWO ITALIAN COPPER LATTICINIO GLASS BOWLS
Makers unknown, c.1930

The first, a footed and straight-sided cylindrical body with applied handles depicting bas-relief faces; the second, a shallow-bodied bowl with an everted rim, both unsigned
The tallest: 2.25in. (Total: 2 Items)
Estimate: 300-600

30488
FOUR COLORED GLASS TUMBLERS
Makers unknown, c.1930

Comprising a Jefferson custard tumbler; a pale blue tumbler with painted enamel roses; a white satin finish tumbler with blue birds; a white cased swirl spatter tumbler, each unsigned
Each approx. 4in. high (Total: 4 Items)
Estimate: 50-100

30486
A NEAPOLITAN SATIN GLASS TUMBLER
Hobbs, Brockunier & Co., c.1880

The cylindrical form Neapolitan pink satin with white casing, unsigned
4.2in. high
Estimate: 100-200

30489
A SET OF SIX AMERICAN CROESUS IMPERIAL GREEN GLASS ITEMS
Riverside Glass Works, c.1910

Comprising a tankard, *together with* a berry set, including a large footed serving bowl and four small footed berry bowls, each unsigned
The tallest: 5.5in. high (Total: 6 Items)
Estimate: 400-600

30487
A BOHEMIAN OVERLAID AND CUT GLASS DECANTER AND RÖMER
Makers unknown, c.1890

The stoppered decanter white cut to clear with lavish gilt banding and polychrome floral decoration; the cobalt cut to opalescent white römer with gilt fleur de lis decoration, unsigned
The taller: 8in. (Total: 3 Items)
Estimate: 300-500

30490
A SET OF AMERICAN GUTATTE PATTERN MILK GLASS ITEMS
Consolidated Lamp & Glass Co., c.1890

The matching set includes a pitcher, creamer, sugar bowl and four tumblers all in white with gilt rims, unsigned
The tallest: 9.2in. high (Total: 7 Items)
Estimate: 200-300

30490

30491
AN AMERICAN ART GLASS VASE
Vineland Flint Glass Works, c.1925

The tapering ovoid form in blue with clear vertical ribbing, signed underside *Durand 1962*
10in. high
Estimate: 300-500

30491

30492
A COLLECTION OF AMERICAN MOLD-BLOWN AND PRESSED GLASS
Makers unknown, c.1870-1930

Comprising a pair of mold-blown steins with leaf etching and thick beveled covers bezel-set in hinged pewter mounts; a square amethyst pressed 'Daisy and Button' ice cream saucer; a pressed tumbler with green thumbprint decoration; and a pressed Argus thumbprint goblet with gilt highlights, possibly by Bakewell, Pears & Co., all pieces unmarked
The tallest: 6.25in. high, 3.5in. rim diameter (Total: 5 Items)
Estimate: 300-500

30493
AN AMERICAN WHITE GUTTATE PATTERN GLASS BUTTER DISH AND SUGAR BOWL
Maker unknown, c.1890

Ivory color with gilt accents, a covered butter dish and covered sugar bowl, unsigned
The sugar: 5.5in. high (Total: 4 Items)
Estimate: 200-400

30494
TWO ART GLASS BOWLS
Makers unknown, Twentieth Century

The first, of shell form in green glass with air bubbles and gold flecks; the second, a low bowl with wide everted tri-corner rim in green and amber, unsigned
7.6in. long and 7in. diameter respectively (Total: 2 Items)
Estimate: 100-200

30495
FIVE AMERICAN 'FRANCESWARE' GLASS ITEMS
Hobbs, Brockunier & Co., c.1880

Comprising three lidded jars, cream and sugar bowl, each with a frosted hobnail body and yellow rim, unsigned
Various sizes (Total: 8 items)
Estimate: 200-400

30496
FIVE ENAMEL DECORATED GLASSES
Various makers, c.1890

Comprising a cushion-footed stemmed cylindrical tumbler decorated with an etched ground, red rose and green garland pattern; a green iridescent carnival glass tumbler, fine rib decoration to the upper third and enamel flower pattern; a dome-footed amber tumbler with enamel decoration depicting gilt flowers, some with red and blue details; a footed amber enameled fluted tumbler decorated with blue enamel flowers; and a pale purple-gold flashed goblet with gilt pattern of flowers, and geometric shapes, gilt detail to foot, unsigned
The tallest: 7.7in. (Total: 5 Items)
Estimate: 100-300

30497
TWO PIECES OF AMERICAN GLASS
Cambridge and maker unknown, c.1900

Including a green tri-sectioned covered candy dish and a custard footed pitcher, unmarked
6.5in. high (Total: 3 Items)
Estimate: 100-200

30498
THREE AMERICAN CASED GLASS TUMBLERS
Maker unknown, c.1900

Comprising a white cased pink body with hand-painted moss rose decoration; a satin cranberry cased satin body sans decoration; and a satin cranberry cased white body with gilt cord-and-tassel decoration beneath simple gilt bands near the rim, each unsigned
The tallest: 4.1in. (Total: 3 Items)
Estimate: 400-600

30499
AN AMERICAN PAINTED AND GILDED GLASS PITCHER
Heisey, c.1897-1905

The tapering cylindrical 'Ivorina Verde' (custard) form with '#1245 Ring Band' decoration above and below the hand-painted spray of roses on the obverse, the notched and scalloped rim with gracious spout, molded handle, molded *Heisey* mark in center of underside
7.25in. high
Estimate: 300-500

30500
AN AMERICAN CRANBERRY PRESSED GLASS PITCHER
Maker unknown, c.1890

A round spreading foot, slender tapering cranberry body with a pinched spout and applied clear glass handle, pressed diamond pattern in four panels, unsigned
6in. high
Estimate: 100-300

30501
A PAIR OF ITALIAN SPANGLED GLASS BOWLS
Maker unknown, c.1950

The matching pair of three-lobed clover shape with controlled-bubble technique and silver-backed gold foil suspended in clear glass graduating to an amethyst rim, unsigned
2.75in. high (Total: 2 Items)
Estimate: 100-300

30502
AN AMERICAN 'WILD ROSE' PEACH BLOW VASE
New England Glass Co., c.1890

The round body tapers at the bottom of the neck, flares and then tapers again at the rim, unsigned
5.7in. high
Estimate: 600-800

30503
TEN ASSORTED GLASS TUMBLERS AND A VASE
Various makers, c.1900

Including a Northwood 'Grape and Cable' pattern tumbler in marigold with a hint of magenta to the rim, raised mark on the inside; a Hobbs Brockunier amber hobnail tumbler; a round footed iridescent column vase with a flared scalloped and asymmetrical rim; and two Indiana Glass Co. tumblers in the 'Gaelic' pattern
The vase: 8.5in. high (Total: 10 Items)
Estimate: 200-300

30504
SEVEN BLUE OPALESCENT GLASS SERVING PIECES
Northwood, Jefferson Glass Co., c.1898

Comprising a Northwood 'Intaglio' pattern cream and open sugar bowl; a Northwood fluted scroll pattern spooner and low bowl; a Northwood vase in the 'Simple Simon' pattern; a Jefferson Glass Co. 'Tokyo' pattern cream and open sugar bowl; each unmarked
The tallest: 5.7in. high (Total: 7 Items)
Estimate: 200-400

30505

30505
A PAIR OF AMERICAN PRESSED GLASS SHAKERS
Maker unknown, c.1900

The domed foot rising to a four-sided form with threaded metal top, each side depicts a medallion design of a coin, unsigned
3.1in. high (Total: 2 Items)
Estimate: 100-200

30506

30506
TWO AMERICAN BLOWN GLASS TUMBLERS AND A CABINET VASE
Northwood Glass Co., c.1890

The etched finish clear to ruby swirling cylindrical tumbler in the 'Royal Ivy' pattern; a clear to ruby cylindrical tumbler in the 'Royal Oak' pattern; and a 'Royal Oak' pattern clear to ruby quartre-foil cabinet vase, unsigned
The tumblers: 3.7in. high, The vase: 2.2in. high (Total: 3 Items)
Estimate: 100-300

30507

30507
ELEVEN PIECES OF AMERICAN GREEN GLASS
Various makers, c.1900

Comprising a Riverside 'Empress' pattern covered sugar; a Riverside 'Croesus' pattern tumbler; a United States Glass Co. 'Lacy Medallion' tumbler; a Northwood 'Memphis' pattern covered butter dish, signed; a Model Glint Glass Co. green 'Anthemion' ('Albany') pattern tumbler; a Northwood 'Gold Rose' pattern covered butter dish, signed; a 'Bohemian' pattern toothbrush holder; a United States Glass Co. 'Florida' ('Emerald Green Herringbone') pattern pitcher
The tallest: 9.75in. high (Total: 11 Items)
Estimate: 200-400

30508

30508
THREE GLASS GOBLETS AND A GLASS MATCH HOLDER
Makers unknown, c.1890

Comprising two Bohemian goblets, one with amber panels and one with green, both with gilt detailing overall; a opalescent Roemer goblet with a ribbed and knobbed stem, three prunts to top knob; a blue glass with enamel vine and flower pattern supported by a metal footed leaf mount and rim, each unsigned
Various sizes (Total: 4 Items)
Estimate: 200-400

30509

30509
FOUR HOBNAIL TUMBLERS
Various makers, c.1890

Comprising an amethyst tumbler, a frosted clear to cranberry tumbler, and one opalescent and one clear 'Thousand Eye' tumbler, all unsigned
The tallest: 4.2in. (Total: 4 Items)
Estimate: 200-300

30511

30511
AN AMERICAN 'ROYAL OAK' LIDDED GLASS DISH
Northwood, c.1900

The low square-shaped dish in a frosted and clear finish with rounded shoulders, frosted cranberry to clear lid depicting oak leaves, acorn finial, unsigned
5.7in. high (Total: 2 Items)
Estimate: 75-150

30510

30510
AN AMERICAN OPALESCENT 'DRAPE' LIDDED GLASS BOWL
Northwood, c.1890

Blue with milky highlights, the low dish with scalloped rim and a high domed cover with shaped finial, stamped with a raised mold mark
5.7in. high (Total: 2 items)
Estimate: 200-400

30512

30512
FOURTEEN RUBY GLASS ITEMS
Various makers, c.1925

Comprising ten ruby goblets with a tri-bulb stem; a Steuben compote, stamped underside; a tri-footed pressed glass low bowl with a star design to the center; a pressed glass bowl with an open lattice rim; an Anchor Hocking vase with a bulbous form
The tallest: 6.3in. high (Total: 14 Items)
Estimate: 200-400

30513
A PAIR OF AMERICAN CRANBERRY GLASS VASES
Maker unknown, c.1900

Each of the ribbed barrel forms with tri-cornered rim, the obverse of each with raised gilt decoration, unsigned
12in. high (Total: 2 Items)
Estimate: 600-800

30516
AN AMERICAN 'HOLLY' AMBER GLASS TUMBLER
Greentown (Indiana Tumbler and Goblet Co.), design by Jacob Rosenthal, production 1902-1903

The cylindrical body with slight concave, and decorated with alternating vertical beaded panels and holly, unsigned
7in. high
Estimate: 200-300

30514
A GROUP OF ENAMELED PRESSED GLASS TUMBLERS
Makers unknown, c.1930

Comprising three similar faceted glass tumblers with red cherries; an enameled tumbler with grapes; a faceted tumbler with flowers, each unmarked
The tallest: 4.2in. high (Total: 5 Items)
Estimate: 50-100

30515
FOUR AMERICAN ENAMELED BLUE GLASS TUMBLERS
Makers unknown, c.1900

One with pink flowers; a pair with pink tulips and gilt rims; one with demi-lune florets and gilded rim, each unsigned
4in. high (Total: 4 Items)
Estimate: 100-300

30517
AN AMERICAN GOTHIC ARCH LACY SANDWICH FLINT GLASS BOWL
Boston and Sandwich Glass Works, c.1850

Possibly a sugar base without a cover, the three-mold, cerulean blue octagonal body with circular foot, the eight panels with four pairs of Gothic-arched window patterns, unsigned
3.5in. high
A similar bowl with lid intact illustrated p.810 *Magazine Antiques* December 1993
Estimate: 200-400

30518
A GROUP OF AMERICAN RUBY AND CRANBERRY GLASS
Makers unknown, c.1900

Comprising four matched ruby red tumblers with ribbing; one ruby tumbler with faceted sides to the lower third; one heavy glass cranberry cased goblet on a clear pedestal foot; a cranberry and clear coin spot tumbler; a ruby flashed and clear goblet; a vase in cranberry to clear short foot bulbous form to a flared rim, Greek key pattern to the mid section, unsigned
The tallest: 6.4in. (Total: 9 Items)
Estimate: 100-300

30520
FOUR BOHEMIAN GLASS GOBLETS
Various makers, c.1900

Comprising a Val St. Lambert goblet, round star pattern foot, faceted stem to faceted knob transition supporting an olive green cut to clear with stars and diamonds; two matching goblets, one amethyst, one green, depicting grapes and diamonds; a purple cut to clear goblet depicting grapes and leaves, the Val St. Lambert signed underside
7.9in. high (Total: 4 Items)
Estimate: 100-300

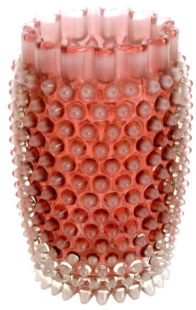

30521
FOUR ENAMELED GLASS TUMBLERS
Makers unknown, c.1930

Each with enamel decoration, three depict flowers, the fourth in an enamel bead scroll pattern with gilt bands and border, unsigned
The tallest: 4.1in. high (Total: 4 Items)
Estimate: 50-100

30519
AN AMERICAN CRANBERRY HOBNAIL GLASS VASE
Maker unknown, c.1900

The swollen cylindrical form raised on a row of hobnail feet and surmounted by an undulating rim, unsigned
6in. high
Estimate: 200-400

30522

THREE PIECES OF ASSORTED GLASS STEMWARE
Cambridge, Moser, and maker unknown, Twentieth Century

Comprising a Moser cordial with gold and white enamel decoration to quatre-foil emerald-green cup; a Cambridge goblet with gold decoration; a Bohemian amethyst cut to clear cordial with faceted and zippered stem; all pieces unmarked
The tallest: 7.75in. (Total: 3 Items)
Estimate: 100-300

30523

FOUR AMERICAN ENAMELED GLASS ITEMS
Mary Gregory style, Twentieth Century

Comprising an octagonal tumbler decorated with a boy holding a letter; a vase decorated with a girl holding a bouquet; a vase decorated with a boy holding a rose; *together with* a small footed vase decorated with a boy flying a kite, each unsigned
The tallest: 5.75in. (Total: 4 Items)
Estimate: 200-300

30524

FIVE AMERICAN PATTERN GLASS ITEMS
Makers unknown, c.1930

Comprising a 'diamond-point-and-panel' pattern goblet in purple slag glass; a 'grape-and-cable' pattern chocolate glass tumbler; a 'cactus' pattern chocolate glass toothpick holder; a 'cactus' pattern chocolate glass salt shaker; a green milk glass toothpick holder, each unsigned
The tallest: 6.5in. (Total: 5 Items)
Estimate: 200-400

30525

FOUR PIECES OF BOHEMIAN GLASS
Makers unknown, c.1890

Comprising a pitcher cranberry cut to clear decoration featuring fox, hound, stag, doe, and castle amid diapered cartouches and rows of coin spot motif; a cylindrical cranberry cut to clear goblet with animal and coin spot decorative motifs; a cranberry cut to clear compote depicting a deer chase in the forest; a miniature covered tankard, each unsigned
The tallest: 8in. (Total: 4 Items)
Estimate: 200-300

30526

A COLLECTION OF AMERICAN OPALESCENT BLUE GLASS ITEMS
Various makers, various dates

Comprising a pair of Jefferson Glass Co. bowls in the 'Many Loops' pattern; a Northwood 'Shell & Wild Rose' pattern footed dish with 'egg and dart' pierced border; a Northwood 'Fluted Scroll' footed spooner, a Northwood 'Intaglio' pattern creamer; a Northwood 'Pearls & Scales' pattern compote, *together with* a 'Desert Garden' compote, all unmarked
The tallest: 5in. (Total: 7 Items)
Estimate: 300-400

30527

AN ETCHED RUBY GLASS DECANTER AND TWO CORDIALS
Maker unknown, c.1880

The ruby flashed etched-to-clear Bohemian-style decanter depicts a castle, deer and various cartouche, with an eight-sided stopper; matching cordials depict deer and cartouche, each unsigned
7.7in. high and 2.4in. high respectively (Total: 4 Items)
Estimate: 100-200

30528

AN AMERICAN PATTERN GLASS LEMONADE SET
U.S. Glass Co., c.1898

Comprising an emerald green pitcher, covered sugar dish, creamer, and a covered round dish, each in the 'Missouri' or 'Palm and Scroll' pattern, unsigned
The tallest: 8.5in. (Total: 6 Items)
Estimate: 100-300

30529

A MIXED LOT OF GLASS ITEMS
Makers unknown, various dates

Comprising a footed and stemmed glass tumbler with an etched bowl decorated in enamel beaded swags and scroll design, glass bead highlights; a clear and white opalescent footed and stemmed rose bowl with a beaded scale pattern with a tightly ruffled rim; a cranberry opalescent coin spot tumbler; a cranberry thumbprint cup with a clear applied handle; two cordial glasses with tapering faceted clear stems supporting a bowl in amethyst and one in cranberry; a pink pressed glass swan; and a cobalt pipe, all unsigned
The tallest: 4.7in. high (Total: 8 Items)
Estimate: 100-300

30530

A MILLE-FIORI GLASS PLATE
Maker unknown, Twentieth Century

The satin finish round foot rising to a wide everted rim primarily in yellow and white with burgundy and green center to the flowers, burgundy threading to the edge, unsigned
6.2in. diameter
Estimate: 100-200

30531

FOUR PIECES OF AMERICAN BLUE GLASS
Northwood and others, c.1920

Comprising a swirled juice glass with gilt rim; a dome-footed and owl-shaped creamer; a boy's molded mug; a Northwood tumbler with daisy decoration and maker's mark
The tallest: 4in. (Total: 4 Items)
Estimate: 100-300

30535
A GROUP OF OPALESCENT AND PRESSED GLASS ITEMS
Makers unknown, c.1900

Comprising a blue pressed glass anvil 'Daisy and button' pattern toothpick holder; a blue and opalescent ribbed bowl; a pale blue opalescent scalloped rim 'Scroll with Acanthus' pattern compote; a blue pressed glass hobnail pattern toothpick holder; a blue pressed glass 'Daisy and Button' toothpick holder with metal rim and foot mounts, unsigned
The tallest: 5in. high (Total: 5 Items)
Estimate: 100-200

30532
AN AMERICAN MOLD-BLOWN RUBY GLASS FINGERBOWL
Maker unknown, c.1890

The deep cup with smooth interior and raised crackle decoration to the exterior, unsigned
3in. high
Estimate: 200-400

30533
A GLASS ROLLING PIN
Maker unknown, c.1890

The deep clear amethyst color pin, cylindrical form with two handles, unsigned
15.2in. long
Estimate: 100-300

30536
A MOTTLED GLASS ROSEBOWL
Maker unknown, c.1910

The three-sided dimpled form with a tri-lobed rim in blue ground with a white and yellow mottled finish, unsigned
4.1in. high
Estimate: 100-200

30534
A GROUP OF RUBY GLASS ITEMS
Various makers, c.1900

Comprising a clear heavily-ribbed celery vase with thumbprints to the ribs flashed in ruby; a ruby Bohemian glass goblet with a faceted cushion foot and eight-panel bowl with gilt threading; a Millard ruby to clear fan design cylindrical syrup pitcher, clear applied handle and a metal hinged lid; a ruby Bohemian goblet with a cushion foot, short stem and cylindrical bowl, ivory enamel floral decoration to front and back with a cartouche of gilt lettering, gilt detail to rim, flowers and base, each unsigned
The tallest: 6in. high (Total: 4 Items)
Estimate: 200-400

30537
TWO AMERICAN GLASS TOOTHPICK HOLDERS
Hobbs & Brockunier Glass Co. and Northwood Glass, respectively, c.1900

The first, with frosted and flattened oval swirl body and yellow-collared rim; the second, with swirled barrel-shaped body with characteristic clear base and ivy patterned waist and ruby top; each unsigned
2.6in. high and 2.4in. high, respectively (Total: 2 Items)
Estimate: 400-600

30538
A COLLECTION OF AMERICAN 'JEWEL AND DRAPERY' BLUE OPALESCENT GLASS TABLEWARE
Northwood, c.1920

Comprising a creamer and sugar set, each piece with hexagonal base and scalloped rim with gilt highlights; a covered butter dish with starburst base and scalloped rim, *together with* a covered bowl with hexagonal base and 'jewel' knob; all pieces with molded maker's mark
The tallest: 7in. high (Total: 6 Items)
Estimate: 200-300

30539
A GLASS CABINET VASE
Maker unknown, c.1920

The molded foot supports a bulbous and ribbed base with a diamond quilt pattern rising to a star-shaped neck, cased in red with a dark red rim, unsigned
3.1in. high
Estimate: 100-200

30540
A PAIR OF AMERICAN BRILLIANT CUT GLASS SALT AND PEPPER SHAKERS
Maker unknown, c.1890

The tapering square shape with faceted corners in a clear and frosted finish and a cut 'Klondike' pattern in amber, metal threaded caps, unsigned (Total: 2 Items)
3.2in. high
Estimate: 100-200

30541
A GROUP OF GREEN PRESSED GLASS SERVING PIECES
Various makers, c.1900

Comprising a swirl column berry set of a large center bowl and six individual bowls in green with gilding; a matching oval swirl column relish dish; a cream and open sugar bowl in green faceted cylindrical form with a gilt scalloped and notched rim depicting a raised gold rose pattern; and a cream and lidded sugar dish in apple green shell pattern with gilt center medallions, gilt scalloped rim, unsigned
The tallest: 6.4in. (Total: 13 Items)
Estimate: 200-400

30543
AN ITALIAN SPANGLED GLASS BOWL
Maker unknown, Twentieth Century

The molded foot supports a tri-fold shallow bowl in a white lace pattern with gold ribbing radiating from the center, unsigned
6.2in. diameter
Estimate: 200-400

30542
AN AMERICAN 'MAIZE' GLASS TUMBLER
Libbey Glass Co., c.1920

The opaque, swollen cylindrical shape modeled in light custard color to depict husks rising up to conceal an ear of corn, unsigned
4in. high
Estimate: 100-200

30544
FIVE MARY GREGORY ITEMS
Maker unknown, c.1915

Comprising a cranberry tumbler depicting a young boy in white enamel; a green bowl depicting an angel in flowers to the front side, gilt rim; a green bud vase with an angel in flowers in white enamel, gilt rim; a green pitcher with applied handle, white enamel depicting a young boy; and a faceted green vase enameled with a young boy in Victorian dress surrounded by grasses, each unsigned
The tallest: 6.9in. (Total: 5 Items)
Estimate: 100-300

30545
TWO BLUE PRESSED GLASS SERVING PIECES
Makers unknown, c.1900

Both items in the 'Daisy and Button' pattern comprising a wheelbarrow form with a metel wheel and axle; and a rectangular tray, both unsigned
9.2in. long and 11in. long respectively (Total: 2 Items)
Estimate: 50-100

30547
FOUR GLASS PAPERWEIGHTS
Murano and Joe St. Clair, Twentieth Century

The Italian pear in clear glass with a deep crimson core, bronze mica leaf and stem, green on base; two apples of red blown glass encased in clear with a clear stem and leaf; the fourth a flat base dome form in clear glass with multicolored glass swirls to the interior; the pear has a Murano sticker to the underside, the apples are stamped underside
The tallest: 5in. high (Total: 4 Items)
Estimate: 100-300

30548
AN OPALESCENT COIN SPOT PATTERN GLASS BOWL
Maker unknown, c.1900

The footed blue glass with a craquelure finish, unsigned
3in. high
Estimate: 100-200

30546
A SET OF 'DRAPE' OPALESCENT GLASS TUMBLERS AND A PITCHER
Makers unknown, c.1900

Comprising a blue opalescent pitcher and five matching tumblers rising from clear blue to a pale milky blue collared rim; three additional tumblers also clear blue rising to a pale blue milky collared rim with gilt accents, unsigned
The pitcher: 8.5in. high (Total: 9 Items)
Estimate: 200-400

30549
AN ITALIAN LATTICINO GLASS BOWL
Maker unknown, c.1940

The footed, shallow cylindrical body with alternating bands of blue and twisted-copper, applied clear double-handles with relief face and gold inclusions, unsigned
2.5in. high
Estimate: 100-200

30551
AN ITALIAN ART GLASS VASE
Maker unknown, Twentieth Century

The double gourd form in clear blue and gold bands with a thin green stripe bordering the gold, unsigned
5.2in. high
Estimate: 100-200

30550
A COLLECTION OF AMERICAN GREEN GLASS ITEMS
Various makers, various dates

Comprising a Northwood 'Northwood Block' pattern opalescent compote; a 'Swags With Brackets' pattern opalescent compote; a 'Beaded and Scales' pattern opalescent and red compote; a domefooted compote with paneled stem flaring to a shallow bowl with three pink roses beneath a scalloped and gilded rim; a Fenton 'Water Lily and Cat Tails' pattern opalescent footed bowl; a Northwood 'Ruffles and Rings' pattern opalescent footed bowl; a Jefferson Glass Co. 'Barbelli' pattern opalescent bowl; a 'Water Lily' pattern opalescent bowl; a 'Spokes and Wheels' pattern blue-green opalescent bowl; a 'Jewel and Fan' pattern opalescent dish; a Northwood 'Regal' pattern opalescent bowl; two 'Daisy and Button' pattern toothpick holders; each unsigned
The tallest: 4.5in. (Total: 13 Items)
Estimate: 300-600

30552
FIVE BLUE OPALESCENT AND PRESSED GLASS ITEMS
Maker unknown, c.1890

Comprising an opalescent blue hobnail footed vase; a pressed glass diamond form lidded butter dish with a relief scroll pattern to base and lid; a blue opal basket in 'Old Man Winter' pattern; an opalescent hobnail toothpick holder on three feet, all unmarked
The tallest: 5.5in. (Total: 5 Items)
Estimate: 100-300

30553
A GROUP OF ENAMELED GLASS ITEMS
Makers unknown, Twentieth Century

Four items in the style of Mary Gregory; *together with* a blue vase with enameled scene of a fisherman, each unsigned
The tallest: 6.7in. high (Total: 5 Items)
Estimate: 100-300

30554
A PRESSED GLASS CREAMER
Maker unknown, c.1900

The yellow round foot supporting a quatre-foil ribbed bulbous form with a circular pattern to each side, round to square neck with a clear applied reeded handle, partially cased in red, unsigned
4.7in. high
Estimate: 100-200

30555
AN IRISH PORCELAIN PITCHER
Belleek, c.1891

The bulbous body tapers to a slender neck with a large flared spout and curved handle, the fluted and medallion pattern body overlapped by applique floral motif, stamped underside in black ink
9in. high
Estimate: 300-500

30556
EIGHT RUSSIAN PATTERN CUT GLASS DISHES AND TRAY
Maker unknown, c.1900

The set includes eight square nut dishes and a rectangular tray with handles, unsigned
4.5in. square and 14.7in. long respectively (Total: 9 Items)
Estimate: 500-700

30557
FOUR AMERICAN BRILLIANT CUT GLASS ITEMS
Various makers, c.1900

Comprising a Libbey bowl cut with stars, fans and fine diamonds, notched scalloped rim; a round bowl cut with hobstars, diamond and fine diamonds, notched scalloped rim; a Hawkes celery dish cut with stars, diamonds and fine diamonds, notched scalloped rim; and a second celery dish cut with stars, notched scalloped rim, Libbey bowl and Hawkes celery dish are both stamped
11.2in. the longest celery bowl, 8.2in. the widest bowl (Total: 4 Items)
Estimate: 300-500

30558
AN AMERICAN GLASS BOWL ATTRIBUTED TO DORFINGER AND A HOBSTAR GLASS BOWL
Makers unknown, c.1900

The first has three hobnails and a pointed and arched notch rim; the second has six hobnails with a scalloped notch rim, unsigned
7.9in. diameter and 9in. diameter respectively (Total: 2 Items)
Estimate: 400-600

30559
TWO ETCHED GLASS VASES
Hawkes; Sabino, c.1920

The first, a classical form with engraved garlands and draped floral design, stamped underside with *Hawkes* hallmark; the second, a footed, short-stemmed fluted trumpet form with an etched finish, engraved underside *Sabino France*
10.2in. high and 5.7in. high respectively (Total: 2 Items)
Estimate: 200-400

30560
THREE AMERICAN BRILLIANT CUT GLASS ITEMS
Makers unknown, c.1900

A tall compote with spreading foot; a bulbous vase with flaring cylindrical neck; a rosewater bowl with etched floral underside,
The tallest: 8.8in. high (Total: 3 Items)
Estimate: 300-500

30561
AN AMERICAN BRILLIANT-CUT GLASS CABINET VASE
Maker unknown, c.1910

The double-handled globular vase with flared neck embellished with Russian-cut decoration
6.5in. high
Estimate: 400-500

30563
AN AMERICAN BRILLIANT CUT GLASS PITCHER
Maker unknown, c.1910

The tankard style pitcher with hobstars and circles and a sterling silver rim with a floral border, monogrammed *G W*
12.6in. high
Estimate: 300-500

30562
SIX AMERICAN BRILLIANT CUT GLASS DISHES
Makers unknown, c.1910

The group consists of four round notched dishes, three with scalloped rims; a square shape notched rim dish; a rectangular scalloped and notched rim dish, various patterns, all unsigned
6in. to 7in. diameter (Total: 6 Items)
Estimate: 300-500

30564
TWO PIECES OF AMERICAN BRILLIANT CUT GLASS
probably Pitkins & Brooks, c.1900

Comprising a stoppered cologne bottle of globular shape with three pinwheel hobstars alternating with three 'diamond-and-button' panels, the shoulder and neck with zippered panels, the stopper faceted, *together with* a tall compote with starburst disc foot under a faceted controlled air bubble stem, the bowl with four hobstars alternating with four fine diamond panels beneath the notched and scalloped rim, unmarked
The tallest: 8.5in. high (Total: 3 Items)
Estimate: 300-500

30565
AN AMERICAN BRILLIANT CUT GLASS BOWL, PLATE AND CONDIMENT SET
Makers unknown, c.1900

The bowl with stars, crosshatching, leaves and a central star; the plate with hobstars, fans and a large central star; the condiment set includes a bowl and plate of hobstar clusters and etched stylized flower and leaf pattern, unsigned
Various sizes (Total: 4 Items)
Estimate: 200-400

30567
NINE ENGLISH ETCHED AND CUT GLASS ITEMS
Thomas Webb & Sons and various makers, c.1890

Comprising two etched cordials signed *Webb Made in England*; a Russian pattern cut glass cruet with a faceted stopper; and five cut glass tumblers
4.2in. high, 5.6in. high, 3.8in. high respectively (Total: 9 Items)
Estimate: 300-500

30566
AN AMERICAN BRILLIANT CUT GLASS DECANTER AND BOWL
Maker unknown, c.1900

The set includes a ship's decanter with a bulbous base rising to a cylindrical neck with a flared rim, hobstars, diamonds and fans; a low wide bowl with a notched scalloped rim, hobstars, fans and crosshatching, unsigned
7.5in. high and 8in. diameter respectively (Total: 2 Items)
Estimate: 200-300

30568
A COLLECTION OF AMERICAN ETCHED GLASS ITEMS
Heisey, Hawkes, Steuben, and Fostoria, c.1925

Comprising an unsigned clear plate with floral and band etching; an unsigned decanter with wreath and floral decoration; a pair of Fostoria candlestick holders with 'June' pattern, a Waverly bowl blank with orchid pattern by Heisey; a small Hawkes marked compote with flower decoration; a Steuben marked peach plate with floral border; respective items with maker's mark of *Hawkes* and *Steuben*
Bowl 3.1in. high, rim 12.5in. diameter (Total: 7 Items)
Estimate: 200-300

30569
FOUR AMERICAN BRILLIANT CUT GLASS GOBLETS
Makers unknown, c.1910

The group consists of two matching wine glasses in the Baker's Gothic pattern, a cordial glass in Russian cut pattern; the third larger goblet has a floral and leaf pattern, all unsigned
4.5in. high, 4.4in. high and 6.1in. high respectively (Total: 4 Items)
Estimate: 100-200

30570
AN AMERICAN BRILLIANT CUT GLASS CREAMER AND SUGAR
Maker unknown, c.1900

The creamer in 'Niles' pattern, the sugar dish in 'Saratoga' pattern, both unsigned
2.5in. high and 2.9in. high, respectively (Total: 2 Items)
Estimate: 100-200

30571
FIFTEEN AMERICAN CUT GLASS BOWLS
Hawkes, Twentieth Century

The group consists of matching pattern of stylized flowers and leaves with small circles on a round flat foot rising to a short stem supporting a wide ovoid bowl, unsigned
4.5in. high (Total: 15 Items)
Estimate: 600-800

30572
AN AMERICAN BRILLIANT CUT GLASS PITCHER
Maker unknown, c.1910

The wide base tapering to the body and flaring to a notched asymmetrical rim with an applied notched handle, hobstars, crosshatching and fan design, unsigned
10.4in. high
Estimate: 200-300

30573
AN AMERICAN BRILLIANT CUT GLASS COMPOTE AND FOOTED DISH
Makers unknown, c.1900

The compote has a cut disc foot rising to a faceted stem and a shallow bowl with notched rim, pattern has stars, fans, and crosshatching; the shallow four footed dish in a Clark's 'Jubilee' pattern, unsigned
7.5in. high and 9in. diameter respectively (Total: 2 Items)
Estimate: 500-700

30574
A PAIR OF AMERICAN BRILLIANT CUT GLASS NAPPIES
Maker unknown, c.1900

The notched scalloped-rim nappies have fans, hobstars and some crosshatching, unsigned
6in. diameter (Total: 2 Items)
Estimate: 200-300

30575
A SET OF TWELVE ENGLISH 'CORBETT' ETCHED GLASS SERVING BOWLS AND UNDERPLATES
Thomas Webb & Sons, c.1925

Each with everted rim and enhanced with scrolling vine and clover-leaf motif, nine with maker's mark near pontil, three without
2.5in. high, 5in. rim diameter (Total: 24 Items)
Estimate: 300-500

30576
A COLLECTION OF AMERICAN BRILLIANT-CUT GLASS ITEMS
Pairpoint, c.1890

Comprising eight assorted tumblers without marker's mark and an 'Estelle' pattern bowl by Pairpoint; all pieces without signature or mark
Bowl 3in. high, 9in. rim diameter respectively (Total: 9 Items)
Estimate: 500-600

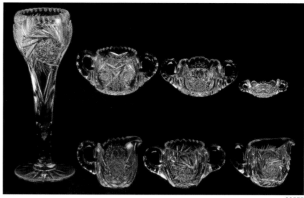

30577
SEVEN AMERICAN BRILLIANT CUT GLASS ITEMS
Various patterns, c.1915

Comprising a footed trumpet form vase; two creamers; three notch-rimmed two-handled sugar bowls; and a two-handled salt cellar, each unsigned
The vase: 12in. high (Total: 7 Items)
Estimate: 200-400

30578
AN AMERICAN BRILLIANT CUT GLASS ROSE BOWL, CELERY DISH AND NAPPY
Makers unknown, c.1900

The group consists of a Russian pattern rose bowl; a Rex variation pattern celery dish; and a Brazilian pattern handled nappy, all unsigned
5.6in. high; 10in. long; and 6in. diameter respectively
Provenance: Maude B. Feld sold items to Mrs. R. A. McMurry sold items to current owner (Total: 3 Items)
Estimate: 400-600

30579
AN AMERICAN BRILLIANT CUT GLASS COMPOTE
Maker unknown, c.1900

The round notch base rising to a faceted and knobbed stem supporting a bowl with hobstars and crosshatching, scalloped notched rim, unsigned
10.6in. high
Estimate: 500-700

30580
A COLLECTION OF AMERICAN BRILLIANT CUT GLASS BOWLS
Tuthill and other makers, c.1910

Comprising three shallow round bowls and a nappy, each with notched and scalloped rim, and a Tuthill rectilinear bowl with canted corners and floral border, Tuthill mark on underside of bowl
Tuthill bowl: 2in. high, 9.25in. long, 6.6in.wide (Total: 5 Items)
Estimate: 600-800

30581
ELEVEN AMERICAN GLASS TABLE ITEMS
Makers unknown, c.1910

Comprising a pair of pressed glass napkin rings with *R* monogram; three unmatched brilliant-cut napkin rings; five matching brilliant-cut tumblers; and a large flower-cut cylindrical vase, each unsigned
The tallest: 11.75in. high (Total: 11 Items)
Estimate: 400-600

30582
A SET OF ELEVEN CUT GLASS PUNCH CUPS
H. P. Sinclaire & Co., 1900

The round foot and short stem supporting a low bulbous form with a flared rim and two applied handles, floral and leaf pattern, acid stamped underside
1.6in. high (Total: 11 Items)
Estimate: 100-300

30583
SIX AMERICAN BRILLIANT CUT GLASS ITEMS
Makers unknown, c.1900

Comprising a cylindrical vase with a floral and leaf cut pattern; a tapering wide notched and scallop rim bowl; four knife rests of various patterns, all unsigned
The vase: 14in. high; The bowl: 8.2in. diameter; The knife rests: various sizes (Total: 6 Items)
Estimate: 300-500

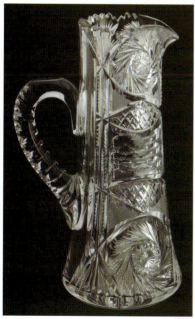

30584
AN AMERICAN BRILLIANT CUT GLASS PITCHER
Maker unknown, c.1900

The pitcher decorated with large hobstars, crosshatching and fans with an applied notched handle and rim, unsigned
11.7in. high
Estimate: 500-700

30585
FOUR AMERICAN BRILLIANT CUT GLASS SERVING PIECES
Makers unknown, c.1910

The group consists of a matching set of cream and sugar with a notched and scalloped rim, hobstar and crosshatching pattern; a low bowl with a scalloped and notched rim with hobstars, crosshatching and fans; and a tri-footed plate with a scalloped and notched edge with hobstars, all unsigned
Various sizes (Total: 4 Items)
Estimate: 300-500

30586
A COLLECTION OF AMERICAN BRILLIANT-CUT GLASS
Hawkes and other makers, c.1900

Comprising a Russian-cut cruet, an octagonal Hawkes bowl with etched floral decoration, a Hawkes footed compote with etched rim, an etched tumbler, a shallow dish with notched and scalloped rim, and a small condiment dish
Bowl and compote with Hawkes mark
Cruet 7.5in. (Total: 7 Items)
Estimate: 400-600

30587
AN AMERICAN BRILLIANT GLASS BUTTER DISH AND LID
Libbey Glass Co., c.1895

The scallop and notched edge dish and domed top with faceted knob handle in the Imperial pattern, unsigned
6in. high (Total: 2 Items)
Estimate: 300-500

30588
EIGHT AMERICAN BRILLIANT CUT GLASS ITEMS
Libbey, Hawkes, and other makers, c.1900

Comprising a tall goblet engraved with floral wreath centering the initials *BW*; a pair of Libbey tumblers with strawberry diamonds below starbursts; a pair of unmarked tumblers with hobstars below fans; a hobstar decorated nappy with notched and scalloped rim; and a tumbler and sherbert in Hawkes' 'Strawberry' pattern; both Hawkes tumblers with *Libbey* mark on interior base; the Strawberry tumbler with *Hawkes* mark
The tallest: 9in. high (Total: 8 Items)
Estimate: 300-500

30589
A GROUP OF ETCHED AND CUT GLASS ITEMS
Various makers, c.1900

Comprising a pressed glass biscuit barrel with lid; an etched gemel bottle; a floral pattern cut glass pitcher; a cut crystal vase signed *Royal Brierley*; a daisy pattern cut glass pitcher and matching tumbler
The tallest: 10.2in. high (Total: 7 Items)
Estimate: 200-400

30590
AN AMERICAN BRILLIANT CUT GLASS PITCHER
Maker unknown, c.1910

Enhanced with overall Russian cut, the swollen base tapering to a notched pattern rim
6.7in. high
Estimate: 300-500

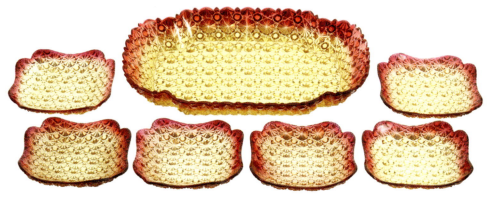

30591
AN AMERICAN 'DAISY AND BUTTON' AMBERINA GLASS ICE CREAM SERVICE
New England Glass Co., c.1920

Comprising a quatre-foil serving dish and six matching plates, each with cranberry red rim surrounding golden-yellow center, unsigned
The serving dish: 2in. high, 14.25in. long, 9in. wide (Total: 7 items)
Estimate: 800-1,000

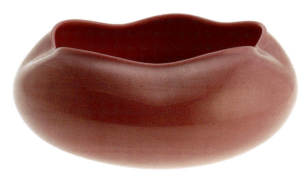

30592
AN AMERICAN 'WILD ROSE' PEACH BLOW GLASS BOWL
New England Glass Co., c.1890

The low, wide bulbous form with a lightly ruffled rim, pale pink transitions to deep pink, unsigned
3.2in. high, 7.7in. diameter
Estimate: 200-400

30593
FOUR AMERICAN ART GLASS PUNCH CUPS
New England Glass Co., c.1890

The amberina inverted thumbprint punch cups in amber to ruby, applied amber handles, unsigned
2.5in. high (Total: 4 Items)
Estimate: 100-300

30594
AN AMERICAN PLATED AMBERINA PUNCH CUP
New England Glass Co., c.1900

Also known as 'Rose Amber', the nonagonal ribbed body shading from pale yellow-amber to a rich ruby, applied amber loop handle, unsigned
2.5in. high
Estimate: 3,000-4,000

30595
AN AMERICAN THUMBPRINT PATTERN AMBERINA GLASS DECANTER
New England Glass Co., c.1890

The bulbous form rising to a slender neck, applied amber handle and amber faceted stopper, unsigned
10.2in. high
Estimate: 300-500

30596
AN AMERICAN THUMBPRINT PATTERN REVERSE AMBERINA PITCHER
Maker unknown, c.1900

The footed, square, and red body with concave sides transitioning to the amber triangular neck and ruffled rim, with applied clear reeded handle
9.75in. high
Estimate: 300-500

30598

TWO PIECES OF AMERICAN AMBERINA GLASS
New England Glass Co., 1890

Comprising a cylindrical tumbler with inverted coin spot decoration and an amber applied handle, *together with* a tapering cylindrical spooner terminating with a square scalloped rim, inverted diamond quilted pattern, both unmarked
The tallest: 4.5in. (Total: 2 Items)
Estimate: 100-200

30597

AN AMERICAN THUMBPRINT PATTERN AMBERINA GLASS CRUET
New England Glass Co., c.1900

The globular amber base gathering to a crimson red collar with tri-cornered rim, applied amber handle and faceted amber stopper, unsigned (Total: 2 Items)
5.75in. high
Estimate: 200-400

30599

AN AMERICAN THUMBPRINT PATTERN AMBERINA GLASS BOWL
New England Glass Co., c.1890

The globular form with warm amber to cranberry tone, unsigned
9.2in. high
Estimate: 100-300

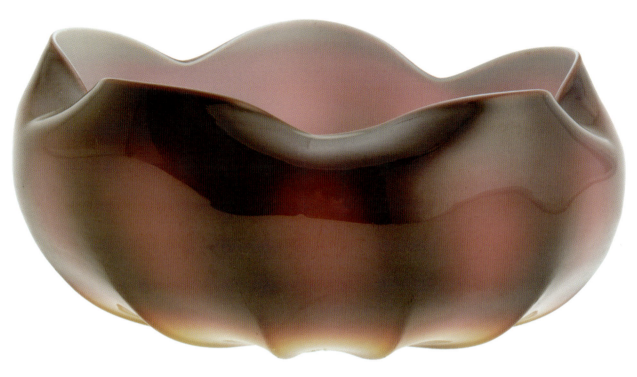

30600
AN AMERICAN PLATED AMBERINA GLASS BOWL
New England Glass Co., c.1890

The cased melon ribbed body rising to a softly undulating rim in amber to deep amethyst, unsigned
3.4in. high, 7.5in. diameter
A similar illustrated in Grover's *Art Glass Nouveau* p.24
A similar sold Early Auction Co., Summer Auction, July 1992 lot 203, hammer $8,000
Estimate: 4,000-8,000

30601
AN AMERICAN THUMBPRINT PATTERN AMBERINA PITCHER
Mt. Washington Glass Co., c.1910

Also known as 'Rose Amber', the baluster form modulates to a square rim, the amber to rose form with applied reeded amber handle, polished oval pontil, unmarked
7.5in. high
Estimate: 300-500

30603
AN AMERICAN AMBERINA GLASS PITCHER
New England Glass Co., c.1890

The amberina bulbous ovoid form in the inverted thumbprint pattern with a quartre-foil neck and applied reeded handle, amber to ruby, unsigned
7.2in. high
Estimate: 200-300

30602
A COLLECTION OF FOUR AMERICAN AMBERINA GLASS TUMBLERS
New England Glass Co., c.1900

Comprising a mold-blown cylindrical coin-spotted standard amberina; a blown cylindrical coin-spotted standard amberina; one blown cylindrical diamond-quilted standard amberina; and one blown cylindrical coin-spotted 'reverse amberina', all four unsigned
The tallest: 4in. high (Total: 4 Items)
Estimate: 300-400

30604
AN AMERICAN DIAMOND QUILT PATTERN AMBERINA GLASS VASE
New England Glass Co., c.1890

The deep amber cylindrical base tapering up to a square ruby neck and scallop rim, unsigned
6.75in. high
Estimate: 300-500

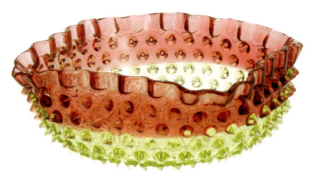

30607
AN AMERICAN HOBNAIL PATTERN AMBERINA GLASS BOWL
New England Glass Co., c.1910

The rounded square form with yellow-green base and sides rising to a cranberry ruffled rim, unsigned
3.25in. high
Estimate: 200-300

30605
AN AMERICAN DIAMOND QUILT PATTERN REVERSE-AMBERINA GLASS PITCHER
New England Glass Co., c.1890

The footed and straight-sided cylindrical red body tapering to a straight-sided cylindrical amber collar with small spout, applied reeded clear handle, unsigned
5.5in. high
Estimate: 100-300

30606
FOUR AMERICAN AMBERINA GLASS TUMBLERS AND A DISH
New England Glass Co., c.1890

Comprising two matching faceted juice tumblers; a dimple juice glass; a dimple tumbler; and an oval dish with a 'daisy and button' pattern, unsigned
The tallest: 4in. high (Total: 5 Items)
Estimate: 100-200

30608
AN AMERICAN 'THUMBPRINT' AMBERINA GLASS PITCHER
New England Glass Co., c.1880

The ovoid form with a cylindrical neck and slightly flared rim to spout in amber and crimson, applied handle in amber, unsigned
5.4in. high
Estimate: 50-100

30609
AN AMERICAN AMBERINA DIAMOND QUILT PATTERN GLASS BOWL
New England Glass Co., c.1890

The quilt pattern transitions from amber to ruby, unsigned
2.6in. high
Estimate: 100-200

30610
TWO AMERICAN THUMBPRINT PATTERN AMBERINA GLASS MUGS
New England Glass Co., c.1890

The cylindrical form transitions from amber to crimson, applied amber handle, each unsigned
3.9in. high (Total: 2 Items)
Estimate: 200-300

30611
AN AMERICAN THUMBPRINT PATTERN AMBERINA GLASS PITCHER
New England Glass Co., c.1890

The bulbous amber body tapering to a four-ruffle rim, the applied amber handle fashioned as a twisted cord looped around the neck, unsigned
6in. high
Estimate: 400-600

30612
AN AMERICAN AMBERINA GLASS SALT AND PEPPER
New England Glass Co., c.1890

The cylindrical form, amber to crimson, with metal tops, unsigned
3.8in. high (Total: 2 Items)
Estimate: 100-200

30613
AN AMERICAN SWIRL PATTERN AMBERINA GLASS PITCHER
New England Glass Co., c.1890

The bulbous form rising to a cylindrical neck in amber to cranberry, applied amber handle, unsigned
7.2in. high
Estimate: 200-400

30614
AN AMERICAN THUMBPRINT PATTERN AMBERINA GLASS PITCHER
New England Glass Co., c.1890

The bulbous form and cylindrical tri-fold neck with an inverted thumbprint pattern gradating from amber to cranberry, applied reeded handle, unsigned
5.8in. high
Estimate: 200-400

30615
AN AMERICAN 'DAISY AND BUTTON' AMBERINA GLASS BERRY SERVICE
New England Glass Co., c.1920

Comprising a square-form serving dish and six matching plates, each with brilliant crimson rim surrounding golden-yellow center, unsigned
The serving dish 2.5in. high, 8.9in. long, 8.9in. wide (Total: 7 Items)
Estimate: 600-800

30616
A PAIR OF AMERICAN WHEELING PEACH BLOW GLASS VASES
Hobbs Brockunier & Co. c.1890

The GLOSSY-FINISH bulbous body tapering to a stick neck, unsigned
8.2in. high (Total: 2 Items)
Estimate: 800-1,200

30617
AN AMERICAN GLOSSY-FINISH PEACH BLOW GLASS BELL
Maker unknown, c.1900

The tightly ruffled rim in cranberry transitions to a tapering peach tone, a satin diamond quilt pattern handle in cranberry, thin white detail to tip of the rim, unsigned
7in. high
Estimate: 100-200

30619
AN AMERICAN WHEELING PEACH BLOW GLASS TUMBLER
New England Glass Co., c.1890

The cased cylindrical form in deep custard to crimson, unsigned
3.6in. high
Estimate: 100-200

30618
AN AMERICAN GLOSSY-FINISH 'WILD ROSE' BOWL
New England Glass Co., c.1890

The low and wide form with a slightly ruffled rim in pale pink primarily to the underside rising to deep rose, pink center to the inside of the foot, unsigned
7.7in. wide
Estimate: 200-400

30620
AN AMERICAN WHEELING PEACH BLOW GLASS BUD VASE
Hobbs, Brockunier & Co., c.1890

The ivory cased bottle form in creamy yellow to deep crimson, unsigned
8.7in. high
Estimate: 400-500

30621
AN AMERICAN ACID-FINISH 'WILD ROSE' LILY VASE
New England Glass Co., c.1885

The circular foot supporting a lily form body with tri-fold rim, unsigned
7in. high
Estimate: 400-600

30623
TWO AMERICAN GLOSSY-FINISH 'WILD ROSE' GLASS TUMBLERS
New England Glass Co., c.1890

The cylindrical forms transition from ivory to rose peach blow coloration, unsigned
3.8in. high (Total: 2 Items)
Estimate: 300-500

30622
AN AMERICAN 'WILD ROSE' GLASS TOOTHPICK AND SATIN GLASS VASE
New England Glass Co., and unknown maker, c.1890

The peach blow 'wild rose' toothpick with an ivory base to rose top; the satin vase with a short neck and tri-fold rim in the style of peach blow 'wild rose' with a slightly mottled surface, both unsigned
The toothpick: 2in. high; The vase: 6.1in. high (Total: 2 Items)
Estimate: 300-500

30624
AN AMERICAN GLOSSY-FINISH WHEELING PEACH BLOW GLASS TUMBLER
Hobbs Brockunier & Co., c. 1890

The straight-sided cylindrical white cased body transitions from golden yellow to red, unsigned
3.75in. high
Estimate: 400-500

30625

30625
AN AMERICAN 'WILD ROSE' PEACH BLOW FINGER BOWL
New England Glass Co., c.1890

The bulbous form rising to a flared and ruffled rim, unsigned
2.7in. high, 5.3in. diameter
Estimate: 300-500

30627
AN AMERICAN GLOSSY-FINISH 'WILD ROSE' LILY VASE
New England Glass Co., c.1885

The circular foot with tapering stem and petal rim, transitions from white to deep rose, unsigned
6.1in. high
Estimate: 300-500

30627

30626

30626
TWO AMERICAN 'WILD ROSE' GLASS TUMBLERS
New England Glass Co., c.1890

Both of cylindrical form, one transitions from ivory to rose, the other from pale pink to rose, unsigned
3.7in. high (Total. 2 Items)
Estimate: 300-500

30628
AN AMERICAN 'WILD ROSE' PEACH BLOW GLASS VASE
New England Glass Co., c.1890

The double gourd form rising to a tapering neck in pale pink to deep rose, thumbprint to each side of the lower and middle gourd, unsigned
6.9in. high
Estimate: 500-700

30628

30630

30630
AN AMERICAN CRANBERRY GLASS SYRUP PITCHER
Maker unknown, c.1890

The mold-blown ovoid form with stripes of opalescent white swirls, applied opalescent handle, surmounted with bezel-mounted and hinged metal cap, the metal bezel marked *PAT.APR. 26 81/PAT. APR. 28 82*
6.25in. high
Estimate: 200-300

30629

30629
AN AMERICAN WHEELING PEACH BLOW MORGAN VASE
Hobbs Brockunier & Co., c.1886

The amber gargoyle holder supports a glossy ivory cased ovoid form vase with a cylindrical neck shading from pale yellow to deep ruby, unsigned
10in. high
Estimate: 1,200-1,500

30631

30632
AN AMERICAN MOLD-BLOWN GLASS CRUET
Maker unknown, c.1890

The tapered and lobed cylindrical base in cerulean-blue with white diamond design extending into the neck and tri-cornered rim, applied cerulean handle, faceted stopper, unsigned
6.75in. high
Estimate: 300-500

30631
AN OPAQUE COLORED GLASS SYRUP PITCHER
Maker unknown, c.1900

The opaque lime-green melon-form body with a tall neck, applied handle, and metal hinged lid and spout, unsigned
5.2in. high
Estimate: 200-400

30632

30633

30633
AN AMERICAN MOLD-BLOWN AND CASED GLASS SUGAR CASTER
Maker unknown, c.1910

The footed and compressed globular body in seafoam-green, the clear casing with quilted pattern punctuated with flowers and buttons, unsigned
4.75in. high
Estimate: 100-300

30635

30635
AN AMERICAN SATIN GLASS SYRUP PITCHER
Maker unknown, c.1900

The bulbous body cased in pink glass with florette-buttoned and diamond-quilted pattern with a short cylindrical neck mounted with white metal collar and hinged lid, applied satin glass handle, unmarked
4.5in. high
Estimate: 200-300

30634

30634
AN AMERICAN MOLD BLOWN PEACH BLOW GLASS TANKARD
Mt. Washington Glass Co., c.1885

The acorn-form body surmounted by a metal hinged cover, applied smooth white glass handle, glass unsigned, white metal cover with impressed mark *PAT.APR.26,81/ PAT.APR.2,82*
7in. high
Estimate: 200-400

30636

30636
AN OPALESCENT GLASS SYRUP PITCHER
Maker unknown, c.1900

The blue bulbous form with a cylindrical neck and applied handle with a coin spot and swirl pattern, metal hinged lid, unsigned
5.9in
Estimate: 100-200

30637

30637
AN AMERICAN LOUIS XV PATTERN GLASS CRUET
Northwood, c.1920

The bulbous form with molded handle and faceted clear stopper, unsigned
6.75in. high
Estimate: 100-200

30639

30639
A SPATTER GLASS VASE AND PERFUME BOTTLE
Maker unknown, c.1900

The cushion foot to cylindrical body spatter pattern in white, cranberry and clear with a spiraling clear rigaree decoration; a cushion foot to bulbous body, wide neck with an inverted rim in spatter pattern of white, pink and clear decorated with gilt enamel flowers, threaded mount to top, unsigned
6in. high and 4.6in. high respectively (Total: 2 Items)
Estimate: 200-300

30638
AN AMERICAN WHALE OIL BLUE GLASS LAMP
Maker unknown, c.1835

The wide-domed disc, clear glass foot tapering to a thick-knobbed stem applied to a cobalt 'light-bulb' shaped oil receptacle capped with copper mount, the underside of foot with large cut pontil, unsigned
10.75in. high
Estimate: 100-200

30638

30640

30640
A GROUP OF THREE AMERICAN SPATTER GLASS ITEMS
Makers unknown, c.1890

Comprising a clear mold-blown sugar caster spattered with red and white, and capped with pierced metal lid; a cranberry straight-sided tumbler with swirled ribbing spattered with white; *together with* a mold-blown cased bulbous vase with ruffled rim with white-spattered interior cased with bands of yellow and pink heightened with random spatters of green and orange, each unsigned
The tallest: 5.6in. (Total: 3 Items)
Estimate: 100-200

30641
A PAIR OF GLASS OIL LAMPS
Sandwich Glass Co., c.1860

Each a blue opaline glass cushion foot stepping up to a collared stem supporting a clam broth ribbed globe and a brass-threaded mount to the top, unsigned
10.5in. high (Total: 2 Items)
Estimate: 100-300

30642
AN OPALESCENT HOBNAIL GLASS SYRUP PITCHER
Maker unknown, c.1900

The ovoid form with a collared neck in cranberry with opalescent hobnails, clear applied handle and hinged metal lid, unsigned
6.7in. high
Estimate: 100-200

30643
A COLORED GLASS SUGAR SHAKER
Maker unknown, c.1900

The acorn form in pale blue opaque glass with a metal threaded top, unsigned
5in. high
Estimate: 100-300

30644
AN AMERICAN STRIPED GLASS CRUET
Maker unknown, c.1900

The globular body and slender neck with tri-cornered rim in cerulean blue and opalescent white swirled stripes, the applied handle and faceted stopper in Prussian blue, unsigned
6.75in. high (Total: 2 Items)
Estimate: 200-300

30645
AN AMERICAN COIN SPOT PATTERN GLASS SUGAR SHAKER
Maker unknown, c.1900

The mold-blown ovoid form ranging from clear to cranberry at the rim, the entire with opalescent white coin spot decoration, covered with pierced metal screw-on cap, unsigned
5in. high (Total: 2 Items)
Estimate: 200-400

30646

30646
A PRESSED GLASS SUGAR SHAKER
Maker unknown, c.1900

The bulbous form with pressed stylized leaf pattern to the body and a guilloche band to the neck, cased in yellow, metal threaded top, unsigned
4.6in. high
Estimate: 100-200

30648

30648
AN AMERICAN MOLD-BLOWN AND CASED GLASS SUGAR CASTER
Maker unknown, c.1890

The globular body in cranberry and white with suspended gold particles cased in clear glass with leaf and petal pattern, unsigned
3.75in. high
Estimate: 300-500

30647

30650

30647
AN AMERICAN 'WILD ROSE' GLASS SYRUP PITCHER
New England Glass Co., c.1890

The ribbed ovoid form with a short cylindrical neck, applied handle in white, metal hinged lid, unsigned
4.2in. high
Estimate: 200-400

30649

30649
AN OPALESCENT GLASS CRUET
Buckeye Glass Co., c.1890

The chrysanthemum blue swirl bulbous-rib base with a tapering form to a cylindrical neck and tri-fold rim, applied handle, faceted stopper, unsigned
6.5in. high (Total: 2 Items)
Estimate: 200-300

30650
AN OPALESCENT GLASS SUGAR SHAKER
Maker unknown, c.1900

The cranberry and opalescent swirl ovoid form with a threaded metal lid, unsigned
5.2in. high
Estimate: 200-400

30651

AN AMERICAN 'ROYAL IVY' RUBINA GLASS SYRUP PITCHER
Northwood, c.1890

The ribbed mold-blown ovoid form with a bulbous collared neck, the lower third in frosted clear rising to cranberry, applied handle and metal lid with tiny checkerboard pattern, unsigned
6.5in. high
Estimate: 200-300

30653

AN AMERICAN 'ROYAL IVY' SPATTER PRESSED GLASS SUGAR SHAKER
Northwood, c.1889

The cylindrical ribbed swirl form depicting the 'royal ivy' pattern, cased in a spatter design of mottled pink, white and yellow, threaded metal lid, unsigned
4.3in. high
Estimate: 200-400

30652

AN AMERICAN COIN SPOT PATTERN RUBINA GLASS SYRUP PITCHER
Maker unknown, c.1890

The mold-blown pear-shaped body with applied clear handle and bezel-mounted and hinged metal lid, unsigned
6.75in. high
Estimate: 200-300

30654

A PRESSED GLASS SUGAR SHAKER
Maker unknown, c.1915

The green bulbous daisy quilted body with a decorative flower and bead neck and threaded metal lid, unsigned
4.7in. high
Estimate: 100-200

30655
AN AMERICAN CHRYSANTHEMUM BASE STRIPED CRANBERRY SUGAR CASTER
Maker unknown, c.1890

The molded white-stripped body with flared and ribbed base, resembling a chrysanthemum, beneath a flat waist and a swirled, ribbed, and tapered upper body terminating with a white metal pierced screw-on cap, unsigned
4.9in. high
Estimate: 300-400

30656
AN AMERICAN CASED HOBNAIL GLASS PITCHER
Maker unknown, c.1900

The footed ovoid form with applied clear reed handle, unmarked
6in. high
Estimate: 100-200

30657
AN AMERICAN AGATA 'WILD ROSE' GLASS VASE
New England Glass Co., c.1890

The bulbous form with tapering slender neck, blue and gold oil spot decoration, unsigned
8.2in. high
Estimate: 1,000-1,200

30658

AN AMERICAN AGATA 'WILD ROSE' GLASS TUMBLER
New England glass Co., c.1890

The cylindrical form in white to rose with gilt mottling and ink spots, unsigned
3.7in. high
Estimate: 300-500

30660

AN AMERICAN AGATA 'WILD ROSE' GLASS VASE
New England Glass Co., c.1890

The pinched form with scalloped four-sided rim, blue oil spots on a finely mottled surface, unsigned
4.6in. high
Estimate: 1,000-1,500

30661

AN AMERICAN AGATA 'WILD ROSE' TUMBLER
New England Glass Co., c.1887

The cylindrical body shading from white to a deep peach blow pink, the glossy exterior with characteristic spattered mottling, unsigned
3.6in. high
Estimate: 500-700

30659

AN AMERICAN AGATA 'WILD ROSE' GLASS TUMBLER
New England Glass Co., c.1886-1887

The cylindrical body shading from pale pink to deep rose, the glossy exterior with characteristic spattered mottling and oil spots, unsigned
3.6in. high
Estimate: 400-600

30662

AN AMERICAN AGATA 'WILD ROSE' GLASS TUMBLER
New England Glass Co., c.1890

The cylindrical form in white to rose with mottling and ink spots overall, unsigned
3.7in. high
Estimate: 300-500

30663
AN AMERICAN AGATA 'WILD ROSE' GLASS VASE
New England Glass Co., c.1890

The squared form with concave sides tapering to a flared and deeply ruffled rim, mottled gilt and ink spot pattern, unsigned
4.4in. high
Estimate: 1,000-1,200

30665
AN AMERICAN AGATA 'WILD ROSE' GLASS TUMBLER
New England Glass Co., c.1890

The cylindrical form in white to rose with gilt mottling, unsigned
3.7in. high
Estimate: 300-500

30664
AN AMERICAN AGATA 'WILD ROSE' TUMBLER
New England Glass Co., c.1887

The cylindrical body shading from pale pink to deep rose, the glossy exterior with characteristic spattered mottling, unsigned
3.75in. high
Estimate: 400-600

30666
AN AMERICAN AGATA 'WILD ROSE' GLASS TUMBLER
New England Glass Co., c.1890

The cylindrical form in white to rose with mottling and ink spots, unsigned
3.7in. high
Estimate: 300-500

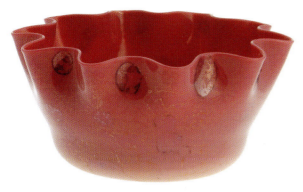

30667

30667
AN AMERICAN AGATA 'WILD ROSE' GLASS BOWL
New England Glass Co., c.1890

The circular body with a slightly flared and ruffled rim, mottled gold and blue ink spot design, unsigned
2.2in. high, 5.2in. diameter
Estimate: 300-500

30669

30669
AN AMERICAN AGATA 'WILD ROSE' GLASS CELERY VASE
New England Glass Co., c.1890

The tapering cylindrical form with a square scalloped rim, lightly mottled gilt pattern, unsigned
6.4in. high
Estimate: 500-700

30668

30668
AN AMERICAN AGATA 'WILD ROSE' GLASS TUMBLER
New England Glass Co., c.1890

The cylindrical form in white to rose with mottling and faint ink spots, unsigned
3.7in. high
Estimate: 300-500

30670

30670
AN AMERICAN AGATA 'WILD ROSE' GLASS TUMBLER
New England Glass Co., c.1890

The cylindrical form in white to rose with mottling and faint ink spots, unsigned
3.7in. high
Estimate: 300-500

30671

AN AMERICAN ACID-FINISH JACK-IN-THE-PULPIT BURMESE GLASS VASE
Mt. Washington Glass Co., c.1890

The round foot to a slender trumpet form flaring to a tightly ruffled rim in custard and salmon, unsigned
17.7in. high
Estimate: 900-1,200

30673

TWO AMERICAN ACID-FINISH BURMESE GLASS CUPS
Mt. Washington Glass Co., c.1890

The first, a lemonade of slightly flared cylindrical form in custard and salmon with a low-set applied handle; the second, a tri-footed ovoid cup with an applied angular handle in pale custard and pale pink, both unsigned
3.3in. high and 3.1in. high respectively (Total: 2 Items)
Estimate: 200-400

30674

AN AMERICAN ACID-FINISH DIAMOND QUILT PATTERN BURMESE GLASS CUP
Mt. Washington Glass Co., c.1890

The cylindrical form in custard and salmon with a faint diamond quilt pattern, unsigned
2.7in. high
Estimate: 300-500

30672

AN AMERICAN TRI-FOLD BURMESE GLASS BOWL
Mt. Washington Glass Co., c.1890

The circular custard-colored basal center rising through a bulging peach-colored body to a triangular rim with a thin band of light custard coloration, unsigned
10.8in. high
Estimate: 200-300

30675

AN AMERICAN BURMESE GLASS VASE
Mt. Washington Glass Co., c.1890

The footed elongated ovoid form with flared tri-ruffled rim, the custard yellow base transitions to salmon pink, unsigned
12.3in. high
Estimate: 400-600

30677

AN AMERICAN ACID-FINISH BURMESE GLASS CUP
Mt. Washington Glass Co., c.1890

The wide-rimmed shallow bowl in custard and salmon with custard rim and applied custard loop handle, unsigned
1.6in. high
Estimate: 200-400

30678

AN AMERICAN GLOSSY-FINISH BURMESE GLASS CUP AND SAUCER
Mt. Washington Glass Co., c.1900

The footed saucer with a thick band of salmon pink surrounding a custard center; the bulbous cup shading from light custard to a peach rim with applied custard loop handle, unsigned
The cup 2.75in. high; The saucer: 5.5in. diameter (Total: 2 Items)
Estimate: 200-300

30676

AN AMERICAN ACID-FINISH JACK-IN-THE-PULPIT BURMESE GLASS VASE
Mt. Washington Glass Co., c.1890

The custard yellow circular foot, disc join and flaring body, the salmon pink everted and outturned ruffled rim with highlighted custard edge, unsigned
12.4in. high
Estimate: 300-500

30679

TWO AMERICAN ACID-FINISH BURMESE GLASS TUMBLERS
Mt. Washington Glass Co., c.1900

Each cylindrical form graduating from custard yellow to peach, unsigned
Each approx 3.8in. high (Total: 2 Items)
Estimate: 500-800

30680
AN AMERICAN GLOSSY-FINISH BURMESE GLASS BOWL
Mt. Washington Glass Co., c.1890

The bulbous bowl with tri-fold rim supported by three rolled and applied feet, primarily in salmon with custard to the lower half, unsigned
9.2in. diameter, 5in. high
Estimate: 400-600

30682
A PAIR OF AMERICAN ACID-FINISH BURMESE GLASS TUMBLERS
Mt. Washington Glass Co., c.1900

Both of cylindrical form, each with differing transitions from custard yellow to salmon pink, unsigned
3.8in. high (Total: 2 Items)
Estimate: 100-300

30681
AN AMERICAN GLOSSY-FINISH BURMESE GLASS CREAMER
Mt. Washington Glass Co., c.1890

The circular footed conical body flaring to a tightly ruffled rim, applied handle, in custard yellow to salmon pink, unsigned
5.4in. high
Estimate: 400-600

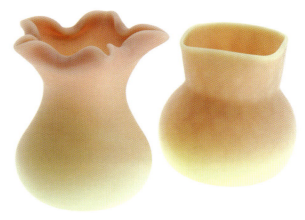

30683
TWO GLASS CABINET VASES
Thomas Webb & Sons; Mt. Washington Glass Co., c.1890

The first a Queen's Burmese bulbous base tapering to the neck and flaring to a floral form rim, stamped underside *Thomas Webb & Sons Queen's Burmese ware*; the second a diamond quilt pattern with a bulbous base rising to a square shaped neck, unsigned
3in. high and 2.6in. high respectively (Total: 2 Items)
Estimate: 500-700

30684

30684
AN AMERICAN ACID-FINISH JACK-IN-THE-PULPIT BURMESE GLASS VASE
Mt. Washington Glass Co., c.1900

The custard yellow foot and body rising to a crimped face in salmon with a pale custard rim, unsigned
6.75in. high
Estimate: 200-400

30687

30687
AN AMERICAN GLOSSY-FINISH BURMESE GLASS CUP AND SAUCER
Mt. Washington Glass Co., c.1900

The footed cup in custard and salmon with an applied handle in custard; matching shallow saucer, both unsigned
The cup: 2.5in. high; The saucer 5.3in. diameter (Total: 2 Items)
Estimate: 400-600

30685

30685
AN AMERICAN GLOSSY-FINISH BURMESE GLASS VASE
Mt Washington Glass Co., c.1900

The straight sided circular base in custard yellow rising to a flared and ruffled rim in deep salmon pink, the side punctuated with a narrow and continuous band of scalloped shells in light custard color, unsigned
2.25in. high
Estimate: 200-400

30688
AN AMERICAN ACID-FINISH BURMESE LILY VASE
Mt. Washington Glass Co., c.1890

The circular base and disc join supporting a slender body with a flaring tri-fold rim in custard and salmon, with yellow highlighted rim, unsigned
14.6in. high
Estimate: 500-800

30688

30686

30686
TWO AMERICAN ACID-FINISH BURMESE GLASS PUNCH CUPS
Mt. Washington Glass Co., c.1900

The first, a flared cylinder body with applied angular handle; the second, of baluster form with applied handle, unsigned
The tallest: 2.75in. high (Total: 2 Items)
Estimate: 200-400

30689
AN AMERICAN BURMESE GLASS FAIRY LAMP
Mt. Washington Glass Co., c.1890

The clear glass diamond pattern base with a domed Burmese custard to salmon shade, base stamped in mold *S. Clarke Fairy Pyramid*
3.6in. high (Total: 2 Items)
Estimate: 100-300

30691
AN AMERICAN ACID-FINISH BURMESE GLASS BOWL
Mt. Washington Glass Co., c.1890

The footed bulbous body tapering to the neck and flaring to a tightly ruffled rim in custard and salmon, unsigned
3in. high
Estimate: 300-500

30692
AN AMERICAN GLOSSY-FINISH BURMESE GLASS BOWL
Mt. Washington Glass Co., c.1890

The tri-footed round form with a tri-fold rim in custard to salmon with custard feet and rim, unsigned
2.3in. high
Estimate: 200-300

30690
AN AMERICAN ACID-FINISH BURMESE GLASS PITCHER
Mt. Washington Glass Co., c.1890

The short circular foot supporting a slightly tapering cylindrical body with an applied handle in custard and salmon, unsigned
7in. high
Estimate: 300-500

30693
AN AMERICAN GLOSSY-FINISH BURMESE LILY VASE
Mt. Washington Glass Co., c.1890

The round custard yellow base with salmon pink ring rising to a slender body flared lily form rim, unsigned
7.9in. high
Estimate: 300-500

30695
AN AMERICAN ACID-FINISH BURMESE GLASS PITCHER
Mt. Washington Glass Co., c.1900

The footed globular form transitions from custard yellow to a pale salmon pink rim, applied angular custard handle, unsigned
8.75in. high
Estimate: 200-300

30694
AN AMERICAN GLOSSY-FINISH BURMESE GLASS CUP AND SAUCER
Mt. Washington Glass Co., c.1900

The footed cup in custard and salmon with an applied handle in custard, matching shallow saucer, both unsigned
The cup: 2.5in. high; The saucer: 5.6in. diameter (Total: 2 Items)
Estimate: 400-600

30696
AN AMERICAN ACID-FINISH BURMESE GLASS VASE
Mt. Washington Glass Co., c.1890

The double gourd form tapering to a slender neck in salmon and custard, unsigned
8in. high
Estimate: 300-500

30697
AN AMERICAN GLOSSY-FINISH BURMESE GLASS CUP
Mt. Washington Glass Co., c.1890

The conical form in custard and salmon with custard handle, unsigned
2in. high
Estimate: 100-200

30699
AN AMERICAN ACID-FINISH BURMESE GLASS VASE
Mt. Washington Glass Co., c.1890

The double gourd gently transitions to a tapering cylindrical neck in custard and salmon, unsigned
8.2in. high
Estimate: 200-300

30698
AN AMERICAN ACID-FINISH BURMESE JACK-IN-THE-PULPIT GLASS VASE
Mt. Washington Glass Co., 1890

The circular base supporting a disc join and slender body with a flared and tightly ruffled rim in custard and salmon, blush of pink to foot, unsigned
12.8in. high
Estimate: 600-900

30700
AN AMERICAN ACID-FINISH BURMESE GLASS RUFFLED BOWL
Mt. Washington Glass Co., c.1890

The footed round bowl with tapered neck transitions from yellow to salmon, the tightly ruffled rim in yellow, unsigned
3.2in. high
Estimate: 400-600

30701
AN AMERICAN ACID-FINISH BURMESE LILY VASE
Mt. Washington Glass Co., c.1900

The custard yellow foot and body rising to a tri-cornered rim with a diffused band of soft salmon below the yellow rim, unsigned
7.25in. high
Estimate: 200-300

30702
AN ENGLISH ACID-FINISH QUEEN'S BURMESE GLASS VASE
Thomas Webb & Sons, c.1890

The bulbous body and tapered neck transitions from custard yellow to salmon pink, with custard highlight along rim, stamped underside *Queen's Burmese Ware/ Patented/ Thos Webb & Sons*
11.5in. high
Estimate: 700-1,000

30703
AN AMERICAN GLOSSY-FINISH BURMESE LILY VASE
Mt. Washington Glass Co., c.1890

The baluster form with short foot and scalloped rim, the custard yellow transitioning to salmon pink
8in. high
Estimate: 200-400

30704
AN AMERICAN GLOSSY-FINISH BURMESE GLASS CUP
Mt. Washington Glass Co., c.1890

The slightly domed round foot supporting an open ovoid form with two applied handles in custard and salmon, unsigned
3.7in. high
Estimate: 200-400

30706
AN AMERICAN ACID-FINISH BURMESE GLASS PITCHER
Mt. Washington Glass Co., c.1890

The footed and tapered cylindrical body with applique handle and tightly ruffled rim in custard and salmon with yellow highlighted rim, unsigned
5.5in. high
Estimate: 300-400

30705
AN AMERICAN GLOSSY-FINISH BURMESE LILY VASE
Mt. Washington Glass Co., c.1890

The circular base and disc supporting a slender trumpet form body with tri-fold rim, custard to salmon with soft yellow highlighted rim, unsigned
6.2in. high
Estimate: 300-500

30707
TWO AMERICAN ACID-FINISH BURMESE GLASS TUMBLERS
Mt. Washington Glass Co., c.1900

Both of cylindrical form, each with differing transitions from custard yellow to salmon pink, unsigned
3.75in. high (Total: 2 Items)
Estimate: 400-600

30710
AN AMERICAN ACID-FINISH BURMESE LILY VASE
Mt. Washington Glass Co., c.1890

The circular foot and disc rising to a slender body with flared lily rim in custard and salmon, unsigned
14.5in. high
Estimate: 400-600

30708
TWO AMERICAN ACID-FINISH BURMESE GLASS SHAKERS
Mt. Washington Glass Co., c.1900

Each with cylindrical ribbed body and custard to salmon coloration, capped with metal collar and pierced, screw-on tops, unsigned
Each 4in. high (Total: 2 Items)
Estimate: 100-300

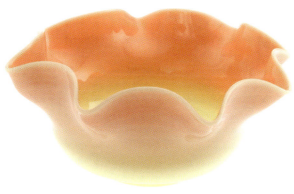

30709
AN AMERICAN ACID-FINISH BURMESE GLASS CUP AND SAUCER
Mt. Washington Glass Co., c.1900

The footed saucer with a broad border of salmon surrounding a custard center; the footed bulbous cup shading from light custard to a deep salmon rim with applied custard loop handle, unsigned
The cup: 2.5in. high; The saucer: 5.4in. diameter (Total: 2 Items)
Estimate: 300-500

30711
AN AMERICAN GLOSSY-FINISH BURMESE GLASS BOWL
Mt. Washington Glass Co., c.1890

A short round foot to a bulbous form with a ruffled rim, custard to salmon with a custard highlight along the rim, unsigned
10.5in. wide
Estimate: 300-500

30712
AN AMERICAN ACID-FINISH BURMESE GLASS CREAMER AND CUP
Mt. Washington Glass Co., c.1890

Both with a bulbous base and tapering cylindrical neck, applied handles in custard and salmon, unsigned
3.6in. high and 2.7in. high respectively (Total: 2 Items)
Estimate: 400-600

30714
AN AMERICAN GLOSSY-FINISH BURMESE TWO-HANDLED GLASS VASE
Mt. Washington Glass Co., c.1890

The ovoid form with a slightly flared four-sided neck, a subtle diamond quilt pattern apparent against the salmon coloration, two applied reeded handles, unsigned
4.2in. high
Estimate: 300-500

30713
AN AMERICAN GLOSSY-FINISH BURMESE GLASS CUP AND SAUCER
Mt. Washington Glass Co., c.1890

The round footed cup rising to an open ovoid form with an applied handle; matching shallow saucer, both in custard and salmon, unsigned
The cup: 2.5in. high; The saucer: 5.4in. diameter (Total: 2 Items)
Estimate: 200-400

30715
AN AMERICAN ACID-FINISH BURMESE GLASS VASE
Mt. Washington Glass Co., c.1885

The custard yellow foot beneath a ribbed bulbous body in soft salmon rising to peach tapering neck and cupped mouth with custard yellow rim, unsigned
4.75in. high
Estimate: 200-400

30716

30716
AN AMERICAN GLOSSY-FINISH BURMESE GLASS CUP AND SAUCER
Mt. Washington Glass Co., c.1900

The deeply dished saucer with thin band of light salmon surrounding custard center; the flaring cylindrical cup with custard base and light salmon rim with applied angular handle, both unmarked
The cup: 2in. high; The saucer 5.25in. diameter (Total: 2 Items)
Estimate: 400-600

30718

30718
TWO AMERICAN ACID-FINISH BURMESE GLASS ITEMS
Mt. Washington Glass Co., c.1890

The first, a vase with round body and flaring flora-form rim; the second, a rose bowl inward crimped rim, each unsigned
The vase: 3in. high; The bowl: 2.3in. high (Total: 2 Items)
Estimate: 200-400

30717
AN AMERICAN ACID-FINISH BURMESE GLASS VASE
Mt. Washington Glass Co., c.1890

The slender ovoid body in custard yellow transitioning to salmon pink with a yellow rim
8.5in. high
Estimate: 400-600

30717

30719
AN AMERICAN ACID-FINISH JACK-IN-THE-PULPIT BURMESE GLASS VASE
Mt. Washington Glass Co., c.1900

The custard yellow foot and body rising to a crimped face in salmon with a pale custard rim, unsigned
6.75in. high
Estimate: 300-500

30719

30720

30720
AN AMERICAN ACID-FINISH BURMESE GLASS BOWL
Mt. Washington Glass Co., c.1890

The round bulbous form in custard and salmon coloration, a shaped rectangular rim in yellow, unsigned
2.1in. high, 5in. wide
Estimate: 300-500

30721

30721
AN AMERICAN GLOSSY-FINISH BURMESE GLASS CUP AND SAUCER
Mt. Washington Glass Co., c.1890

The footed cup in custard and salmon with an applied handle in custard; matching shallow saucer, both unsigned
The cup: 2.5in. high; The saucer: 5.5in. diameter (Total: 2 Items)
Estimate: 200-400

30722

30722
AN AMERICAN GLOSSY-FINISH BURMESE GLASS TWO HANDLED CUP
Mt. Washington Glass Co., c.1890

The footed form with two applied custard handles, unsigned
3.5in. high
Estimate: 400-600

30723

30723
AN AMERICAN ACID-FINISH BURMESE GLASS BOWL
Mt. Washington Glass Co., c.1890

The bulbous body with a ruffled rim in satin finish of custard yellow transitioning to salmon pink, unsigned
2.6in. high
Estimate: 300-500

30724
AN AMERICAN ACID-FINISH BURMESE GLASS VASE
Mt. Washington Glass Co., c.1900

The footed bottle form with custard base and long salmon neck with light custard rim, unsigned
6in. high
Estimate: 200-300

30726
AN AMERICAN ACID-FINISH BURMESE FAIRY LAMP
Mt. Washington Glass Co., c.1890

The semi elliptical form in custard and salmon with subtle swirling, resting on a molded clear glass base, the base is stamped *S. Clarke Fairy Pyramid*
3.8in. high (Total: 2 Items)
Estimate: 200-400

30725
AN AMERICAN ACID-FINISH BURMESE LILY VASE
Mt. Washington Glass Co., c.1890

Round pedestal base with disc join tapering stem with petal rim in muted custard and pink, unsigned
6.2in. high
Estimate: 200-400

30727
AN AMERICAN ACID-FINISH BURMESE GLASS CUP AND SAUCER
Mt. Washington Glass Co., c.1890

The cup on a short foot rising to an open ovoid form with applied handle; the matching saucer with a deep rise, both pieces in custard and salmon, unsigned
The cup: 2.1in. high; The saucer: 5.2in. diameter (Total: 2 Items)
Estimate: 400-600

30728
AN AMERICAN ACID-FINISH BURMESE LILY VASE
Mt. Washington Glass Co., c.1890

The round disc foot rising to a slender standard with a lily form rim, in custard to salmon, slight pink bloom to base and yellow rim, unsigned
14.2in. high
Estimate: 800-1,000

30730
AN AMERICAN ACID-FINISH BURMESE GLASS VASE
Mt. Washington Glass Co., c.1890

The double gourd form with a tapering cylindrical neck, gradual transition from custard yellow to deep salmon, unsigned
7in. high
Estimate: 300-500

30729
AN AMERICAN ACID-FINISH BURMESE GLASS CREAMER AND TOOTHPICK HOLDER
Mt. Washington Glass Co., c.1890

The creamer with applied wishbone feet supporting an ovoid form with a short neck in custard and salmon, applied handle; the quilt pattern toothpick with a bulbous body rising to a square slightly flared rim in custard and salmon, both unsigned
4.2in. high and 2.6in. high respectively (Total: 2 Items)
Estimate: 200-400

30731
AN AMERICAN ACID-FINISH BURMESE GLASS BOWL
Mt. Washington Glass Co., c.1900

The squat form custard yellow body rising to a pale salmon pink neck with tightly ruffled rim, unsigned
3in. high
Estimate: 300-500

30732
AN AMERICAN ACID-FINISH JACK-IN-THE-PULPIT BURMESE GLASS VASE
Mt. Washington Glass Co., c.1890

The circular base and disc rising to a slender stem flaring to a tightly ruffled everted rim in custard and salmon, unsigned
11in. high
Estimate: 300-500

30734
AN AMERICAN ACID-FINISH BURMESE GLASS VASE
Mt. Washington Glass Co., c.1890

The bulbous body with a long cylindrical neck, subtle transition from custard yellow to salmon pink with yellow highlight to rim, unsigned
10.5in. high
Estimate: 300-500

30735
AN AMERICAN ACID-FINISH BURMESE LILY VASE
Mt. Washington Glass Co., c.1900

The delicately domed foot with disc join supporting a long stem form with a tri-fold yellow highlighted rim, in custard yellow and salmon pink, unsigned
9.7in. high
Estimate: 400-600

30733
AN AMERICAN GLOSSY-FINISH BURMESE GLASS PITCHER
Mt. Washington Glass Co., c.1890

The cylindrical form transitions from custard to salmon with an applied custard handle, unsigned
8.9in. high
Estimate: 500-700

30736

30736
AN AMERICAN ACID-FINISH BURMESE GLASS PITCHER
Mt. Washington Glass Co., c.1890

The footed and short-stemmed pedestal supporting an elephant ear body with applied handle, color transitions from custard yellow to salmon pink, unsigned
12.7in. high
Estimate: 600-800

30737

30737
AN AMERICAN NAPOLI GLASS BRIDES BOWL ON STAND
Mt. Washington Glass Co., c.1900

The nouveau Pairpoint four-footed round base rising to a baluster form stem to a flared scalloped rim in silver plate, flower and leaf relief pattern to entire stand; a silver plate mount fitting into the stand supports the low wide Napoli glass bowl in a flashed cranberry ground with an enamel pattern of peaches on branches, gilt highlights to the pattern on the inside of the bowl and to the rim, stand stamped underside *Pairpoint Mfg. Co. New Bedford, Mass. Quadruple Plate B4704*
11in. high overall; the bowl 10in. diameter (Total: 2)
Estimate: 1,500-2,000

30738

30738
AN AMERICAN ENAMELED ACID-FINISH BURMESE GLASS CABINET VASE
Mt. Washington Glass Co., c.1900

The globular custard body rising to a salmon flared and ruffled rim, the obverse enameled with a flowering bough, unsigned
3in. high
Estimate: 400-600

30740

30740
AN AMERICAN 'ROYAL FLEMISH' LIDDED GLASS CRACKER JAR
Mt. Washington Glass Co., c.1890

The barrel-form gold Roman Coin design on a brown and tan ground outlined in heavy gold enamel decoration, silver plate rim and lid, cover and bail handle
7.6in. high
Estimate: 1,200-1,500

30739

30739
AN ENGLISH GILT PEACH BLOW GLASS VASE
Thomas Webb & Sons, c.1890

The cased urn form with a short neck decorated with gilt prunus branches, blossoms and a bee, unsigned
4.2in. high
Estimate: 300-500

30741

30741
AN AMERICAN ETCHED POMONA FIRST-GRIND GLASS LEMONADE
New England Glass Co., c.1885

Etched cornflower pattern with staining, scalloped border, applied handle, unsigned
5.7in. high
Estimate: 100-300

30743

30743
A CASED AND GILT-DECORATED GLASS VASE
Maker unknown, c.1900

The cylindrical foot supporting a bulbous form with a slightly flaring neck, burgundy with gilt decoration depicting flowers, leaves and a bird, ivory casing, unsigned
4.5in. high
Estimate: 100-300

30742

30742
AN AMERICAN CORALENE DECORATED VASE
Maker unknown, c.1900

The ovoid form with a cylindrical neck and a ruffled rim cased in pink with a white ground and applied coralene decoration in amber depicting seaweed, unsigned
6.1in. high
Estimate: 100-300

30744

30744
AN ENAMELED SATIN GLASS VASE
Maker unknown, c.1930

The straight cylindrical form rising to a shouldered neck in white to lemon yellow, decorated with white enamel flowers on gilt vines, clear etched and applied handles, unsigned
8.7in. high
Estimate: 100-200

30745
AN AMERICAN ENAMELED ACID-FINISH GLASS SUGAR SHAKER
Mt. Washington Glass Co., c.1890

The ivory ground egg form enameled with multicolored leaves and red berries, metal top, unsigned
4.4in. high (Total: 2 Items)
Estimate: 200-400

30747
AN ENGLISH DECORATED 'QUEEN'S BURMESE' GLASS VASE
Thomas Webb & Sons, c.1890

The ovoid body rising to a slender neck with a flared rim in custard and salmon depicting hazelnuts, flowers and leaves, stamped underside
7.6in. high
Estimate: 900-1,200

30746
A DECORATED CORALENE GLASS VASE
Maker unknown, c.1900

The ovoid form rising to a slightly flared cylindrical neck, blue ground and ivory coralene floral pattern with gilt border, enamel artists stamp on underside
6in. high
Estimate: 300-500

30750
A DIAMOND QUILT PATTERN SATIN GLASS CORALENE BOWL
Maker unknown, c.1900

The ivory cased quatre-foil form with a butterscotch to ivory diamond quilt pattern and coralene fleur de lis in yellow, unsigned
2.6in. high
Estimate: 200-300

30748
AN AMERICAN ART GLASS BRIDE'S BASKET
The stand: Pairpoint, c.1880

The glass with a heavily ruffled rim, white exterior decorated with a faint ivy pattern, a salmon pink interior and enameled design of small white flowers, leaves and purple scroll work, silver plated footed holder with stylized floral handle, monogram at the top of handle *D H G* reverse engraved with *Flore '95,* signed underside of holder *Pairpoint Mfg Co. Quadruple Plate* and *4731*
11.7in. high
Estimate: 300-500

30751
AN ENAMELED RUBINA VERDE GLASS VASE
attributed to Moser, c.1900

The salmon-colored foot resembling an upturned flower, creating an irregular and oblong foot extending upwards into a eight-sepaled calyx within which rest the tapering quatre-foil body of pink-to-green glass embellished with arabesque and polychrome flowers terminating with a gilt rim, unsigned
9.1in. high
Estimate: 300-400

30749
AN AMERICAN ENAMELED ART GLASS VASE
Mt. Washington Glass Co., c.1890

The 'Crown Milano' bulbous body tapering to a short flared neck with small gilt-ribbed applied handles, depicting acorns and leaves in soft brown, blue and red with gold threading, gilt decorative border to neck, stamped underside
8.2in. high
Estimate: 500-700

30752
AN AMERICAN 'CROWN MILANO' GLASS PITCHER
Mt. Washington Glass Co., c.1890

Of melon ribbed form, shaped spout, twisted and applied rope handle, cactus flower design with heavy gilt threading and scroll pattern around rim, enamel signature underside
7in. high
Estimate: 1,500-2,000

30753
AN AMERICAN ENAMELED ACID-FINISH 'WILD ROSE' GLASS BOWL
New England Glass Co., c.1890

The bulbous shape with ruffled rim, enameled daisy design, unsigned
3.6in. high
Estimate: 300-400

30754
AN AMERICAN CORALENE AND ENAMELED GLASS PITCHER
Maker unknown, c.1910

The ovoid amber body decorated with a naturalistic bird perched in a flowering magnolia tree rendered in clear beads over polychrome enamels, applied deep peridot green handle, unsigned with *Patent:* painted within the polished pontil
7.25in. high
Estimate: 400-600

30755

30755
A DIAMOND QUILT PATTERN CORALENE SATIN GLASS VASE
Maker unknown, c.1890

The tapering ovoid form in a satin mother-of-pearl diamond quilt pattern with coralene decoration of stylized flowers, unsigned
4.9in. high
Estimate: 100-200

30756

30756
AN AMERICAN DANA ALDEN CHRISTMAS CONDIMENT SET
Alden Griffith Co., c.1880

Comprising three barrel-shaped opalware glass shakers with pierced metal covers, housed in a tri-sectioned metal stand with ring handle, one metal cover impressed *DANA K. ALDEN, BOSTON/PAT. DEC. 25 1877*, the metal stand with impressed mark *ALDEN, GRIFFITH & CO/BOSTON, MASS.*, glass unsigned but probably by Boston & Sandwich Glass Co., although Alden used other glass companies when Boston & Sandwich Glass Co. could not keep up with production needs of this popular product
The stand: 4.5in. high (Total: 4 Items)
Estimate: 400-800

30757

30757
A CZECHOSLOVAKIAN GILT AND ENAMELED GLASS VASE
Moser, c.1890

The blue opaque ovoid body with a four-lobed rim, enamel decoration depicting flowers, beading and threading detail to border, unsigned
3.9in. high
Estimate: 100-200

30758
AN AMERICAN CORALENE 'CROWN MILANO' GLASS BISCUIT JAR
Mt. Washington Glass Co., c.1890

Modeled in imitation of a sea urchin and painted with aquatic swirls in pastel green, blue, ecru and pink, the obverse encrusted with bright red, green and white coralene beads set in gold enamel seaweed design, the reverse with a Burrowing Brittle Star Fish naturalistically rendered in gold, pink, rust, and white enamel decoration, the rim with gilt-metal bezel collar attaching a coiled bail handle over a repoussé floral lid with figural butterfly knob, underside of lid with incised mark and number *M - W/4418/c*
8.5in. high with handle raised, 5in. rim diameter
Estimate: 1,000-1,500

30759
AN ENAMELED ACID-FINISH BURMESE GLASS VASE
possibly Thomas Webb & Sons, c.1890

The body decorated with leaves, berries and vines, ruffled top with applied ruffled base, unsigned
4in. high
Estimate: 200-400

30760
A CONTINENTAL ENAMEL DECORATED GLASS VASE
Peloton, c.1880

The dome footed and short-stemmed vase in clear glass with blue filaments enameled with leaves and small white flowers, unsigned
10in. high
Estimate: 200-400

30761

30761
AN AMERICAN ENAMELED ART GLASS VASE
Mt. Washington Glass Co., c.1890

The 'Crown Milano' cylindrical form flaring to a ruffled rim in an ivory ground with pale blue flowers overlaid with a gilt floral pattern, footed open work silver plate base, silver base stamped underside *Pairpoint*
6.7in. high
Estimate: 400-600

30763

30763
AN AMERICAN DAISY PATTERN BURMESE GLASS BOWL
Mt. Washington Glass Co., c.1890

With applique wishbone feet and a flared rim, in custard and salmon with enameled design, gilt threading to rim and feet, unsigned
2.6in. high
Estimate: 200-300

30762

30762
TWO PIECES OF AMERICAN GLASS
Northwood, c.1900

Including a 'Royal Ivy' pattern spatter ware bowl with pink and yellow on white ground *together with* a multi-colored dish with ruffled rim and upturned sides centering floral decoration, unsigned
The tallest: 3.25in. (Total: 2 Items)
Estimate: 200-300

30764

30764
A CORALENE DECORATED ART GLASS BOWL
Maker unknown, c.1900

The bulbous form with a ruffled rim in white to blue, yellow seaweed coralene decoration, unsigned
3.3in. high
Estimate: 100-200

30765

30765
AN AMERICAN ENAMELED 'CROWN MILANO' GLASS BOWL
Mt. Washington Glass Co., c.1890

The satin ivory ground with twisted fluting, enamel and beaded decoration in a floral design with gilt thread, enameled *Crown Milano* stamp underside
4in. high
Provenance: Maude B. Feld sold item to Mrs. R. A. McMurry sold item to current owner
Estimate: 400-600

30767
A CONTINENTAL BLOWN GLASS AND ENAMEL VASE
In the style of Moser, c.1900

The quatre-foil body with cobalt ground and applied floral rococo gilt and enamel decoration, unsigned
12.2in. high
Estimate: 200-400

30767

30766

30766
AN AMERICAN ENAMELED ACID-FINISH BURMESE GLASS CABINET VASE
Mt. Washington Glass Co., c.1900

The pale custard yellow ovoid body with straight collar rim enhanced with floral and leaf enamel decoration, unsigned
2.75in. high
Estimate: 300-500

30768

30768
A DECORATED 'CUT VELVET' GLASS VASE
Maker unknown, c.1900

The white cased ovoid form to tapering cylindrical neck in a pink diamond quilt pattern with an enamel decoration of branches, gilt leaves and small white flowers, unsigned
10in. high
Estimate: 200-400

30769

AN AMERICAN 'ROYAL FLEMISH' GLASS BISCUIT JAR
Mt. Washington Glass Co., c.1892

The shallow circular foot uplifting the cubed body decorated with thistle foliage and blooms in muted tones of celadon and aubergine heightened with white and outlined in raised gold over a frosted ground, the thin circular neck bezel-set with white metal collar with ruffle rim, bail handle and fitted domed lid with repoussé decoration and shaped knob; the underside with iron-red hand-painted 'reverse *R*' in diamond mark of Mt. Washington over the number *523*, the interior of the domed lid with impressed *M - W* over stamped number *4413K*
With handle up 9.75in. high (Total: 2 Items)
Estimate: 2,500-3,000

30770

AN AMERICAN GLASS EGG SUGAR SHAKER
Mt. Washington Glass Co., c.1890

The pale pink to ivory ground with enameled daisy pattern overall, silverplate top
3.7in. high
Estimate: 200-300

30771

30771
AN AMERICAN 'CROWN MILANO' ART GLASS VASE
Mt. Washington Glass Co., c.1890

The bulbous form stick vase rising to a tapered neck in an ivory ground with a design of gilt roses and a cobweb with raised gilt beading and thread, stamped underside
12.1in. high
Estimate: 1,000-1,500

30772

30772
AN AMERICAN HAWTHORN DESIGN BURMESE GLASS VASE
Mt. Washington Glass Co., c.1890

The ovoid body with tapering cylindrical neck, custard and salmon pink colors with enamel decoration in the Hawthorn Design, unsigned
12in. high
Estimate: 1,800-2,500

30773
AN AMERICAN GILT AMBERINA MUG
possibly Cambridge, c.1900

The cylindrical body with molded and swirled ribs, transitions from a squat amber base to a slightly flared rose rim, the obverse gilded with a spray of chrysanthemums, applied reeded amber handle, unsigned
5.25in. high
Estimate: 200-300

30775
AN AMERICAN CORALENE AND ENAMELED AMBERINA GLASS VASE
New England Glass Co., c.1890

The footed octagonal faceted tapering form rising to a ruffled rim in a clear amber to cranberry with coralene and enamel decoration depicting flowers and leaves, gilt detail to foot and rim, unsigned
6in. high
Estimate: 200-400

30774
AN AMERICAN OPALWARE GLASS SHAKER AND CORALENE VASE
Mt. Washington Glass Co., c.1900

Comprising a tomato-shaped salt shaker with floral decoration and a screw-on, pierced metal cap *together with* a coralene-beaded cabinet vase of footed globular form, unsigned
The vase: 2.75in. high (Total: 2 Items)
Estimate: 300-600

30776
AN AMERICAN ENAMELED 'CROWN MILANO' GLASS EWER
Mt. Washington Glass Co., c.1890

The flattened spherical form with a short cylindrical neck and cupped rim in a pale yellow ground with enameled decoration depicting acorns, leaves and branches in green, rust and gold, applied twisted rope style handle in aqua, stamped underside
10.5in. high
Estimate: 1,200-1,500

30777
AN AMERICAN 'CROWN MILANO' ENAMELED GLASS VASE
Mt. Washington Glass Co., c.1890

The three-sided form tapers to a slender cylindrical neck, applied decorative handles at base of neck, decorated with pansies and gilt enamel ornamentation, enamel *Crown Milano, 563.* stamp underside
7.7in. high
Estimate: 500-700

30779
AN AMERICAN DECORATED BURMESE GLASS LIDDED JAR
Mt. Washington Glass Co., c.1890

The acid-finish and beaded enameling floral design in yellow to salmon, silver plate lid with floral pattern,
5in. high
Estimate: 500-700

30778
AN ENGLISH ENAMELED QUEEN'S BURMESE GLASS VASE
Thomas Webb & Sons, c.1890

The round foot rising to a slender trumpet body with a seven-pointed floral form top in custard and salmon with a GLOSSY-FINISH enameled decoration of a grapevine with fruit, stamped underside
5.9in. high
Estimate: 500-700

30780
AN AMERICAN DECORATED ACID-FINISH BURMESE GLASS VASE
Mt. Washington Glass Co., c.1890

The bulbous body with long cylindrical neck in custard and pale pink enameled with stylized floral design in gilt thread, unsigned
9.6in. high
Estimate: 500-700

30781
AN AMERICAN THREADED GLASS MUG
Boston & Sandwich Glass Co., c.1920

The cylindrical body with cobalt threading to simulate water out of which grows the etched water lilies and cat tails, applied clear glass loop handle, unsigned
5.5in. high
Estimate: 100-200

30782
AN AMERICAN CORALENE BELLEWARE GLASS JEWELRY BOX
Carl V. Helmschmied, c.1905

Raised on four shaped metal feet with lion's mask, the cylindrical glass body swells to a high, flat shoulder bezel-mounted with hinged metal collar, the conforming flat-topped glass lid opening to reveal a silk-lined interior, the exterior decorated with polychrome enamel depiction of bearded blue iris beneath a continuous covering of coralene bead, hand-painted maker's mark to underside: *Belle/Ware*.
5.5in. high
Estimate: 1,000-1,500

30783
AN AMERICAN ENAMELED 'CROWN MILANO' GLASS VASE
Mt. Washington Glass Co., c.1890

The fern patterned chestnut and ivory ground overlaid with heavy gilt enamel decoration depicting ferns and blossoms, strong border decoration around neck and scalloped rim, maker's mark in black enamel
6.5in. high
Provenance: Maude B. Feld sold item to Mrs. R. A. McMurry sold item to current owner
Estimate: 1,500-1,800

30784

30784
AN AMERICAN ENAMELED ACID-FINISH BURMESE GLASS SUGAR SHAKER
Mt. Washington Glass Co., c.1890

The egg-shaped body with a peach to white ground depicting a pattern of small white and blue enamel flowers with twigs and leaves, metal top, unsigned
4.3in. high
Estimate: 200-400

30785

30786

30786
AN AMERICAN ACID-FINISH ENAMELED BURMESE TWO-HANDLED GLASS VASE
Mt. Washington Glass Co., c.1890

The footed round body with angular sloped sides rises to a slender cylindrical neck and two applied gold tone handles, raised gilt and enameled abstract floral design, unsigned
12in. high
Estimate: 2,000-3,000

30785
AN AMERICAN ENAMELED 'CROWN MILANO' GLASS VASE
Mt. Washington Glass Co., c.1890

The footed globular body with swirled fluting terminates in a narrow neck with pinched, down-turned rim, enameled floral decoration in blue, green, pink, white and orange colors, unsigned
6.5in. high
Estimate: 400-600

30787
AN AMERICAN DECORATED GLASS VASE
Smith Bros., c.1890

Burmese-style custard and salmon colored, four-sided with a ship design on front and back, raised gilt tracing of the ship name 'Santa Maria' and decoration to the rim, stamped underside with rampant lion in a shield
9.6in. high
Illustrated: Albert Christian Revi's *Nineteenth Century Glass. Its Genesis and Development* New York, Galahad Books, 1967
Provenance: Maude B. Feld sold item to Mrs. R. A. McMurry sold item to current owner
Estimate: 400-600

30788
A FRENCH MOLDED FIGURAL GLASS PLATE
René Lalique, c.1930

An Art Deco motif, high relief nude in motion amongst radiating vines and blossoms, molded signature, *Lalique,* etched *France*
6.7in. diameter
Estimate: 300-500

30789
A DIAMOND QUILT PATTERN SATIN GLASS PITCHER AND TWO TUMBLERS
Mt. Washington Glass Co., c.1890

The pitcher of baluster form with an applied handle; the two pink tumblers are cased in white, one tumbler has gilt 'buttons' at quilt points, each unsigned
The pitcher: 7.2in. high; The tumblers 3.7in. high (Total: 3 Items)
Estimate: 200-400

30790

30790
A FRENCH OVERLAID AND ETCHED GLASS VASE
Emile Gallé, c.1900

Tapering lobed shape with frosted white and blue ground, double overlaid in pink and olive green and etched to depict a field of poppies, cameo signature *Gallé*
10.9in. high
Estimate: 1,500-2,000

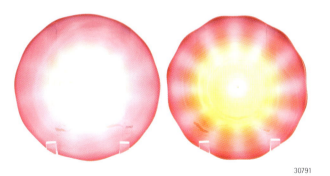

30791

30791
TWO AMERICAN FUCHSIA AMBERINA GLASS PLATES
New England Glass Co., c.1890

Each with gently undulating rims and unmatching reds transitioning to golden yellow centers, unsigned
The largest: 7in. diameter (Total: 2 Items)
Estimate: 200-400

30792

30792
AN ENGLISH OVERLAID AND ETCHED GLASS VASE
Thomas Webb & Sons, c.1890

The frosted cranberry ground overlaid in ivory and etched to depict blossoming branches and foliage with a beetle and two dragonflies on reverse, unsigned
10in. high
Estimate: 4,000-6,000

30793

AN AMERICAN GLASS VASE
Mullein, c.1890

The double gourd pull-up pattern in pink and yellow on a clear satin finish, unsigned
8in. high
Estimate: 200-400

30795

A FRENCH OVERLAID AND ETCHED GLASS VASE
Emile Gallé, c.1900

The frosted peach and ivory footed bulbous form and cylindrical neck overlaid in green and purple, etched to depict flowers and leaves, cameo signature *Gallé*
3.6in. high
Estimate: 400-600

30794

AN AMERICAN GLASS COMPOTE
Steuben, c.1940

The solid circular base surmounted by four applique legs supporting a shallow bowl with a gradually spreading rim, each engraved under foot
4.9in. high
Estimate: 300-500

30796

A CZECHOSLOVAKIAN ART GLASS VASE
Maker unknown, mid-Twentieth Century

The bulbous form with a small flared rim in a red ground with mottled purple striations around resembling agate stone, stamped underside (illegible)
7.6in. high
Estimate: 100-200

30797

30797
AN AMERICAN FAVRILE GLASS PITCHER
Tiffany & Co., c.1900

The iridescent gold cylindrical form tapers mid-section and flares to the spouted rim, applied handle, the underside with etched signature *L. C. Tiffany – Favrile*
4.25in. high
Estimate: 300-600

30798
A FRENCH ETCHED AND ENAMELED GLASS VASE
Daum Nancy, c.1900

An autumn sunset harbor scene with orange and yellow acid-cut-back mottled ground and black enameled sailing vessels, enamel signature *Daum Nancy* with the *Cross of Lorraine* and artist initials
1.5in. high
Estimate: 800-1,200

30798

30799
A SWIRLED MATSU-NO-KE SATIN GLASS VASE
attributed to Stevens and Williams, c.1885

The inverted ovoid form with swirled, ribbed rose satin glass and applied frosted glass feet, vines, leaves and flowers, everted ruffle rim, Maude B. Feld retail sticker affixed, unsigned
7in. high
Estimate: 300-600

30800
AN OVERLAID AND ETCHED GLASS BOWL
Maker unknown, Twentieth Century

The low bulbous form with a short neck and flared rim, frosted ground depicting a floral pattern in dark purple and white, signature on side illegible
3.5in. high
Estimate: 200-400

30801
AN AMERICAN 'CLUTHRA' GLASS VASE
Steuben, c.1928

The blue and white mottled color over a clear 'Cluthra' ground, flared rim, unsigned
6.5in. high
Estimate: 700-1,000

30802

30802
AN AMERICAN ART GLASS CANDLESTICK HOLDER
Kew-Blas (W. S. Blake at the Union Glass Works), c.1890

The iridescent-gold form broad disc foot rising to a baluster swirled stem with ring collar beneath a deep cup socket and wide everted rim, etched underside *KEW-BLAS* within the polished pontil
8.4in. high
Estimate: 400-500

30803

30803
A SATIN GLASS EWER
Maker unknown, c.1930

The round foot rising to a collared stem supporting a tapered ovoid form with a collared and tapering neck in ivory to purple with a gilt rim, applied handle, unsigned
9.9in. high
Estimate: 100-300

30804

30804
AN OPALESCENT ART GLASS VASE
Maker unknown, c.1900

The red disc foot rising to a short stem supporting a milky divided elliptical form uniting to a tapered neck and a flared rim, applied red 'scale' pattern to the sides and applied red raspberry stamp to the inside of the ellipse, unsigned
9.5in. high
Estimate: 300-500

30805

30806

30806
AN AUSTRIAN IRIDESCENT ART NOUVEAU GLASS VASE
Pallme Koenig, Austria, c.1910

Round squat base with a slender neck that terminates in a crimped flora-form, purple to black irregularly shaped ribbon applique, what appears to be an original factory or retail sticker on the base,
10.7in. high
Estimate: 600-900

30805
AN AUSTRIAN IRIDESCENT GLASS VASE
Loetz, c.1900

The white cased bulbous body to cylindrical collar in a pale green ground, pulled design along bottom edge, with a mottled green and brown base, unsigned
4.1in. high
Estimate: 300-500

30807
AN OVERLAID AND ETCHED SILVER-MOUNTED BISCUIT JAR
attributed to Thomas Webb & Sons, c.1895

Tapering cylindrical body mounted with a silver plated handle and lid, the lid with ivory finial, fine cranberry colored ground with etched ivory flowers, leaves, vines and a butterfly, unsigned
8.5in. high with handle in an upright position
Estimate: 2,000-3,000

30808
AN AMERICAN IRIDESCENT FAVRILE GLASS COMPOTE
Tiffany & Co., c.1902

The round domed foot rising to a slender swelled stem supporting a stepped ovoid form bowl to a short flared rim, gold iridescence with magenta highlights, paper *Maude B. Feld* sticker to inside, signed underside *L. C. Tiffany-Favrile*
9.6in. high
Estimate: 1,000-1,200

30809
AN AMERICAN ART GLASS PITCHER
Steuben, c.1925

The bristol yellow ovoid form with a cylindrical neck and applied handle, acid stamped underside
12.9in. high
Estimate: 300-500

30809

30810
A DIAMOND QUILT PATTERN SATIN GLASS ROSE BOWL
Thomas Webb & Sons, c.1890

The tri-footed bulbous form with a trifold rim in rainbow and mother of pearl, raspberry pontil, acid stamped *Webb* to inside
6.2in. high
Estimate: 800-1,000

30810

30811
A FRENCH OVERLAID AND ETCHED GLASS VASE
Emile Gallé, c.1900

The ovoid form with a short cylindrical neck overlaid in shades of yellow and green and etched to depict leaves and seed pods, with cameo signature *Gallé* after a star
2.7in. high
Estimate: 400-600

30813
A FRENCH MOLD-BLOWN OPALESCENT GLASS VASE
René Lalique, c.1920

The barrel form with a short cylindrical neck molded in a vine pattern with a satin milky opalescent finish, no lid, stamped underside *R. Lalique France*
4.6in. high
Estimate: 100-200

30812
A HOBNAIL PATTERN JACK-IN-THE-PULPIT GLASS VASE
Maker unknown, c.1910

The frosted cylindrical form rising to a clear neck with a ruffled cranberry Jack-in-the-Pulpit rim, unsigned
10.4in. high
Estimate: 200-400

30814
A GLASS AND SILVER PLATE CLARET JUG
Maker unknown, c.1890

The ovoid body, tapering shoulders and short cylindrical neck in clear and purple glass swirls with four vertical ribs mounted with a silver plate decorative hinged lid and handle, hallmark to the hinge *JRM*
10.9in. high
Estimate: 700-900

30815
AN AMERICAN ETCHED AND ENAMELED LIDDED GLASS BOX
St. Louis, c.1910

The etched frosted ground with scrolled borders, cranberry floral motif, lid with center shield and gilt threading on rim, unsigned
6.6in. high (Total: 2 Items)
Estimate: 200-400

30816
AN ENGLISH 'DRAPE' SATIN GLASS VASE
Thomas Webb & Sons, c.1920

The white barrel shape cased in frosted white and cranberry, raised on crimped flora-form feet, the underside with acid-stamped maker's mark *Webb*
5.5in. high
Estimate: 200-300

30817
A SIX-PIECE PLACE SETTING OF AMERICAN 'GRAPE' BRISTOL YELLOW GLASS
Steuben, c.1925

Comprising an ice tea glass, water goblet, wine goblet, champagne and sherbet, each with hexagonal-cut foot, *together with* a plate, all pieces with a band of scrolling and fruiting grape vine engraved near the rim, each piece with block letter acid-stamped signature within the polished pontil, except for the pontil-free plate, stamped on the outer edge of the underside
The tallest: 6in.
Literature: this pattern illustrated in Thomas P. Dimitroff's *Frederick Carder and Steuben Glass: American Classics* on p.182, Fig.8.12 (Total: 6 Items)
Estimate: 400-600

30818
AN ENGLISH GLASS FLASK
Nailsea, c.1890

The ovoid form flattened on either side with a short cylindrical neck in a white ground with red and blue swirl pattern, unsigned
7.5in. high
Estimate: 100-300

30819
AN OVERSHOT IRIDESCENT ART GLASS VASE
Maker unknown, Twentieth Century

The quatre-foil bulbous base rising to a cylindrical column with a flared rim, overshot 'ice glass' decoration overall in blue green, unsigned
8.6in. high
Estimate: 200-300

30821
A DIAMOND QUILT PATTERN MOTHER-OF-PEARL SATIN GLASS VASE
Maker unknown, c.1890

The double gourd form with scalloped rim in a mother-of-pearl satin finish with a rainbow diamond quilt pattern, unsigned
11.5in. high
Estimate: 200-300

30822
AN OVERLAID AND ETCHED GLASS VASE
Emile Gallé, c.1900

The round foot supporting an inverted pear form body, the frosted ground overlaid in amethyst and etched in a floral motif, cameo signature *Gallé*
5.7in. high
Estimate: 500-700

30820
AN AMERICAN IRIDESCENT BLUE AURENE GLASS VASE
Steuben, c.1900

Of organic form, the round base rising to a fanned rim with four pinched openings, signed underside *Aurene 2762*
7.2in. high
Estimate: 700-1,000

30823
AN ENGLISH MATSU-NO-KE CASED GLASS VASE
possibly Stevens and Williams, c.1885

The blue cased, footed, rouleau form transitions from white to robin's egg blue terminating with an opal folded and ruffled amber crest rim, the obverse decorated with applied branches of flowering cherry, unmarked
9.5in. high
Estimate: 100-200

30825
A FRENCH OVERLAID AND ETCHED GLASS CABINET VASE
Emile Gallé, c.1900

The flattened pear form with frosted ground overlaid with emerald-green and etched to depict hibiscus, with cameo signature *Gallé*
3.5in. high
Estimate: 100-300

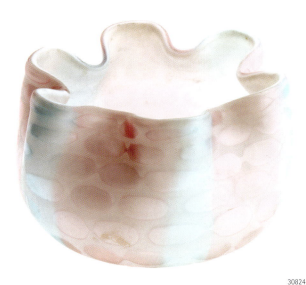

30824
A SATIN GLASS MOTHER-OF-PEARL ROSE BOWL
Maker unknown, c.1900

The rainbow mother-of-pearl bulbous form to a ruffled rim in pale pink and pale blue satin coin spot pattern, white casing, *Maude B. Feld* sticker to underside, unmarked
2.8in. high
Estimate: 200-400

30826
A SATIN GLASS VASE
Maker unknown, c.1920

The cased double gourd form with a slightly flared rim in ivory to cranberry, gilt detail to rim, unsigned
10.5in. high
Estimate: 100-200

30827
A FRENCH OVERLAID AND ETCHED GLASS LAMP BASE
Emile Gallé, c.1910

The frosted white ground overlaid with etched grapes, leaves and vines in auburn and brown, lamp lights internally, electrified with modern cord, etched signature near foot
11in. high
Estimate: 300-600

30828
AN ENGLISH OVERLAID AND ETCHED PEACH BLOW GLASS VASE
Stevens and Williams, c.1890

White cased interior, the transitioning salmon pink to deep peach ground overlaid in ivory and etched to depict hibiscus blossoms and a butterfly, unsigned
5.7in. high
Provenance: Maude B. Feld sold item to Mrs. R. A. McMurry sold item to current owner
Estimate: 2,000-3,000

30828

30829
A FRENCH ETCHED AND OVERLAID GLASS VASE
Richard, c.1925

Round tapering foot with gourd-shaped body, tangerine ground overlaid with indigo leaves vines and flowers, cameo signature *Richard*
5in. high
Estimate: 300-500

30829

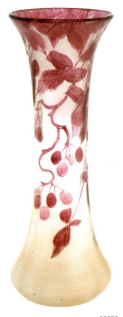

30830
AN AMERICAN GLASS SAUCE BOAT
Steuben, Twentieth Century

The round disc base rising to a knobbed stem supporting a bowl with a slanted rim, applied handle and spout decoration, signed underside
8.5in. high
Estimate: 300-500

30831
AN AMERICAN ART GLASS CANDLESTICK
Tiffany & Co., c.1910

The cushion foot rising to a spiral stem with a flared cup and scalloped rim in iridescent gold finish, signed underside *L. C. T.*
5.1in. high
Estimate: 500-800

30832
A FRENCH OVERLAID AND ENAMELED GLASS VASE
Legras, c.1915

The bulbous base to cylindrical body and flared rim in a peach ground with an enameled burgundy vines with grapes, signed in relief *Legras* on the side, stamped underside *Ovington New York/France*
10.5in. high
Estimate: 500-700

30833
AN ENGLISH OVERLAID, ETCHED AND SILVER-MOUNTED GLASS PERFUME BOTTLE
The Glass: Thomas Webb & Sons, c.1890

The globular form with frosted yellow ground double overlaid in carnelian red and ivory and etched to depict a floral motif, silver top with English hallmarks, cameo glass unsigned
3.5in. high
Estimate: 1,200-1,800

30834
A SATIN GLASS VASE
Maker unknown, c.1890

The blue diamond quilted mother-of-pearl with a bulbous base rising to a cylindrical neck flaring to a tightly ruffled yellow rim, unsigned
9.4in. high
Estimate: 200-400

30836
AN AMERICAN HOBNAIL PLUM GLASS PITCHER
Maker unknown, c.1920

The spherical body rising to square flared neck, applied frosted handle, unsigned
6.75in. high
Estimate: 100-300

30835
A FRENCH OVERLAID AND ETCHED GLASS VASE
D'Argental, c.1900

The ovoid form with frosted blue to indigo ground overlaid in purple and etched to depict a pastoral scene, cameo signature *D'Argental*
9.7in. high
Estimate: 1,500-1,800

30837
THREE AMERICAN ART GLASS ITEMS
Makers unknown, c.1930

Comprising an enameled cylindrical lidded yellow mottled glass jar; a blue satin lily form vase; a cranberry vase with a rigaree rim; all unsigned
7.6in. high (Total: 3 Items)
Estimate: 100-200

30838

30838
A PAIR OF AMERICAN FROSTED CHAMPAGNE GLASSES
Steuben, c.1920

Each with a disc foot beneath twisted stem and pink conical cup, unsigned
5.5in. high (Total: 2 Items)
Estimate: 200-400

30839

30839
TWO AMERICAN DIAMOND QUILT PATTERN MOTHER-OF-PEARL VASES
Maker unknown, c.1900

The first, a yellow double gourd form; the second, a cinnamon-colored with ovoid form and flared neck, unsigned
7.5in. high (Total: 2 Items)
Estimate: 100-200

30840

30840
AN AMERICAN FAVRILE GLASS VASE
Tiffany & Co., c.1908

The tapering cylindrical form frosted and etched with grapes and leaves in green and purple, color only to the mid section, Maude B. Feld sticker on underside, etched signature underside *L. C. Tiffany-Favrile 7025 C*
12.3in. high
Provenance: Maude B. Feld sold item to Mrs. R. A. McMurry sold item to current owner
Estimate: 4,000-6,000

30841
AN ENGLISH CORALENE SATIN GLASS VASE
Stevens and Williams, c.1890

The footed bulbous form tapering to a cylindrical neck in rainbow satin and ivory decorated with coralene seaweed beading, unsigned
9in. high
Estimate: 700-1,000

30842
AN ENGLISH OVERLAID AND ETCHED GLASS VASE
Thomas Webb & Sons, c.1890

The footed bulbous form tapering to a flared rim with a cranberry ground overlaid in ivory etched to depict grape vines and foliage, stamped *Thomas Webb & Sons/ Cameo*
11in. high
Estimate: 3,000-4,000

30843
AN AMERICAN OPALESCENT HOBNAIL GLASS PITCHER
Hobbs Brockunier & Co., c.1880

The bulbous form with a quartre-foil neck and rim in cranberry with opalescent hobnails, applied clear handle, unsigned
8.2in. high
Estimate: 200-300

30844
A BELGIAN OVERLAID AND ETCHED GLASS BOWL
attributed to Val St. Lambert, c.1910

The circular foot with cranberry-cut-to-clear starburst centering the square-shaped form with cut corners and delicate cranberry floral sprays against an acid-etched ground of small leaves, unsigned
2.5in. high
Estimate: 300-400

30846
AN AMERICAN COIN SPOT PATTERN SATIN GLASS PITCHER
possibly Mt. Washington Glass Co., c.1900

The baluster form transitions from mother-of-pearl white to deep crimson in the neck and ruffled rim and spout, applied frosted reeded handle, unsigned
8.5in. high
Estimate: 100-200

30845
AN ENGLISH SATIN GLASS HINGED BOX
Stevens and Williams, c.1890

The pale blue ovoid form with a round lid and brass hinge in a diamond quilt mother-of-pearl finish, unsigned
4.7in. high
Estimate: 200-400

30847
AN AMERICAN GLASS VASE AND NUT DISH
Steuben, c.1945

The first, with George Thompson double-swirl stem; the second with swirl-shaped handle; each with script signature *Steuben* on underside
The vase 8.5in. high, 4.6in. rim diameter (Total: 2 Items)
Estimate: 500-700

30848

A PAIR OF AMERICAN ART NOUVEAU GLASS CANDLESTICKS
Tiffany & Co., c.1902

The round base rising to a floral form top in amethyst, one signed underside *L. C. T.*
3.5in. high
Estimate: 1,200-1,800

30848

30849

AN ENGLISH OVERLAID AND ETCHED GLASS VASE
Thomas Webb & Sons, c.1887

The simulated ivory bulbous low footed bowl with a short neck depicts a floral pattern with a rope design to the rim and foot, stamped underside
3.2in. high
Provenance: Maude B. Feld sold item to Mrs. R. A. McMurry sold item to current owner
Estimate: 1,500-2,000

30849

30850
AN AMERICAN DIAMOND QUILT PATTERN CASED SATIN GLASS JUG
Mt. Washington Glass Co., c.1900

The baluster form with pink ground and mother-of-pearl diamond pattern, applied frosted handle, unsigned
4.5in. high
Estimate: 200-400

30852
AN AMERICAN OVERSHOT CRANBERRY GLASS TOOTHPICK HOLDER
Maker unknown, c.1880

The diminutive cranberry body with rolled-collar rim, white, pale blue and yellow 'ice' decoration throughout, unsigned
2.5in. high
Estimate: 200-300

30853
AN AMERICAN IRIDESCENT BLOWN GLASS TAZZA
Steuben, c.1920

A small ribbed tazza with blue iridescent color inside the dish and ivory calcite on the exterior, with applied round pedestal foot, unsigned
2.7in. high
Estimate: 400-600

30851
A BOHEMIAN IRIDESCENT GLASS VASE
PalmeKonig, c.1915

The bulbous base tapering to a long cylindrical neck in a milky iridescent ground overlaid with iridescent purple threading, unsigned
7.7in. high
Estimate: 400-600

30854

30854
AN AMERICAN GLASS PERFUME BOTTLE
Maker unknown, c.1890

The globular form in mottled white and cranberry, screw-on brass cap, unsigned
4in. high
Estimate: 200-250

30855

30855
A FRENCH OVERLAID AND ETCHED GLASS VASE
Emile Gallé, c.1900

The frosted ground overlaid in periwinkle and etched to depict columbine, cameo signature *Gallé*
5in. high
Estimate: 500-700

30856
AN AMERICAN ART GLASS VASE
Steuben, c.1925

The flint white round foot supports a light blue jade ovoid form vase tapering at the top to a short, wide neck and flared rim, unsigned
10.8in. high
Estimate: 1,200-1,500

30857

30856

30857
AN OPALESCENT COIN SPOT PATTERN CRANBERRY GLASS PITCHER
Maker unknown, c.1910

The ovoid body with cylindrical neck and ruffle rim, applied clear loop handle, unsigned
9in. high
Estimate: 100-200

30859
AN AMERICAN ART NOUVEAU OVERLAID AND ETCHED GLASS VASE
Honesdale, c.1900

The opalescent ground with a clear golden stylized tulip pattern with detailed gilt design, enamel signature *Honesdale*
12.1in. high
Estimate: 300-500

30858
AN AMERICAN FAVRILE GLASS MINIATURE VASE
Tiffany & Co., c.1900

The iridescent gold bulbous body with double pulled handles rising to a cylindrical neck and mouth with rolled rim, the underside with etched initials *L. C. T.* and number *Y8422* around the polished pontil
2in. high
Estimate: 400-500

30860
AN AMERICAN GLASS DISH, PITCHER AND VASE
Various makers, c.1900

The Mt. Washington leaf mold dish in a white and pink spangled pattern; a satin pitcher, clear etched 'thorn' handle, cased in white; a millefiori vase, each unsigned
The tallest: 8.5in. high (Total: 3 Items)
Estimate: 50-150

30861
AN ENGLISH OVERLAID AND ETCHED GEM CAMEO GLASS VASE
Thomas Webb & Sons, c.1885

The frosted cranberry glass overlaid in ivory and etched to depict wild roses and ferns with two butterflies, impressed stamp *Thomas Webb & Sons Gem Cameo*
6.7in. high
Estimate: 1,000-1,500

30862

30862
AN AMERICAN IRIDESCENT BLUE AURENE GLASS VASE
Steuben, c.1900

The circular foot upswept and joined to a graduating cylindrical body with hearts and vine decoration, signed underside *Steuben Aurene 6298*
10.1in. high
Publication: A similar illustrated in *Frederick Carder and Steuben Glass* by Thomas P. Dimitroff, fig.10.120 p.247
Estimate: 4,000-6,000

30863
A SATIN GLASS VASE
Maker unknown, c.1890

The cushion foot ovoid body with a double molded neck ring and heavily ruffled rim in pale blue mother-of-pearl herringbone pattern, white casing, unsigned
10.2in. high
Estimate: 200-400

30863

30864

30864
AN AMERICAN ART GLASS PITCHER
Steuben, c.1930

The alabaster baluster form with a flared cylindrical neck and short spout, applied handle in black, unsigned
9.6in. high
Estimate: 200-400

30865
A FRENCH OVERLAID AND ETCHED GLASS VASE
Emile Gallé, 1904

The round base transitions to a slender form with a high collar, the frosted ivory and peach ground overlaid in lavender and olive, cameo *Gallé* signature after a star
10.7in. high
Estimate: 1,000-1,200

30865

30866
A SET OF SEVEN AMERICAN IRIDESCENT FAVRILE GLASS GOBLETS
Tiffany & Co., c.1900

Each, the round foot rising to a straight stem supporting an inverted bell form bowl in lime green iridescence with flaring rim, each signed underside *L C T Favrile 5*
6in. high (Total: 7 Items)
Estimate: 1,500-2,000

30867
AN AMERICAN SPATTER GLASS VASE
Maker unknown, c.1910

The cylindrical body with ribbed spiral rising to swollen shoulder flowing into flared and ruffled rim, the entire with mottled white, pink, cranberry, and burgundy, unsigned
8.8in. high
Estimate: 200-300

30868
AN AMERICAN 'HEART AND VINE' GLASS VASE
attributed to Durand, c.1920

The wide ovoid iridescent pearl-white body with repeating green and gold heart pattern beneath a profusion of iridescent gold threading, unsigned
6.25in. high (Total: 2 Items)
Estimate: 900-1,200

30869

30869
AN ENGLISH OVERLAID AND ETCHED GLASS VASE
Thomas Webb & Sons, c.1890

The frosted cranberry ground overlaid in ivory and etched to depict a floral design with fern leaves on reverse, unsigned
8.5in. high
Estimate: 3,000-4,000

30870
AN OPALESCENT COIN SPOT PATTERN GLASS PITCHER
Maker unknown, c.1900

The clear ovoid form with a short cylindrical neck and milky ruffled rim, applied handle, unsigned
8.9in. high
Estimate: 200-400

30871
AN AMERICAN GLASS DRESSER BOX
Wavecrest, c.1890

The square form with tri ribbed corners in pale blue with a ivory cartouche depicting delicate pink flowers, metal hinged mount with matching glass lid, stamped underside
4in. high
Estimate: 300-500

30872
AN AMERICAN MINIATURE FAVRILE GLASS ROSE BOWL
Tiffany & Co., c.1910

The d'or verde globular form punctuated with pulled prunts and vertical ribbing, unsigned, the underside with etched number 'J2753'
1.25in. high
Estimate: 200-400

30873
AN OPALESCENT COIN SPOT PATTERN SATIN GLASS VASE
Maker unknown, c.1900

The pinched bulbous form rising to a tri-fold neck in white to rose, opalescent coin spot pattern, frosted applied handle, white casing, unsigned
10in. high
Estimate: 100-300

30874

30874
AN AMERICAN 'DRAPE' HINGED GLASS BOX
Northwood, c.1900

Of cylindrical form in ivory, pink and yellow drape pattern, the gradual tapered hinged lid with metal banded border, unsigned
5in. high
Estimate: 600-900

30875

30875
AN ENGLISH OVERLAID AND ETCHED GLASS VASE
Thomas Webb & Sons, c.1890

The frosted cranberry ground overlaid in ivory and etched to depict raspberry vines, scalloped pattern bordering the rim, unsigned
5.7in. high
Provenance: Maude B. Feld sold item to Mrs. R. A. McMurry sold item to current owner
Estimate: 1,500-2,000

30876
A DIAMOND QUILT PATTERN SATIN GLASS BOWL
Stevens and Williams, c.1900

The five clear applied feet support a bulbous form with a pinched square and heavily ruffled rim, cased in deep pink with a butterscotch diamond quilt satin finish, double pontil floral stamp to underside
4.2in. high
Estimate: 200-400

30876

30877

30877
AN AMERICAN IRIDESCENT ART GLASS VASE ON BRONZE BASE
Steuben, c.1920

The domed gold encrusted bronze base mounted to an elongated baluster form blue glass vase with a flared rim, highlights of green and magenta, underside stamped *Silver Crest*
10.9in. high

Estimate: 300-500

30878

30878
AN AMERICAN JACK-IN-THE-PULPIT GOLD AURENE GLASS VASE
Steuben, c.1904

The round foot supporting a trumpet form body with flora-form rim, signed underside *Aurene*
6.1in. high

Estimate: 400-600

30879

30879
AN AUSTRIAN ART GLASS BUD VASE
Loetz, c.1900

The round pinched form rising to a slender cylindrical neck with a flared rim in a lemon iridescent ground overlaid with champagne opalescent marbling, signed underside *Loetz Austria*
7.2in. high (Total: 3 items)

Estimate: 1,000-1,500

30880

30880
FOUR AMERICAN CASED PINK SATIN GLASS ITEMS
Makers unknown, c.1910

Comprising a footed bulbous vase with a tightly ruffled bi-cornered rim; a pitcher with applied 'thorn' handle; two footed vases with applied 'thorn' handles and tightly ruffled quadre-cornered rims, unsigned
The tallest: 6.75in. high (Total: 4 Items)

Estimate: 400-600

30881
AN ETCHED GLASS BOWL
attributed to Val St. Lambert, c.1920

The round foot supporting a quatre-foil bowl, heavily decorated with an etched fern pattern and a floral design, rim and base flashed in green, unsigned
5.6in. diameter (Total: 1 Items)
Estimate: 200-300

30882
A FRENCH ACID-ETCHED AND ENAMELED GLASS VASE
August J. F. Legras, c.1900

The oblong foot beneath conforming acid-etched and frosted body with tapering sides rising to a blue-bordered rim, the obverse with a stylized spray of flowers rendered in polychrome and gold enamels, with gilt cameo signature *Legras*
3.25in. high
Estimate: 200-300

30883
AN ENGLISH SATIN GLASS VASE
Stevens and Williams, c.1890

The footed melon form body with tapered neck and bulbous rim, cased in ivory, mottled and swirled decoration throughout, unsigned
6.2in. high
Estimate: 200-400

30884
A FRENCH BLOWN AND MOTTLED GLASS VASE
Daum Nancy, c.1915

The footed trifold shaped rim in etched reds and orange, incised signature in side *Daum Nancy* with *Cross of Lorraine*
4.1in. high
Estimate: 300-500

30885
AN ENGLISH OVERLAID AND ETCHED GLASS BISCUIT JAR
Thomas Webb & Sons, c.1890

The frosted cranberry bulbous form overlaid in ivory and etched to depict seashells and seaweed, brass mounted rim and handle, brass lid with designed scroll work to the top, unsigned
6in. high (Total: 2 Items)
Estimate: 4,000-6,000

30886
AN ENGLISH DIAMOND QUILT PATTERN SATIN GLASS VASE
Stevens and Williams, c.1890

Of baluster form with flared rim, rainbow mother-of-pearl diamond pattern, marked underside *PATENT*
7in. high
Estimate: 600-900

30887
AN AMERICAN IRIDESCENT FAVRILE GLASS PLATE
Tiffany & Co., c.1900

The ivory ground with an ultramarine blue border and cerulean blue pulled feather design, signed underside *L. C. Tiffany-Favrile*
8in. diameter
Estimate: 1,000-1,500

30888
A FRENCH OVERLAID AND ETCHED GLASS CABINET VASE
Emile Gallé, c.1900

The tri-lobed barrel form with frosted ground, overlaid with mauve and etched to depict the tendrils, leaves and buds of a sweet pea vine, cameo signature *Gallé*
3.4in. high
Estimate: 400-600

30889

30889
AN AUSTRIAN IRIDESCENT GLASS VASE
Loetz, c.1900

The double gourd form with 'Papillon' oil spot technique flaring to a double pointed lip, unsigned
6.6in. high
Estimate: 400-600

30891

30891
AN AMERICAN PRESSED GLASS SUGAR SHAKER
Maker unknown, c.1915

The cylindrical clear to rose body in the 'Royal Ivy' Rubina pattern, threaded metal lid, unsigned
4.2in. high
Estimate: 100-300

30890

30890
AN AMERICAN ROUND GLASS DRESSER BOX
Wavecrest, c.1890

The footed basin with raised decoration on the sides and floral designs on obverse and reverse with yellow metal mount at the shoulder, the top with a square painted cartouche centered with raised decoration opening to reveal a lined interior, stamped underside *WaveCrest* in black
3.5in. high
Estimate: 300-400

30892

30892
A FRENCH OVERLAID AND ETCHED GLASS CABINET VASE
Emile Gallé, c.1900

The mottled frosted amber and pink ground overlaid in olive green, and etched with pendant berried vines, with cameo signature *Gallé*
3in. high
Estimate: 400-600

30893
AN ENGLISH OVERLAID AND ETCHED GLASS VASE
attributed to Woodall for Thomas Webb & Sons, c.1885

The six-paneled form with blue ground overlaid in ivory, each panel etched with a unique foliate design, one panel with a bird, one with a moth, rim and shoulder with oriental design, unsigned
6in. high
Estimate: 3,000-5,000

30894

30894
AN AMERICAN IRIDESCENT GOLD AURENE GLASS GOBLET
Steuben, c.1900

The circular ribbed foot with a cylindrical stem supporting an inverted bell form bowl in gold iridescence, applique detail to the stem, signed underside *Steuben Aurene 5067*
5.4in. high
Estimate: 500-700

30896

30896
A FRENCH OVERLAID AND ETCHED GLASS VASE
Croismare, c.1900

The frosted ground overlaid with olive and amethyst, etched to depict leaves, vines and berries, cameo signature at edge of foot
3in. high
Estimate: 200-400

30895

30895
A GROUP OF GLASS ITEMS
Makers unknown, c.1900

Comprising a two-handled vase; a white satin hobnail pattern bowl cased in pink; a pitcher with a rigaree foot; a 'Jack-in-the-Pulpit' vase; each unsigned
The tallest: 6.5in. (Total: 4 Items)
Estimate: 200-400

30897
AN ENGLISH OVERLAID AND ETCHED GLASS VASE
Thomas Webb & Sons, c.1890

The double gourd form with frosted yellow ground double overlaid in red and white, and etched to depict morning glories and a moth, stamped underside
6.5in. high
Provenance: Maude B. Feld sold item to Mrs. R. A. McMurry sold item to current owner
Estimate: 1,500-2,000

30897

30898
A PAIR OF SATIN AND OPALESCENT DIAMOND QUILT PATTERN GLASS BOWLS
Makers unknown, c.1900

Comprising one cranberry and one blue of the same form and pattern, unsigned
3in. high (Total: 2 Items)
Estimate: 200-400

30899
TWO GLASS VASES
Maker unknown, c. 1885

The pair of spangled floriform 'End of Day' pattern with metallic inclusions one in brown, green, and white, the second in pink, green, and white
Both 8in. high (Total: 2 Items)
Estimate: 200-300

30900
AN AMERICAN FAVRILE GLASS CABINET VASE
Tiffany & Co., c.1900

The iridescent violet-gold bulbous body tapering to a cylindrical neck, decorated with small pulled prunts and vertical ribbing, the underside with etched initials *L. C. T.* and number *N986* around the polished pontil and with original paper label
2in. high
Estimate: 300-500

30901
A PAIR OF APPLIED AND DECORATED GOBLETS
Flint, c.1890

The Tree of Life design with red applique snake on stem over stylized craquelure ground with gold enamel, unsigned
7.7in. high (Total: 2 Items)
Estimate: 200-300

30902
AN AMERICAN SATIN GLASS VASE
Maker unknown, c.1900

The white cased pale pink cushion foot and stem rising to a cranberry four point ruffle body and flared rim, diamond mother-of-pearl pattern, unsigned
8.7in. high
Estimate: 100-300

30903
AN AMERICAN HERRINGBONE PATTERN SATIN GLASS BASKET
Maker unknown, c.1910

The white mother-of-pearl short circular foot supporting a globular body with flaring ruffled rim in butterscotch, applied frosted twisted twig form handle, unmarked
9.5in. high, 10in. long, 7in. wide
Estimate: 500-700

30904
AN OVERLAID AND ETCHED SILVER MOUNTED GLASS EWER
attributed to Thomas Webb & Sons, c.1890

A round pedestal foot with threaded decoration, the body of tapering cylindrical form with a silver plated spout, hinged cover and handle, cranberry ground with etched ivory morning glory design, butterfly in flight on one side, lid engraved 'Dot and Ross from Clara', unsigned
11.75in. high
Estimate: 2,000-3,000

30905
AN AMERICAN DECORATED GLASS LAMP SHADE
Quezal, c.1900

Pulled feather, iridescent floral-form lamp shade in ivory, green, gold and yellow hues, etched and enameled signature
6.5in. high
Estimate: 100-300

30907
A FRENCH OVERLAID AND ETCHED GLASS VASE
Le Verre Francais, c.1920

The footed bulbous form with a flaring pinched neck in mottled pale apricot and orange depicting a stylized floral pattern, candy cane twist to underside
3.2in. high
Estimate: 200-300

30906
A FRENCH ETCHED AND ENAMELED GLASS VASE
Daum Nancy, c.1910

The mottled orange and brown ground etched and enameled to depict a snowy winter forest scene in shades of ivory, chestnut and grisaille, enameled signature *Daum Nancy* with the *Cross of Lorraine* and *B*..
1.5in. high
Estimate: 600-800

30908
AN AMERICAN PUFFY DRESSER BOX
Wavecrest, c.1890

The shaped and molded opal body fitted with gilt metal hinged bezel mounts and pierced pendant floral corners, the conforming lid with four pink enamel reserves of forget-me-not flowers in yellow and blue beaded enamel centering a small pink reserve, unsigned, possibly made by the C.F. Monroe Co., New Bedford M.A. for Wavecrest
3.5 high, 7in. square
Estimate: 300-400

30909
AN ENGLISH OVERLAID AND ETCHED GLASS VASE
Thomas Webb & Sons, c.1890

The rounded conical body with flaring rim, chartreuse ground overlaid in ivory and etched to depict cherry blossoms, leaves and vines, unsigned
6.7in. high
Estimate: 1,800-2,500

30910
A SILVER-MOUNTED SATIN GLASS PERFUME BOTTLE
Maker unknown, c.1876

The melon ribbed globular form in ochre, Birmingham sterling silver hallmarks to side of cap
1.7in. high
Estimate: 200-400

30911
A FRENCH GLASS VASE
René Lalique, c.1930

The outward cylindrical form with six rectilinear recessed panels of champagne color, each with a standing female figure in profile, the underside with etched signature *R. Lalique/France*
3.9in. high
Estimate: 600-900

30912

30913

30913
THREE BLUE SATIN GLASS ITEMS
Various makers, c.1930

Comprising a diamond quilted mother-of-pearl cased satin glass vase of barrel form with high collar; a satin finish rose bowl; a carafe with swirled blue and white stripes; each unsigned
The tallest: 7.75in. high

Provenance: the rose bowl formerly in the Maude B. Feld collection, retaining a Feld sticker numbered *28 1F* (Total: 3 Items)
Estimate: 300-400

30912
A FRENCH OVERLAID AND ETCHED GLASS VASE
Daum Nancy, c.1900

The cylindrical form with opalescent ground overlaid with mottled rose vines in autumnal colors of orange and green, signed underside *Daum Nancy* with the *Cross of Lorraine*
5.2in. high
Estimate: 900-1,200

30914
A FRENCH OVERLAID AND ETCHED GLASS VASE
Daum Nancy, c.1900

The slightly tapered cylindrical form with an orange ground depicting boats in brown and black, signed underside *Daum Nancy 14* with the *Cross of Lorraine*
1.5in. high
Estimate: 300-500

30914

30915
AN AMERICAN GOLD IRIDESCENT GLASS PLATE
Quezal, c.1910

The undulated edge of the circular body with thick gold iridescent border surrounding magenta center, the underside with etched signature *Quezal* and number *2992-34* in polished pontil
6.6in. diameter
Estimate: 100-300

30915

30916
A FRENCH WHEEL-ETCHED GLASS PITCHER
Muller Croismare, early Twentieth Century

The late Art Nouveau form with a mottled ground in soft yellow and ivory, overlaid and etched to depict a floral and leaf pattern in red, brown, yellow and black, applique handle, carved and applied cabochons, enamel signature *Muller Croismare* to underside
6in. high
Estimate: 3,000-5,000

30918
FOUR SATIN GLASS VASES
Makers unknown, c.1890

Comprising a pair of pink 'Jack-in-the-Pulpit' vases with a diamond quilt pattern; a double gourd form vase in a diamond quilt pattern mother-of-pearl finish fading from pink to cinnamon; a melon lobed body with a cylindrical neck in a herringbone mother-of-pearl finish fading from pink to cinnamon; each unsigned
The tallest: 7.5in. (Total: 4 Items)
Estimate: 200-400

30917
AN AMERICAN SATIN GLASS VASE
Boston and Sandwich Co., c.1900

The baluster form transitions from pink to a slightly deeper pink, the tightly ruffled rim in frosted clear, two frosted clear applied handles, unsigned
8.2in. high
Estimate: 200-400

30919
AN AMERICAN IRIDESCENT 'AURENE' GLASS VASE
Steuben, c.1905

The bulbous form with flared and scalloped rim, gold Aurene ribbed design, magenta and blue highlights, engraved signature *Aurene 569*
4.3in. high
Estimate: 800-1,200

30920
AN ENGLISH OVERLAID AND ETCHED GLASS VASE
Thomas Webb & Sons, c.1890

Of baluster form, the yellow frosted ground overlaid in ivory and etched to depict a single stem double blossom flower, banded at rim and base, unsigned
3.5in. high
Estimate: 600-900

30922
AN AMERICAN THREADED ART GLASS PERFUME BOTTLE
Steuben, c.1927

The square form with curved shoulders to a short cylindrical neck and flared rim in clear glass with black threading, black pointed and faceted stopper, unsigned
5in. high (Total: 2 Items)
Estimate: 200-300

30921
A FRENCH OVERLAID AND ETCHED CABINET GLASS VASE
Gauthier, c.1910

The ovoid white ground overlaid with chartreuse, etched to depict flowering daisy, with cameo signature *Gauthier*
3in. high
Estimate: 200-300

30923
A CONTINENTAL ENAMELED AND APPLIQUE GLASS VASE
Moser, c.1885

The blue urn-form with ruffled rim and applied frosted 'icicle' enamel floral design to body and neck, unsigned
5.7in. high
Estimate: 300-400

30924
AN ENGLISH OVERLAID AND ETCHED GLASS VASE
Thomas Webb & Sons, c.1890

The cranberry ovoid form with a flared rim overlaid in ivory depicting hibiscus on their stems, leaves and a butterfly on the reverse, border around the rim and base, stamped underside
5.7in. high
Estimate: 1,800–2,200

30924

30925
A FRENCH OVERLAID AND ETCHED GLASS VASE
Daum Nancy, c.1900

The squat form with mottled brown and yellow ground overlaid and fire polished with yellow, green and red autumnal rose vines, etched *Daum Nancy* signature with *Cross of Lorraine*
4.3in. high
Estimate: 1,500-2,000

30926
AN AMERICAN IRIDESCENT FAVRILE GLASS VASE
Tiffany & Co., c.1913

The bulbous form rising to a tapering slender neck in an iridescent finish of a ribbed pattern in brown and gold, signed underside *L. C. Tiffany-Favrile 3323 H*
12.4in. high
Estimate: 3,000-5,000

30927
AN ENGLISH OVERLAID, ETCHED AND SILVER-MOUNTED GLASS PERFUME BOTTLE
The glass: Thomas Webb & Sons, c.1900

The long tapering form in a blue ground overlaid in ivory and etched to depict passion flowers and leaves, sterling silver top, monogram *M E C*, unsigned
10.5in. long
Estimate: 1,500-2,000

30928
A FRENCH TRIPLE OVERLAID AND ETCHED GLASS VASE
Muller Freres, c.1900

The frosted mottled ground ranging from pink up to aqua, overlaid and etched to depict a wooded landscape with rivers and mountains in the background, with cameo signature *Muller Fres/Luneville*
7.5in. high
Estimate: 1,300-1,600

30929
AN ENGLISH OVERLAID AND ETCHED GLASS VASE
Thomas Webb & Sons, c.1900

The frosted amber ground overlaid in ivory and etched to depict a fern and leaf motif, unsigned
6.5in. high
Estimate: 1,200-1,800

30930
AN ENGLISH TRIPLE OVERLAID AND ETCHED GLASS VASE
Thomas Webb & Sons, c.1890

The angular bulbous body cased in white, the frosted canary yellow ground overlaid in carnelian red and etched to depict plums, cherries and pears in fire polished high relief resting on low relief matte branches, foliage and trailing blossoms, engraved design on foot and etched design along rim, unsigned
8.6in. high
Estimate: 10,000-15,000

30931

30931
AN ENGLISH OVERLAID AND ETCHED GLASS VASE
Thomas Webb & Sons, c.1900

The frosted blue ground overlaid in ivory and etched to depict pendant-flowering jasmine vines on the obverse and a butterfly on the reverse, the underside with circular acid-stamped maker's mark *THOS. WEBB & SONS' CAMEO*
9.25in. high
Estimate: 3,500-4,000

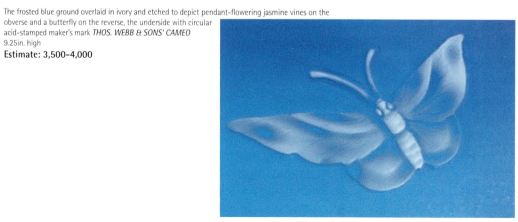

30932

30932
AN ENGLISH TRIPLE OVERLAID AND ETCHED GEM CAMEO GLASS VASE
Thomas Webb & Sons, c.1885

The interior cased in white, the exterior a canary yellow ground overlaid in white and rose and etched in a swirling stylized floral design, the underside with impressed signature *Thomas Webb & Sons Gem Cameo*
4.2in. high
Provenance: Maude B. Feld sold item to Mrs. R. A. McMurry sold item to current owner
Estimate: 1,000-1,800

30933
AN ENGLISH OVERLAID AND ETCHED GEM CAMEO GLASS VASE
Thomas Webb & Sons, retailed by Tiffany & Co., c.1889

The footed ovoid form with frosted blue ground overlaid in ivory and etched to depict fuchsia and a butterfly, the foot and rim with stylized banding, stamped underside *Tiffany & Co/ 1889/ Thomas Webb & Sons/ Gem Cameo*
6.2in. high
Estimate: 3,000-4,000

30934

AN AMERICAN OVERLAID AND ETCHED GLASS BOWL
Steuben, c.1925

Plum Jade, 'Canton' pattern, shape #2687, with narrow foot and high broad shoulder executed in smooth plum glass, the waist with alternating stylized medallions of flowers and 'shou' characters over an acid-etched ground of stylized scrolling cloud motif; acid-stamp *Steuben* within the polished pontil
4.2in. high, 8in. diameter
Estimate: 4,000-6,000

30935

AN ENGLISH OVERLAID AND ETCHED GEM CAMEO GLASS VASE
Thomas Webb & Sons, c.1885

The interior cased in ivory, the yellow ground deeply carved and acid etched in a tree bark texture, carnelian red overlay etched to depict leaves, berries, vines and blossoms, *Maude B. Feld* retail sticker affixed to base, impressed signature *Thomas Webb & Sons Gem Cameo*
10.2in. high
Estimate: 3,000-5,000

30936

AN ENGLISH ETCHED AND PAINTED GLASS VASE
Thomas Webb & Sons, c.1890

The globular form with simulated ivory ground etched and painted to depict pendant rose bush branches, the underside with stamped bas-relief mark *Thomas Webb & Sons*
3.5in. high
Estimate: 700-800

30937

30937
AN AMERICAN FAVRILE PAPERWEIGHT GLASS VASE
Tiffany & Co., c.1917

The cushion foot rising to a slender tapering ovoid form with an inverted rim depicting paper white flowers, the stems and leaves in shades of green with the flowers in white with yellow centers, Maude B. Feld sticker on side, engraved signature underside *L. C. Tiffany-Favrile 8021 K*
15.2in. high
Provenance: Maude B. Feld sold item to Mrs. R. A. McMurry sold item to current owner
Estimate: 15,000-20,000

30938
A CHINESE PORCELAIN PLATTER
Maker unknown, c.1900

The oval rose medallion platter with figural medallions and floral medallions, gilt detail circle to middle and rim, unsigned
14.7in. wide
Estimate: 200-400

30940
AN ASIAN CLOISONNE VASE AND AN ENAMEL VASE
Makers unknown, c.1900

The silver foil ovoid form decorated with liver foil cloisonne depicting pink and red flowers, green leaves and branches over a brass substrate, stamped with a Japanese mon underside; the red ovoid form vase decorated with mother-of-pearl depicting birds and flowering branches with a ru yi border, unmarked
5.9in. high and 6.9in. high respectively (Total: 2 Items)
Estimate: 200-400

30939
A CARVED FIGURAL IVORY STATUE
Maker unknown, c.1900

A carved ivory Buddhist deity with 18 extended arms, hands carrying objects such as a knife, a teapot, bottle, a flaming orb, a necklace and more, seated upon an ornately carved lotus pedestal
10.5in. high
Estimate: 300-600

30941
TWO ASIAN STONE SNUFF BOTTLES
Makers unknown, Twentieth Century

The first, a flattened ovoid form in green jade with a smooth coral lid; the second, a flattened ovoid form in lapis lazuli with a relief carving of flowers on a branch and stylized handles to the sides, orange stone lid carved as a flower, unsigned
2.5in. high and 2.2in. high respectively (Total: 2 Items)
Estimate: 200-400

30942
A CHINESE PEKING GLASS CABINET VASE
Maker unknown, c.1890

The elongated ovoid, opaque-pink body acid-etched with equestrian motif *lian ge ma*, unsigned
4.9in. high
Estimate: 500-700

30943
A COLLECTION OF THREE JAPANESE NETSUKE
Japan, c.1900

Comprising a carved-bone figural grouping of two tigers; a finely carved ivory figure of a seated, smiling Hotei with fan; *together with* a carved and inked ivory Noh figure with revolving face, depicting either the mysterious and handsome youth character mask of 'Doji', or the fierce male deity character mask of 'O-obesimi', the two ivory human figures with incised artist signature to underside
The tallest: 1.95in. high (Total: 3 Items)
Estimate: 200-400

30944
A CHINESE CELADON GINGER JAR
Maker unknown, Twentieth Century

The ovoid form rising to a short cylindrical neck, celadon ground with enamel decoration depicting multicolored flowers and leaves, gold leaf rim, white porcelain insert lid with gilt detail to rim, smooth slightly domed wooden lid, signed underside in Chinese characters
6in. high
Estimate: 100-200

30945
A CONTINENTAL PORCELAIN FIGURAL GROUP
Capo di Monte, c.1930

The platform supporting a male and female figure in late Eighteenth Century attire, stamped underside
9.2in. high
Estimate: 100-300

30946

30946
FOUR CHINESE SNUFF BOTTLES
Makers unknown, Twentieth century

Comprising a flattened round form with a brass neck and lid, black ground with blue silver foil and enamel detail depicting flowers; a flattened ovoid form with a domed lid in a yellow ground with multicolored flowers; a flattened double gourd form with lid primarily in yellow with blue panels of floral decorations; a rectangular form with domed lid, front and back panel depict deer and a heron; all with cork and bone inserts, two signed with Chinese characters
The tallest: 3in. (Total: 4 Items)
Estimate: 300-500

30947

30947
A COLLECTION OF CHINESE FAMILLE ROSE ENAMEL PORCELAIN ITEMS
Late Qing Dynasty, c.1860-1910

Including an assembled group of six late Nineteenth Century export cups and saucers in the 'Rose Medallion' pattern, *together with* a Tongzhi period (1862-1874) octagonal footed bowl decorated in the 'Thousand Antiques' pattern in 'famille rose' enamels, the underside of the bowl with iron-red overglaze six-character archaic-style seal mark and of the period
The tallest: 7in. (Total: 11 Items)
Estimate: 400-600

30948

30948
A CHINESE PORCELAIN AND WOODEN TABLE SCREEN
Maker unknown, c.1900

The late Ching Dynasty rectangular tile decorated with two cranes standing upon a leafy, gnarled pine tree, in greens, whites, blues and browns; the wooden stylized wave stand in dark wood with a rectangular support with scroll work, unsigned
9.5in. high
Estimate: 400-800

30949

30949
A COLLECTION OF CHINESE CLOISONNE ITEMS
Makers unknown, c.1920

Comprising a metal-mounted covered box with turquoise mosaic surface; a copper-wire cloisonne vase of lobbed ovoid form; a copper-wire cloisonne vase of footed bottle form with pink flowers on a black geometric ground, unsigned; *together with* a carved green nephrite model of an archaic ritual vessel
The tallest: 9.5in. high (Total: 4 Items)
Estimate: 300-500

30950

30950
TWO ORIENTAL PLIQUE-A-JOUR BOWLS
Chinese, c.1880

The first begins with a filigree base rising to a multi-colored floral design on a clear ground in the center, bird and floral pattern and border design at rim. The other bowl has a multicolored floral pattern on a green ground with a border pattern at the rim,
3in. high and 2.7in. high (Total: 2 Items)
Estimate: 200-400

30952

30952
TWO ASIAN SNUFF BOTTLES
Makers unknown, Twentieth Century

The first footed flattened ovoid form with a flared rim and domed lid carved in ivory depicting two gold fish with grass script and artists signed, the reverse depicts Chinese characters; the second snuff bottle in cast resin depicts figures, unsigned
2.5in. high and 2.7in. high respectively (Total: 2 Items)
Estimate: 100-200

30951

30951
A PEKING OVERLAID AND ETCHED GLASS VASE
Maker unknown, c.1920

Of baluster form, the ivory ground overlaid in cherry red and etched to depict Chinese images for 'good luck', unsigned
9.2in. high
Estimate: 300-500

30953

30953
AN ORIENTAL GLASS SNUFF BOTTLE
Maker unknown, c.1925

The four-sided slightly tapering form with rounded shoulders and a short cylindrical neck depicting a signed reverse painting of female figures in a pastoral setting, the bottle top in red enamel over white glass with an ivory scoop, signed in characters
3.8in. high
Estimate: 300-500

30954
THREE CLOISONNE VASES, A TOOTHPICK HOLDER AND NAPKIN RING
Makers unknown, c.1880

Comprising a baluster form vase with cobalt ground, multicolored floral pattern and a green scale border; the second ovoid form with a tapered neck and flared rim in yellow ground with a multicolored floral pattern and blue border; the third vase a baluster form with mauve ground and multicolored flowers, a yellow band to the shoulders, blue and white border to the foot, shoulder and rim, cerulean blue interior; the toothpick holder in a mottled cerulean and viridian ground with a stylized daisy pattern; a blue ground napkin ring; two stamped underside *China*
The tallest: 6.1in. (Total: 5 Items)
Estimate: 300-500

30956
FOUR CLOISONNE PIECES AND ONE ENAMEL LIDDED BOWL
Makers unknown, c.1890

The enamel bowl decorated with a pink ground and multicolored floral and foliage design with birds, border to top and bottom, the inside a vibrant green, the cloisonne lidded triangular box in pale yellow ground with stylized floral design with cobalt interior, the cylindrical blue ground cloisonne vase with small white floral design, the cloisonne vase in red, green and ivory ground with an intricate design of birds and stylized flowers, unsigned
Various sizes (Total: 7 Items)
Estimate: 400-600

30957
TWO PAIRS ASIAN CLOISONNE VASES
China/Japan, c.1940

The first pair consists of a red fish scale background overdecorated with multicolored rose design, metal rim at top and bottom, signed *Sato*. The second pair of intricately designed brass substrate with a white ground and intricate multicolored floral design, unsigned
7.3in. high, 9in, high (Total: 4 Items)
Estimate: 300-400

30955
A JAPANESE METAL VASE
Maker unknown, Taisho Period

The cylindrical metal vase with a short neck and flared rim in a dark grey ground cut to depict cranes flying over waves in front of a full moon, trees in the background, signed in Japanese characters to the side
18.1in. high
Estimate: 200-400

30958
A CLOISONNE LIDDED JAR AND TUBE
Makers unknown, c.1875

The jar, a tri-footed gourd shape body in alternating blue, bronze and deep green ground with an intricate pattern of multicolored flowers and butterflies; the tube with a cobalt blue ground and detailed pattern of multicolored spires with stylized flowers and scale border, unsigned
3.7in. high and 6in. high respectively (Total: 3 Items)
Estimate: 300-500

30960
AN ANGLO-INDIAN ENAMELED DISH
Maker unknown, c.1980

The demi-spherical brass body with pierced wall, shaped rim and polychrome enamel decoration, underside retaining original paper label *MADE IN INDIA*
9.5in. diameter
Estimate: 30-50

30959
FOUR ASIAN ENAMEL ITEMS
Makers unknown, c.1900

Comprising an articulated brass fish with red and amber enamel eyes; an enameled perfume bottle with an ivory application stick, signed underside in characters; a champleve and brass candlestick; a brass lion with a removable head in turquoise and coral
The lion: 4.2in. high (Total: 4 Items)
Estimate: 200-400

30961
A CHINESE CLOISONNE CAPPED URN
Maker unknown, c.1920

The high-shoulder baluster shape with all-over brass wire and polychrome floral decoration on black ground, the banded neck receiving the domed cover surmounted with shaped brass knob; brass underside with incised mark *China*
17in. high (Total: 2)
Estimate: 400-600

30962
FIVE CLOISONNE ITEMS
Makers unknown, various dates

Comprising a rectangular box with black ground and heavy floral decoration on a brass hinged substrate; the second a rectangular box depicting a peacock surrounded by multicolored flowers; the third a cylindrical lidded jar displaying an intricate multicolored dragon, bird and floral design; the fourth an ovoid form vase with copper mica powder ground and multicolored floral cartouches; the fifth an elongated ovoid form viridian green vase with pink and yellow flowers; each unmarked
The tallest: 6in. (Total: 6 Items)
Estimate: 200-400

30963
AN IRISH 'ABERDEEN' PORCELAIN PITCHER
Belleek, c.1926

The ivory baluster form rises to a tapered neck and large flared spout with a stylized handle, applique flowers over a fluted and medallion design body, stamped underglaze with Belleek mark in black ink
9.5in. high
Estimate: 300-500

30964
AN AMERICAN ARMCHAIR
The Sheraton Co., 're-made' 1960

In Queen Anne style, the elm frame features shell-carved crest rail and splat, shepard's crook arm rests, gracious slip seat with shaped front, shell-carved seat frieze, and four cabriole legs joined by fancy 'H' stretcher, the underside of the upholstered seat with paper label indicating that the chair was 'remade' on 10-10-60 by The Sheraton Co.
back 39.5in. high, seat 18in. high, seat 24in. wide
Estimate: 800-1,000

30965
AN ENGLISH EDWARDIAN HEPPLEWHITE-STYLE MAHOGANY VITRINE
Maker unknown, c.1905

The flat-top breakfront superstructure fitted with beveled glass side panels centering the single door that opens to a single glass shelf, over hinged lift-top table substructure with beveled glass in the top, front, and curved sides, on four tapering legs with spade feet joined with shelf and shaped stretchers, the superstructure with Twentieth Century electric light, unmarked
48in. high, 26.5in. wide, 15.5in. deep
Estimate: 600-800

30966
AN AMERICAN WALNUT CENTRE TABLE
Maker unknown, c.1875

The rectangular white marble insert framed with conforming step molding over deep continuous frieze with four carved female heads, each between columns and over three pendant spheres, each of the two legs comprising a capped urn between square columns on arched support raised on two metal casters, the legs joined by medial stretcher centered with architectural carving, unmarked
28.5in. high, 43in. wide, 27in. deep
Estimate: 1,200-1,500

30967
AN AMERICAN WALL CLOCK
Ephraim Downs, active from 1811 to 1843

The two-weight works striking on the hours, the dial with roman numerals and gilt spangles in the four corners, the mahogany case with ebonized and gilt-stenciled decoration, the door fitted with clear glass over a large eglomisé panel, the interior with original paper label *Patent Clocks, Invented by Eli Terry, manufactured by Ephraim Downs, Bristol, Conn./Warranted, If Well Used./P. Canfield, Printer Hartford*
32in. high
Estimate: 700-900

30968
AN AMERICAN EASTLAKE WALNUT ARMCHAIR
Maker unknown, c.1870

The bowed rail with upturned ends, the button-upholstered back over tight seat raised on turned tapering front legs on original wooden casters, recently replaced pink Jacquard upholstery, unmarked
The back 39.5in. high, The seat 15in. high, seat 24in. wide
Estimate: 600-800

30969
A VITRINE TABLE
maker unknown, c.1980

In the Louis XV style, the hinged lift-top with rectangular glass inset panel opening to a green damask-lined case with glass side panels above shaped frieze and cabriole legs, the entire with brass mounts, unsigned
30in. high
Estimate: 600-900

30970

30970
A LOUIS XV STYLE GILT-FRAMED LOOKING GLASS
Maker unknown, c.1890

The quatre-foil beveled mirrored glass mounted in a conforming gessoed wire frame with asymmetrical cartouche at top and bottom, the sides with symmetrical floral cartouches, the interior with a row of beading, frame unmarked, original back with stamped black *B & M* mark
46.5in. long, 28.5in. wide
Estimate: 800–1,000

30971

30971
AN AMERICAN EASTLAKE WALNUT CHAIR
Maker unknown

The bowed crest rail with lambrequin-decorated over button-upholstered back flanked by carved armrests over round tight-upholstered seat, raised on wooden casters, exposed frame unmarked
back 39.5in. high, seat 15in. high, seat 24in. wide
Estimate: 800–1,000

30972

30972
A MAHOGANY VITRINE TABLE
Maker unknown, c.1985

In Louis XV style with metal mounts and round Sèvres-style porcelain tiles, the hinged square lift-top with outset sides and conforming glass inset opening to a gold moiré-lined case, raised on four cabriole legs joined by shaped frieze, unmarked
29in. high, 28in. wide, 28in. deep
Estimate: 600-800

30973
AN ENGLISH CHIPPENDALE MAHOGANY PEMBROKE TABLE
Maker unknown, c.1790

The rectangular bevel-edged top with hinged, shaped, satinwood-strung, and beveled leaves above a conforming case with satinwood stringing, one end fitted with a drawer, on square tapering legs with satinwood stringing, unmarked
27in. high
Estimate: 500-600

30973

30974
AN AMERICAN WALNUT CENTRE TABLE
Maker unknown, c.1875

The rouge marble insert framed with rectangular molding with canted corners over conforming deep continuous frieze, each of the two legs comprising three columns on arched support raised on two wooden casters, the legs joined by medial stretcher centered with turned finial and pendant carving, unmarked
29.5in. high, 35in. wide, 22in. deep
Estimate: 600-800

30974

30975
FOUR CHINESE LATE QING DYNASTY TABOURETS
Makers unknown, c.1900

Each of the drum-shaped stands with inset marble tops, pierced and carved decoration, 'X' stretcher, and four cabriole legs, unmarked
the tallest 36in. high (Total: 4 Items)
Estimate: 800-1,000

30975

30976
A CHINESE LATE QING DYNASTY TAOIST SHRINE
Maker unknown, c.1900

The rectangular *hong-mu* (blackwood) case with carved backplate over flat top extending to portico, the pierced frieze and door intricately carved with Taoist symbols, the facade carved with the Eight Taoist Immortals carved in bas-relief flanking the door, unmarked
36.5in. high
Estimate: 600-900

30977
A LATE QING DYNASTY SOFA-BED
Maker unknown, 1900

The hong-mu (blackwood) frame with three 'picture' marble inserts in the back, arm rests flanking plank seat, raised on cabriole legs, unmarked
back 41.5in. high, 68.5in. wide, 22.5in. deep
Estimate: 800-1,000

End of Auction

INVITATION TO CONSIGN

to our next
Fine and Decorative Arts Auction

Fall 2005

Heritage Galleries & Auctioneers is currently accepting consignments for our upcoming sale this Fall 2005. Heritage offers an internet presence of over 140,000 registered unique members, prominent marketing in several major arts and antiques publications, and one low consignment fee, with free illustration and full insurance coverage.

Call now for further information.

Bryan Abbott
Director of Acquisitions
1.800.872.6467 ext. 320

Lucas Rigby
Consignment Director
1.800.872.6467 ext. 379

Ed Jaster
Consignment Director
1.800.872.6467 ext. 288

HERITAGE
Galleries & Auctioneers

HeritageGalleries.com   HeritageGalleries.com   HeritageGalleries.com

HERITAGE
Galleries & Auctioneers

The Heritage family is the world's leading auctioneer of fine collectibles, and now America's third largest auction company (over $300 million annual sales).

HERITAGE Numismatic Auctions, Inc.

Heritage Numismatic Auctions, Inc. is the world's #1 numismatic auctioneer with more than $750 million of rare coins sold at auction since 1976. HNAI offers 100+ auctions each year, with our flagship Signature Auctions held at America's leading conventions. Annual 2004 results exceeded $300 million! Visit HeritageCoins.com

HERITAGE World Coin Auctions

Heritage World Coin Auctions offer the finest in ancients, world coins, and world paper money, through signature catalogs at major conventions and on the Internet. Visit HeritageCoins.com

HERITAGE Rare Coin Galleries

Heritage Currency Auctions of America is the world's most respected auctioneer of paper money, holding three annual Signature Auctions at leading conventions, and bi-monthly Internet auctions. Visit HeritageCurrency.com

HERITAGE CURRENCY AUCTIONS OF AMERICA

Heritage Sports Collectibles is a leader in rare and collectible sports cards, uniforms, equipment, and related vintage sports memorabilia. HSC presents monthly Internet Amazing Sports Auctions and Signature Auctions at national conventions. Visit HeritageSportsCollectibles.com

HERITAGE SPORTS COLLECTIBLES

Heritage Comics Auctions is the world's undisputed leader in auctioning quality comics and comic art, with more than $40 million sold since 2001 and two Guinness World Records! HCA presents Signature Auctions and Internet auctions for consignees like Stan Lee and Nicolas Cage. HCA also sold the original G.I. Joe prototype for $200,000. Visit HeritageComics.com

HERITAGE COMICS

Heritage Vintage Movie Posters has sold millions of dollars of classic movie posters, from the golden age of movie-making through more modern classic and collectible movie art. Visit HeritageMoviePosters.com

HERITAGE Vintage Movie Posters

Heritage-Odyssey Celebrity Memorabilia Auctions are becoming the leading source for Hollywood, entertainment, and celebrity collectibles, from Elton John's $160,000 piano to rare Beatles' records. Visit HeritageOdyssey.com

HERITAGE-ODYSSEY Music & Entertainment Memorabilia

Heritage Fine & Decorative Arts auctions feature Silver, Art Glass, and Paintings, from names like Tiffany, Gorham, Shiebler, Daum, Gallé, Rockwell, Parrish, Croegaert, Frazetta, Prendergast, Rouault, Vargas and Frishmuth. Visit HeritageGalleries.com

HERITAGE-SLATER AMERICANA

Heritage-Slater Americana auctions a wide range of historical and popular-culture collectibles: Presidential autographs, vintage toys, antique advertising, and much more! Visit HeritageGalleries.com

Heritage Galleries & Auctioneers enjoys the collector interest and bidding demand of more than 185,000 registered bidder-members.

What Do You Collect?
Take our survey at HeritageGalleries.com
You could qualify for free auction catalogs, or win $250 cash.

HeritageGalleries.com
Visit today for your free membership, and our latest survey prizes.

3500 Maple Avenue • Dallas, Texas 75219
Phone 214-528-3500 • 800-872-6467